Autumn

Loneliness

..

A HARDSCRATCH PRESS BOOK

The front cover photograph of Kiyoko Tokutomi c. 1955 is from the
Haiku Archives of the California State Library, photographed in turn
by June Hopper Hymas. The 1963 photograph of Kiyoshi Tokutomi
on the back cover is courtesy of Yukiko Tokutomi Northon.

Printed in the United States of America.

First printed August 2009.

Hardscratch Press, 2358 Banbury Place,
Walnut Creek, California 94598-2347.

Library of Congress Control Number: 2009932096

ISBN: 978-0-9789979-4-6

2   4   6   8   9   7   5   3   1

Autumn

Loneliness

The Letters OF *Kiyoshi & Kiyoko Tokutomi*

[JULY–DECEMBER 1967]

· ·

TRANSLATED *by*

Tei Matsushita Scott

AND

Patricia J. Machmiller

Contents

Acknowledgments

THE TRANSLATORS ARE MOST GRATEFUL TO Yukiko Tokutomi Northon for her openness and support of this project. We appreciate her generosity as well as that of other members of the families of Kiyoko and Kiyoshi Tokutomi, especially Mitsuyo Shibata Tao, Hisayo Shibata Tao, Sumie Shibata, and Mitsuye Tokutomi Hoshino for the time they have given searching for photographs and identifying the people pictured.

We also thank the following people who have given of their time and expertise in helping us with technical matters in the letters: Dr. Betty Arnold and the late Dr. James Arnold, Lothar Schicker, Emiko Miyashita, and Nardin Gottfried for their help in identifying medicines and medical terminology; June Hopper Hymas and John T. Blakney for information on 1967 camera technology; and Mayumi Taniguchi for her review of the Japanese and romaji texts.

The staff of the California State Library Haiku Archives, especially Director of Special Collections Gary Kurutz, were very generous in the furtherance of this project. Additional thanks to June Hopper Hymas, who photographed images from the Archives for inclusion in the book.

We thank also the Yuki Teikei Haiku Society for their enthusiastic support throughout.

Introduction

MUCH IS KNOWN ABOUT THE ACTIONS the U.S. government took to help repair the damage done to its former adversary, Japan, in World War II and to speed its recovery, but less is known about how thousands of ordinary people on both sides of the Pacific made the transition. Kiyoshi Tokutomi and Kiyoko Shibata were two people who as teachers met and fell in love in post-war Japan. He was an American; she was Japanese. In 1951 Kiyoshi returned to the United States and entered a hospital to be treated for tuberculosis, which he had contracted in Japan in 1949. Kiyoko followed in 1954. They were married in 1957 and 10 years later were making their life in Northern California when Kiyoshi suffered severe hearing loss attributed to medication prescribed for the tuberculosis. Seeking a cure for the hearing loss he went to Japan for extended treatment while Kiyoko stayed in the United States working at Fairchild Semiconductor and caring for their 10-year-old daughter, Yukiko.

In letters written over a five-month period at this time of great personal duress, these two people confide freely and intimately in each other, with details of their daily activities and of their personal concerns, desires, and dreams, and often expressing their deep mutual love. But these letters also give us a close look at the world that the Tokutomis are part of creating: a world in which there is cooperation between the U.S. and Japan, where the Vietnam War looms large, where the rise of Silicon Valley is on the horizon, and where they, like parents everywhere, worry about instilling in their daughter the values that will make for a good and happy life.

We see through Kiyoshi's eyes the life and customs of the new modern Japan. We catch glimpses of the medical practices of Japan in the late 1960s and see hints that the scientific collaboration between Japan and Germany in the war years has been continued in medical research, pharmaceuticals, and education in the post-war years.

Kiyoko, meanwhile, is a transplanted Japanese in an American society. She and daughter Yukiko live with Kiyoshi's mother in an extended family arrangement—two houses side-by-side in Japantown in San Jose, California. Besides her mother-in-law the family includes her sister Hisayo, who has come from Japan to study mathematics at San Jose State University, and Mitsuko, a cousin of Kiyoshi's from Japan who is finishing high school in the United States.

Both Kiyoko and Kiyoshi had been teachers in Japan immediately after the war. Kiyoshi taught English; Kiyoko taught Japanese literature and culture. The letters include poems that he remembers and haiku that she writes. These literary references foreshadow the extraordinary gift that they together will give America: the Yuki Teikei Haiku Society, which they go on to found in 1975.

The order of the letters has been determined either from the dates in the originals or from the postmark when a date is lacking. On July 30 Kiyoshi began numbering his letters; those numbers have been useful for ordering multiple letters written on the same day. Most mentions of his numbers have been deleted from the letters reproduced here, but there are a few such references left.

For the sake of today's reader, and for space considerations, we have attempted to trim some of the redundancies in the letters without sacrificing the tone and flavor of the writing. Many letters begin with a "How are you?" or a comment on the day's weather and end with "Remember me to Hisayo," for example. Because of the limited space in the aerograms they used, the two often closed without signing their names, although there are also instances when they wrote a closing phrase ("To Kiyoshi-san, who needs Kiyoko-san, from Kiyoko, who needs Kiyoshi-san," for example). We have retained some of these as well.

A few letters are missing from the original collection, and sections have been cut from others. Any excisions by the Tokutomis are noted as such. References that Kiyoko and Kiyoshi make elsewhere in the letters cause us to surmise that these were passionate, sexually explicit passages that they chose to keep private. Because of this evidence of their preference and respecting their clear wishes, the few passages that they overlooked, while not entirely deleted, have been carefully edited. These deletions and any others by the translators are indicated with the customary ellipses.

. . .

These letters are extraordinarily rich in detail and in heart. The insight they give us into the personal world of the writers is rare and touching. They make real the lives of people who were part of healing the chasm of war, part of the transition of two societies from adversaries to allies, and part of the economic and cultural growth of California. The originals of these letters have been donated by the Tokutomis' daughter, Yukiko Tokutomi Northon, to the Haiku Archive in the California State Library.

—Patricia J. Machmiller

About the Project

HONEST, COMPELLING, COURAGEOUS, AND LOVING—these letters, by turns lyrical and realistic, document married life with a delicacy of feeling characteristic of the Japanese way of life. *Autumn Loneliness* reads like an epistolary novel, a fusion of life and art, telling a story of separation and longing within the context of two cultures, Japan and the United States, enriching each.

—Kevin Starr, UNIVERSITY *of* SOUTHERN CALIFORNIA

WHAT IS REMEMBERED OF CIVILIZATION is its art; what is remembered of our lives are the moments of connection with others—and the trees, rocks, birds and stars. Kiyoshi and Kiyoko Tokutomi are remembered for their warmth as haiku teachers and for their contribution in transmitting genuine "haiku spirit" from Japan to America, as part of the historical arc of our international planetary culture. Through this book of letters, Tei Matsushita Scott and Patricia Machmiller have kindly given us an intimate look into the Tokutomis' "personal haiku world" that we can all ultimately mirror and share through appreciation of haiku moments in our lives, down to our last breath.

—Patricia Donegan, POET, TRANSLATOR, and AUTHOR OF *Haiku Mind*

THIS BOOK WILL BE OF INTEREST to anyone fascinated by the cultural relations between Japan and the United States in the decades after Pearl Harbor and Hiroshima. What is unexpected is that, while it tells some part of that story—a story of healings, border crossings, cultural cross-breeding—it does it in the form of letters that are an intimate and moving portrait of a marriage, as absorbing and delicate as a Japanese novel or a film by Ozu.

—Robert Hass, PROFESSOR *of* ENGLISH, UC BERKELEY
U.S. POET LAUREATE, 1995–1997

Early History

KIYOKO SHIBATA, *eighth grade, Saga Girls' School, 1943-44.*
The armband indicates that she is a student volunteer at the iron works.
Photo courtesy of Mitsuyo Shibata Tao.

Kiyoko Shibata
December 28, 1928—December 25, 2002

KIYOKO SHIBATA WAS BORN to Matsue (Miyazaki) and Hideji Shibata in Nabeshima, Saga, Japan, on December 28, 1928. She was the second child of seven in a family of rice farmers working the land on the southern island of Kyushu, about 40 miles from Nagasaki near the Sea of Ariake. She was named by her grandfather for her happy personality. In Saga City she graduated from Saga Girls' High School in the spring of 1945 and immediately enrolled in Saga Teachers' College, where she majored in Japanese literature.

That summer her father, heeding the warnings in leaflets dropped by American pilots over Saga, bundled his children in their winter jackets and sweaters and took them to hide in a cave that he had dug in their garden. Kiyoko's mother and one of Kiyoko's sisters were on their way home when they saw planes flying overhead and hid in a deep ditch at the side of the road. In this way the whole family survived the bombing of and subsequent atomic fallout from Nagasaki.

After graduating from college, Kiyoko taught Japanese literature and music at Nabeshima Middle School where she met Kiyoshi Tokutomi, who was teaching there also. She traveled to the United States in 1954, and she and Kiyoshi were married in 1957. They had one daughter, Yukiko, born that same year. She worked part-time at a gift store in San Jose's Japantown while she attended San Jose City College. Eventually she went to work for Fairchild Semiconductor, where she was employed when the letters begin.

THE MIYAZAKIS, *Kiyoko's mother's family in Japan, 1946. Front row, parents Masashichi and Sano Miyazaki; middle row, from left, sisters Masae Koga, Mitsue Miyazaki Shibata (Kiyoko's mother), and Yuki Miyazaki; back row, brothers Bunji, Masao and Tatsuji Miyazaki. (Not pictured: the youngest brother, Hisao, who was in Burma at the time.) Photo courtesy of Mitsuyo Shibata Tao.*

KIYOKO'S MOTHER, *Mitsue Miyazaki Shibata, and oldest brother, Masayuki, on their farm in Nabeshima, Japan. Photo courtesy of Yukiko Tokutomi Northon.*

HIDEJI SHIBATA, *Kiyoko's father, in Nabeshima, Japan, 1956.*
Photo courtesy of Mitsuyo Shibata Tao.

FACULTY AT NABESHIMA MIDDLE SCHOOL, *1947–48: From left, Nobuyoshi Hariguchi, Shigeaki Mutō, Kiyoko Shibata, Shizuko Yukitake, Mr. Harada (music teacher), Kiyoshi Tokutomi, school nurse (name not known). Photo courtesy of Yukiko Tokutomi Northon.*

KIYOKO'S FAMILY, *the Shibatas, with Kiyoshi at the Dazaifu Tenman Shrine, 1951.*
From left, Kazume, Kiyoko, Hiroyuki, Kiyoshi, Masayoshi, Hisayo, and Mitsuyo.
Mitsuyo later wrote about the day: "This shrine is in Dazaifu, Fukuoka-ken. We went
on one-day trip by train with future brother-in-law. Kiyoko made fancy lunch box
and we ate in the garden. It is a good memory." Photo courtesy of Mitsuyo Shibata Tao.

FROM THE SHIP *on the day Kiyoko left Japan for the United States, 1954.*
Photo courtesy of Yukiko Tokutomi Northon. (A Ceremony of Ribbons: Travelers leaving
Japan via ocean liner were given a roll of ribbon at check-in. At departure time, signaled by
the sound of the steam whistle, passengers would throw one end of the ribbon to well-wishers
on the dock. With the ribbon as the only tie between the water and the land, friends and
family prayed for a safe voyage while the passengers waved sayonara.)

Kiyoshi Tokutomi, *Miyaki High School, Saga, Japan, c. 1940.*
Photo courtesy of Yukiko Tokutomi Northon.

Kiyoshi Tokutomi

October 3, 1923–June 6, 1987

KIYOSHI TOKUTOMI WAS BORN in Watsonville, California, on October 3, 1923, the second child of Sada Haraguchi of Takakise, Saga, Japan, and Tatsuichirō Tokutomi of Yae-machi, Saga. The couple had come to California seeking a new life; eventually they purchased land to farm in Berryessa (now part of San Jose), and Tatsuichirō built their farmhouse there. In November 1931 Tatsuichirō died suddenly. Sada had recently lost a child, and a month after Tatsuichirō's death she lost another baby. She decided to send her three older children to Japan to be raised by her brother while she stayed in the United States and worked to support them. Kiyoshi was nine.

Mitsuye and Yoshimitsu, his brother and sister, had returned to the U.S. before the bombing of Pearl Harbor, but Kiyoshi, about to graduate from high school, was considering college when the war began. He lost touch with his mother, who was interned at Heart Mountain in Wyoming along with his sister and brother and other Japanese Americans. Kiyoshi's sister left the camp to work as a maid at the Navy Language School in Boulder, Colorado. His brother entered the U.S. Army. Kiyoshi, meanwhile, decided to get a degree in education and enrolled at Saga Teachers' College in 1942.

In May 1945, even though he was an American citizen, he was forced into the Japanese Army and taught how to become a human bomb as part of the defense against the American invasion. His assignment was to strap dynamite to his arm, dig a foxhole in the road to hide in, and blow himself up under an advancing tank.

After the war ended, he began teaching at the grammar school where he had studied when he first arrived in Japan. In 1948, when the U.S. was introducing a new curriculum in the Japanese schools, he got a job teaching English at Nabeshima Middle School, where he met his future wife, Kiyoko Shibata.

After the war, food was scarce; Kiyoshi often gave his young students whatever food he acquired for himself. Kiyoko would admonish him: "You are not the Buddha; you have to eat." By 1949 he had contracted tuberculosis, and with no medical help in Japan he became extremely ill. Thanks to the Red Cross he was able to reconnect with his mother. She sent him penicillin, which most likely saved his life, while she petitioned the U.S. government to reinstate his U.S. citizenship. His conscription into the Japanese military had marked him as a traitor, but in 1951 his mother's petition was successful. She arranged for his return to the States, where he was admitted to a sanatorium for treatment of advanced tuberculosis. Before he left Japan, he invited Kiyoko to come to America. She arrived in 1954.

After a lengthy hospitalization Kiyoshi's condition had not improved; the next step was surgical removal of one lung and some chest muscles. Kiyoko was there for the first surgery and for a second surgery to fix the first—and for a long succession of hospitalizations thereafter. They married in 1957.

As a consequence of the first surgery his remaining lung had to be irrigated daily for the rest of his life, and he was unable to lift one of his arms above heart level. Still under treatment for tuberculosis in 1967, he suffered profound hearing loss as a result of the medication, streptomycin, he was being given. In hopes of regaining his hearing he decided to enter a hospital in Japan for treatment unavailable in the United States. This was the reason he and Kiyoko were separated for five months in 1967. Kiyoshi at this point is totally deaf; he speaks, but others communicate by writing notes to him.

KIYOSHI'S GRAMMAR SCHOOL CLASS, *Takakise, Japan, c. 1935.*
Kiyoshi is third from left in the top row. Photo courtesy of Yukiko Tokutomi Northon.

TOP ROW, FROM LEFT: *Saidokoro, Tsukanaga, Tokutomi, Matsumoto,*
Yamamoto, Ōishi, Mitsuno, Fukushima, Arima, Shimomura, Okamoto;

NEXT ROW DOWN: *Moriyama, Yoshida, Takeda, Nakajima, Ishigaki,*
Ōtomi, Koga, Yokoyama, Katae, Narusawa, Fujikawa;

MIDDLE ROW: *Noguchi, Seki, Hara, Tateishi, Ishimaru,*
Yamauchi, Nishizuka, Ide, Terasaki, Ashiya, (name illegible);

SECOND ROW: *Nakajima, Funatsu, Tsunetomi, Hirai, Morokuma,*
Koga, Takashima, Miyazaki, Koga, Inoue;

SITTING IN FRONT: *Nishimura, Tanaka, Nakayama, Koga, Nakamura,*
Murata, Kaniyama, Itō, Fukui. ABSENT: *Shiroshima, Tagami.*
The teacher's name is not known.

On the back of this photo is a date, "Feb. 7, 1940," and a paragraph of explanation in Japanese:
"WHEN KIYOSHI WAS IN THE SIXTH GRADE *of Takakise Elementary School,*
their gymnastic class took first place in the competition held by all schools in Saga Prefecture.
The report of the event was made public [in the OSAKA MAINICHI *newspaper] and Takakise*
School received a huge championship cup from the Minister of Education. The photo of Kiyoshi
diving became a postcard. It appears that one of the copies was sent to Mother [in the U.S.]
and many duplicates were made from it. Unfortunately the original photo is lost."
Photo courtesy of Yukiko Tokutomi Northon.

KIYOSHI'S MOTHER, SADA TOKUTOMI *(right),* AND SISTER, MITSUYE TOKUTOMI, *in San Jose, California, 1939. Mitsuye recalls that after graduating from high school in Japan she returned to the United States in November 1939. Her mother bought her a new dress and they had this photo taken in December. She then dated it on the back—December 20, 1939— and sent it to Kiyoshi, who was still in high school in Japan.*
Photo courtesy of Yukiko Tokutomi Northon.

KIYOSHI WROTE A CHINESE PROVERB *and a prayer for his mother and siblings on the back of the photo, probably in 1942; he and his mother had been separated in 1931 after his father's death:*

"Mother, Sister … don't worry! 'Little swallows and sparrows cannot comprehend the intention of a big bird.' It's been so long since Mother and I were separated—at least 10 years. I wonder how she is doing now. I grew up without knowing her love or the love of my father who was gone forever before I got to know him—I felt so sad, so miserable, all these years. But I am going to be strong, live strong, praying for the good health of Mother, Sister and Brother—divine power in Heaven, let them know of my determination!"

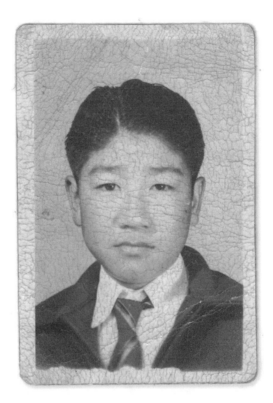

YOSHIMITSU TOKUTOMI, *Kiyoshi's younger brother, in San Jose, California, March 11, 1941. Yoshimitsu had returned to the United States in October or November 1939 after graduating from eighth grade in Japan. The back of the photo is inscribed: "Year 2601 [the emperor's year for 1942], March 11, Received Tokutomi, Yoshimitsu," and "Brother, Do not worry!" Photo courtesy of Yukiko Tokutomi Northon.*

A DINNER HONORING KIYOSHI
AT THE TOKUNAGA HOME *before
his departure to the United States
in 1951. From left: Mr. Tokunaga's
mother; a man whose name is not
known; the mayor of Nabeshima;
Kiyoshi; Mr. Tokunaga's father;
Mr. Tokunaga with young daughter;
Mrs. Tokunaga with their son.
Kiyoshi lived with the Tokunaga
family when he was teaching.
Photo courtesy of Yukiko
Tokutomi Northon.*

KIYOKO SHORTLY AFTER HER ARRIVAL *in the United States, c. 1955.*
Original photo in the Haiku Archive of the California State Library, photographed
in turn by June Hopper Hymas.

KIYOSHI WITH DAUGHTER YUKIKO, 1958.
Photo courtesy of Yukiko Tokutomi Northon.

THE TOKUTOMI RESIDENCE *at 490 Fifth Street, Japantown, San Jose, California, c. 1965. Photo courtesy of Yukiko Tokutomi Northon.*

The Letters

MRS KIYOKO TOKUTOMI

490 N 5TH ST.

SAN JOSE, CALIF 9...

U. S. A.

つぎに ここを おる　　　　　Second fold here

差出人住所氏名
Sender's name and address　K. TOKUTOMI

CHUO-5-BYOTO , KYUDAI RYOTO

July

..

[*Month* of the *Sizzling Cicadas*]

From KIYOKO, *Sunday, July 16, 1967.*

IT IS ABOUT 3:00 P.M. ON Monday in Japan. . . .

I hope you had a good trip. Although I was glad that the nine crew members of Japan Airlines were with you, still I worried that because you are so modest and reserved, you might suffer in pain alone without telling anybody. The long walk to Customs in Haneda must have been difficult. I am anxiously waiting to hear from you.

On the 15th I was watching the passengers boarding the plane. I could see the crew waving their hands, but I wasn't sure if you were near them. Someone was waving a hand from the door in the center. The plane you boarded was called *Asama* and the crew, including the captain, looked to be all Japanese. Since the plane was parked at a right angle to the window where we were watching, with the nose of the plane pointing at us, we could see the cockpit clearly. The captain opened the window and waved his hand to Yukiko. We wanted to shout, if we could, "Daddy is in your plane!" The departure time was 9:30 a.m., but it was finally in the air at 9:45 a.m. After watching the plane taxiing the runways, we went down to the lower level together with Tsukiji-san and others. The plane took off when I was walking by myself to the parking lot. I went to work for about five hours, then went to Yukiko's *bon-odori* and took a few photos. I will mail them to you later. . . .

How warm is it there—is it more than you thought? Brace yourself, and try to eat nourishing food to fight against the heat. Noodles won't help you. Tomorrow I'll start collecting what you need in a box and will mail it within a week. Send me a list of what you want.

Although I would like to keep writing, I'll have Yukiko use the space left. Don't strain yourself—take care of yourself, please!

Daddy, was it fun to ride in the airplane? Yukiko is lonely, Daddy. Maybe I can't go swimming without Daddy. Daddy, I'm waiting for you to get well and come home, Daddy. —YUKIKO

From KIYOSHI, *July 17, 1967.*

ARRIVED SAFELY IN Fukuoka. Watanabe-sensei and Mrs. Watanabe helped me so much.

The people of JAL took good care of me. Matsumura-san and Kōno-san stayed till the plane took off from Tokyo. JAL assigned a special person to assist me at the entry point and at Customs. I can't say enough to express my gratitude. Please call Mr. Tsuge, Mr. Yanase, and Mr. Kasuya of the San Francisco office and thank them for their help.

As you warned me, it is hot here! It was the end of the rainy season and the hottest day was when I arrived in Tokyo. Thanks to Watanabe-sensei, I'm staying in the air-conditioned Nikkatsu Hotel (2,800 yen a night—about $8?). I'll be here until a room becomes available at the hospital. It will cost around 2,000 yen ($5.50) and it is air-conditioned. Watanabe-sensei and his wife did everything for me, including shopping. I'm grateful for their help.

I am expected to stay in the hospital for a long time so the hospital wants to be paid every week or every 10 days. (I cannot stay in the hospital for two or three months without payment.) They suggest that you get payments from the insurance company in exchange for the receipts from the hospital. Please ask the insurance company if this works, and let me know as soon as possible.

Watanabe-sensei is going to take me to the hospital today. I'm writing this since I woke up early. I bought Chanel No. 5 in Honolulu and gave it to Mrs. Watanabe as a gift from you. She was very happy and wants me to tell you how grateful she is. Chanel No. 5 costs $15 without tax. Sensei and his wife are grateful for the jewelry from my sister and her husband—please tell them.

I am leaving for the hospital soon. I'll write again. Tell Mother that I will write her after the visit to the hospital. Remember me to Yukiko and Hisayo-san.

P.S. Sensei is very happy with the electric razor that you gave him.

From KIYOSHI, *July 18.*

I WROTE TO YOU THIS MORNING. I'm writing again, this time from the hospital—I registered as an in-patient today.

I came to the hospital with Watanabe-sensei to see Dr. Harada, the head of the staff as well as the section of Ear and Nose Treatment. Dr. Harada himself gave me a checkup and made an audiogram; then he took me to a professor (the authority in Ear and Nose Treatment and a specialist in the hard of hearing), who examined me. Watanabe-sensei presented his card, and there was an instant recognition of each other as graduates of Kyushu University. This professor immediately decided to check me in to the hospital. So here I am in my hospital room.

I am here as a private patient so that the best medicine will be administered freely. Japanese insurance does not cover advanced medicine. But I will be treated differently. Earlier I wrote about the cost of hospitalization, but there will be some changes. The hospital cost will be a little over 3,000 yen (about $9.00) with air-conditioning and meals, and each treatment will cost between $7.00 and $9.00. This means that the cost is back to the estimate that Watanabe-sensei was telling me. The treatment will last for three months. My physician-in-charge [was] one of the students of Watanabe-sensei at the University of Kyushu. Being the head of the staff, Dr. Harada is extremely busy so that he cannot take charge of my treatment, but he will supervise everything; and Watanabe-sensei's former student, Dr. Yasuda, will be my physician-in-charge and will see me every day. I had a preliminary examination by him today. The treatment will start tomorrow.

Watanabe-sensei took charge of distributing the gifts that I brought. Johnny Walker and a Gillette shaving set went to Dr. Harada; a Parker fountain pen was given together with the razor to Dr. Yasuda, who will be the closest physician to me from now on. He was very pleased. The Napoleon Cognac will be given to the head of the professors later. (I gave Watanabe-sensei a Napoleon which is much better than Johnny Walker.) I left it with Watanabe-sensei. He took care of me from 8:30 a.m. to five p.m. today. I don't know how to thank him enough. Please write him and Mrs. Watanabe and thank them. Sensei's mother is over 90 years old and lives in Hokkaido. She is not going to last long. Sensei postponed a visit on account of me and will fly to Hokkaido as soon as I settle down. He did so much for me—I must show my gratitude somehow. He will be here tomorrow to confer with Dr. Yasuda about me and fly to Hokkaido after that.

I'll write again. Take care and give my love to Yukiko.

P.S. The hospital is a newly built annex. I'm in a private room with a sofa. I think this is close to a first-class room in American hospitals—very spacious and with a bathroom. But the bed is not electrical like most American hospital beds are. It goes into the wall when it is not used. It is not necessary to hang a mosquito net or spread it over the mattress. There are no mosquitoes here.

From KIYOSHI, *July 19.*

... MY TREATMENT STARTED TODAY. Last night I was given an injection of vitamin B_1 (50 mg), ATP (20 mg), and dextrose (20 mg), all in one. This noon I started to take multiple vitamins and a hormone pill. I started on the inhalation of carbonic acid gas around five o'clock this evening. It lasted for about five minutes, but the duration of inhalation will increase gradually. I will be on this treatment for 10 days. The doctor said that my symptom could have been prevented or cured if I had taken a large quantity of vitamin B_1 right at the beginning of this hearing problem. I didn't know that!

Kyushu University is the most advanced in the world regarding cases of hearing difficulties. Watanabe-sensei was really happy to hear that. Inhalation of carbonic acid gas stimulates the blood circulation in the brain which is closely connected to [circulation in the] ears. ATP is also to stimulate blood circulation. If I don't show any improvement in 10 days, I will be given another treatment. They will use advanced medicine since I can pay for it. I am so grateful for your help and Mother's. Watanabe-sensei came back today and talked with Dr. Yasuda about my case. ... Dr. Yasuda has a thick beard. Please send five Gillette shaving kits with the razors on a belt. Also could you get refills for the Parker pen?

It is very hot here. The air-conditioning in the room is not fully working, but it's better than nothing. I am eating well and drinking six bottles of milk a day. I didn't know this, but Watanabe-sensei signed as my guarantor—I don't know how to thank him. The money is kept in a safe in the hospital.

Remember me to Hisayo-san. I'll write to Hiroyuki-san some day. Take care!

From KIYOKO, *July 21.*

HOW ARE YOU? ON THE 17TH I wrote a thank-you note to Prof. and Mrs. Watanabe and mailed it together with the one to you. I'll bet Yukiko's letter hit you at home in your heart. She started to write about herself and ended the letter the way she did since I said, "We've got to cheer him up." She went swimming on Monday with Melanie and her dad. [Yukiko] stayed home from summer school since yesterday due to a stomachache. She was home alone resting. I called her from work about 11:30. She wanted to see her grandmother. She did lock the house as I told her to do. She has grown quite a bit compared to those days when she walked around carrying a blanket and called Lily on the phone because she was lonely.

I phoned Takeda-san at CYS last night after work. I said, "English may be hard, but there shouldn't be any problem with Japanese." He was happy to hear that. The estimate by the printing office of North America was $40, and $37 with tax by C.B. Printing. There is not much difference in pricing so I've decided to use C.B. Printing because it is closer. Since CYS hopes to have it done for $25, let's donate the $12 difference.

I still have to write a thank-you note to the staff of Japan Airlines, and to Hiroyuki, and send a package to you. I can finish these things by this Saturday the 22nd. I'll write to the staff after reading your letter which should come in a couple of days. The San Jose column in the newspaper is now empty. I should write something, but I have other urgent things to do first.

Yesterday's paper reported that on the 16th severe heat waves hit everywhere in Japan except the northeast region. I'm worried about you. Now it is 15 minutes after one. I'll write more from home.

· · ·

I was hoping that a letter from you would be waiting for me, but it didn't come today. I'm very anxiously awaiting your letter, so much so that my neck seems to be getting longer and longer. Yukiko is better now and can eat regular food. I got candies to add to the package. I chose a kind that had many individually-wrapped pieces in a bag so that you can give some to people who help you.

About changing the dressing of your incision—we were so busy before your departure that I had no time to talk to you about it. If you are not in the hospital, why don't you go to a clinic in the neighborhood or to the surgery department of Kyushu University? I'm afraid that the rubber might become slack due to the excessive heat. Besides, it's difficult to remove the safety pin by yourself. It's better to spend some money to be safe—if it becomes festered, it will affect your physical strength, so please think about it. Tell me what you need aside from the bags that I'm going to mail. . . .

We went shopping today for cashews to add to your package. Yukiko picked peanuts labeled French something saying, "Daddy likes these." Please enjoy them.

I hope your letter comes today. I'm anxious to know how you are doing. If nothing comes by this weekend, I'm going to phone you. Today is the 20th, Thursday. I started this letter on the 19th. You compliment my handwriting, but I'm afraid this one may be hard to read.

From KIYOSHI, *July 21.*

HOW ARE YOU, KIYOKO-SAN? How are Yukiko and Hisayo-san? Does Yukiko go to the pool by herself? I am doing all right. It's very hot here. You go one step outside the room and you perspire instantly. The room is supposed to be air-conditioned, but it's not working well. I have to use a fan. But compared to the hallway, it's much better. As you step out of the door, you are immediately attacked by steamy hot air.

I've spent three nights here—today is the fourth day. I've had the inhalation of carbonic acid twice so far. I haven't had it yet today. I went through different tests all day yesterday—tests on balancing, dizziness, direction, putting water in my ears and rotating my eyeballs, reaction to sounds, etc. Compared to this, the test at Stanford was nothing!

Maybe I'm imagining it, but I feel that the ringing in my ears is reduced. I hope the ringing keeps disappearing. I'm concentrating all my energy on the treatment. I'm alone in a large room (more than twice as big as the room in our county hospital) and stay here quietly. No one comes to visit me, and I like it. Watanabe-sensei agrees with me.

I was going to pay Watanabe-sensei for the purchase of slippers and hangers, but he turned it down, saying, "You should not worry about anything." I feel bad because he spent a lot on taxis, too. The other day I told him that I can't ask him to get anything if he doesn't take some money, and I gave him 10,000 yen. I told him that I'll have a nurse call him when I need something. He insists that the bedside clock is his gift to me.

Yesterday Matsumura-san came with a gift (it's heavy—maybe it's some sweet bean cakes). He has done so much for me already. He said he will come see me again before going back to Sendai. He really has a tender heart.

Please send me cotton balls, gauze, and plastic bags as quickly as possible. Because I'm hard of hearing, I depend on the nurses' help very much. There are eight nurses here. I would like to give one Camay and one Dove to each nurse. Could you send me 10 of each brand? I'm scheduled to stay here for three months—I would like to treat them well. Also please send two or three pajamas.

I'm sorry to ask you for so much when you are busy in the office as well as at home. But I think these will take care of me for a while. Give my love to Yukiko and Hisayo-san. Do take care of yourself, Kiyoko-san.

From KIYOKO, *July 22.*

YOUR FIRST LETTER ARRIVED THIS Friday. I hoped I would get another one today, the 22nd, and it came. It seems this is the first time that you went into the hospital with a happy feeling surrounded by well-wishers and good opportunities. Don't you think so? At times we thought that luck was not on our side. But I've never felt this happy, noticing that you stand on the brighter, warmer side of life and feel blessed in spite of being hospitalized. Because of Watanabe-sensei, you have been given this good opportunity and are happily receiving treatment—I've never felt this blessed—although we are separated, I feel more content than the times when I would visit you every other day in the hospital and get to talk with you every night. Can you understand? Let's make the best of this regardless of the result.

By the way, before I forget, I'd like to give you some advice. You were so happy that you wrote 主侍医, which means the Emperor's chief physician. The Imperial Household Agency may not like it! It may be safer to call your doctor 主治医 (physician-in-charge). It would be funny if you use 主侍医 in any letters to others. I recommend sincerely that you give up the duties of the Emperor immediately and become a commoner!

Also, you are mixing up Japan and America completely. For example, you wrote, "It's been four days since I left Japan . . ." and "I feel better than those days when I was in Japan. . . ." If you speak this way to other people, they won't understand you. Maybe I worry too much, but when you can't hear your own voice, you don't understand what you are saying. I'm telling you this now so that you'll be careful not to get mixed up in your conversation.

I couldn't help but smile at the image of you stretched comfortably on the sofa in that first-class hospital room. I laughed imagining you laboriously turning the handle of the manually adjustable bed.

Today is Sunday, the weekend of the Summer Festival. After Lily danced in the festival on Saturday, Yukiko went with her and stayed over one night. We went to Sunnyvale to pick her up. They showed us Henry's photos of his vacation in Tokyo. He has long hair like you and looks handsome like you. I'm going to ask for a copy and send it to you. Also I'll send you a list of addresses. Probably you should write to Henry by air mail because his address is listed in the States.

Yesterday morning (Saturday) I mailed a package. In it you'll find two waterproof pads, one large and one small. You might pin the small one to the sheet or to the larger one with its smooth side down using safety pins on all four corners. After using it let me know what you think—I bought two boxes.

I'll send you a regular, sealed letter again. A letter to Hiroyuki was sent in care of the Fukuoka Storage *[where Kiyoko's brother Hiroyuki was employed]*. The package was sent to Watanabe-sensei's address. Can you call him on the phone? Have Hiroyuki carry the package from Sensei's house to the hospital.

From KIYOSHI, *July 22.*

HOW ARE YOU, KIYOKO-SAN? It is Saturday, my fifth day in the hospital and the fourth day of treatment. Yesterday the density of the carbonic acid gas was raised higher, and starting today I inhale the gas twice a day. Also I get an intravenous injection every day. The heavy noise in my ears seems to have decreased. Dr. Yasuda didn't say anything much when I told him about it the day before yesterday. He asked me about it yesterday; I said, "Not much change because I was exhausted after going through so many examinations." But I rested all day yesterday so that I could tell him that the ringing was reduced. Then he told me that it was a good sign of recovery; I was surprised as well as pleased. Although that stormy sound in my ears is gone, the steady noise is still there. I tell myself that it is too soon to celebrate.

Kiyoko-san, you took care of me so well and gave me strength. I don't know how to thank you. As my wife you poured your devotion over me, loved me, took care of me tenderly—sometimes at night tears run over the brim of my eyes just to think of it. Can I ever take care of you as you take care of me, from the depth of my heart, with a tender touch, with love, like you do to me? I know I can't match your compassion, your tender care—but if our situation were reversed (I pray it won't happen), I am going to try very hard to take care of you as you have done for me. When we are apart like now, I feel your devotion so strongly that I realize how lucky I am.

How is Yukiko? Is she still swimming? Tell her that Daddy said she should get two A's. Are you still working Saturdays? Please don't work too much. . . .

The air-cooler helps a great deal. I'm amazed that I stay in one room from morning to night doing nothing. I'm lonely because you are not here—but once I say to myself that this is the way it should be, it is easier to bear. This reminds me of the two years that we had to live apart. I try not to waste energy as much as possible.

I'll stop writing now. Take good care of yourself. I'll be happy if you write me when you have time. I'll be waiting. Please remember me to Yukiko and Hisayo-san.

From KIYOSHI, *July 23.*

HOW ARE YOU, KIYOKO-SAN? Is Yukiko all right? . . . This is Sunday and Dr. Yasuda is off. Another doctor is on duty. I had the inhalation of carbonic acid gas only once today. There is no improvement in my hearing. I'm telling myself to be patient.

I had a talk with Dr. Yasuda yesterday after I wrote to you. He explained that the inhalation of carbonic acid gas is to stimulate the circulation of blood in the brain; the blood vessels in the brain are closely connected to the ears. I told Dr. Yasuda that I had a prescription of a similar kind, but I didn't finish taking it. He said if I still have it, he would like to see it. It is kept in between cellophane covers. He sounded as though he would add it to the carbonic acid gas inhalation if it is good. Could you ask Dr. Childrey to write the prescription again, and you send it to me by air mail along with the leftover pills? Also send the one that is in a glass container. I think I left that on the dresser by my bed. It was good for the inner ear. Dr. Yasuda wants to check everything that I used to take, and if it is good, add them to the present treatment. I remember the line on the label saying that it was to stimulate blood circulation. Please ask Dr. Childrey for the prescriptions of these two medicines and send me one or two months supply. Those were trial pills. They were supposed to be good and new. Dr. Yasuda can check it out.

Matsumura-san and Miyazaki-san came to see me today. They are going to leave for Sendai soon. Matsumura-san gave me some cakes and grapes; Miyazaki-san brought me a magazine and a book of cartoons. I owe so much to the employees of JAL for their boundless attention. The other day Matsumura-san brought half a dozen bottles of soft drinks.

I intend to write to Hiroyuki-san. . . . I think he is on a business trip for a month and will be home in a week.

Take good care of yourself, Kiyoko-san. I have not written to Cecilia and her husband yet. Say hello to them for me. I wrote only to Tsukiji-san for now because I try not to become too tired. Starting tomorrow I may write one thank-you note every day. I'll write to you again—I'm getting lonely. Please write to me when you have time. I'll be waiting.

From KIYOKO, *July 24.*

. . . THIS MORNING I SENT A LETTER to the hospital for the first time. I wrote a short note on the 17th, and the next day I wrote about CYS and the pins. But it reached you late because it was in care of Watanabe-sensei. I received a phone call from the hospital, but please do not worry over a simple matter like this—I am trying my best, believe me. I thanked the nurse who made the call for you. But I wished I could have heard your voice—next time can't you talk on the line so that I can hear you, and let the nurse receive my answer for you? That nurse was so tense from having to relay your message over the international line—poor girl! I felt she was shaking just as I was once—but don't tell her this.

Today I received the second and the third letter that you wrote after checking in to the hospital. I've made a shopping list and have just come home with new pajamas for you. I'll finish the shopping and send a package by the end of this week. I'm thinking of asking a favor of Kasuya-san and send it by JAL.

I received a very courteous letter today from Watanabe-sensei. He writes, "We decided to introduce Tokutomi-san to the staff of Kyushu University . . . because of his magnetism and his reliable personality." I have told this in detail to your mother. She was very moved by such nice comments given by Sensei who himself is a fine gentleman. . . .

As I mentioned in my air letter that I mailed this morning, the package sent on the 22nd weighs about 22 pounds. It is so heavy that I hate to ask Watanabe-sensei to deliver it to the hospital. I think it is better to have Hiroyuki deliver it to you. . . . Please let him know about this by phone.

Enclosed is a money order for you from Satō-san, a member of the church and your mother's friend. She is the lady who speaks very politely—remember her? She also gave us *botamochi,* and we ate it. . . . I accepted her gift because she was so thoughtful to prepare a money order that you can use—this gift was so different from just a box of chocolates.

I also enclose a copy of a photo. You can show it to the people in the hospital. Yukiko is behaving very well. After you left, I bought a record of *The Sound of Music* which she has wanted for so long. She now can sing it just like the original on the record. I hesitate to talk to you about sound, but please bear with me. Yukiko's singing thrills me with joy. You may get better and hear her sing someday—but if not, her voice must still be in your head. She read 90% of your letter by herself—isn't she great? I can't guarantee an immediate reply from her because writing is harder than reading.* There will be a Japanese folk dance performance starting this Monday in San Francisco. I suggested to Hisayo that we should all go see it, taking Mother also. They say the performance includes *Nagamochi-uta* from Saga Prefecture.

I'm afraid it will be difficult for me to write every day. I have one correspondence still left to send to JAL in Sendai. I've written to Hiroyuki. I wrote a quick note to Watanabe-sensei once and sent it together with my first letter to you. I will take more time and write a courteous letter to Sensei although he said he didn't expect a reply. I'll send it before he comes back from Hokkaido on August sixth.

Hirose-san called last Saturday and offered us his help. Hisayo took that call. I gave him your address at the hospital. When I buy the tickets for the folk dance, I'll call him and see if he wants to join us.

I was so busy in the office because my partner was on sick leave, and I forgot to go to the insurance company. From now on, I must write down things to do on a special memo card to remind myself. . . .

*Yukiko has started taking Japanese lessons and writes to Kiyoshi in Japanese.

From KIYOSHI, *July 25.*

. . . YOUR FIRST LETTER HAS BEEN forwarded to me. I'm back to life now! Every day I waited for this. Like in the song of the blue-eyed doll that was imported to Japan from America, I felt tears welling up in my eyes. I was so anxious for your letter. It was like those days 13 or 14 years ago when I was waiting for your letter. I felt my heart beating fast when the nurse handed your letter to me. I read it many times. Thank you so much, Kiyoko-san. This is like the days when we were young and in love.

It is the eighth day since I checked in to this hospital and seventh day of the treatment. The ringing in my ears has reduced quite a bit, and the stiffness around my neck and head is gone, but the difficulty of hearing has not changed. The doctor said that the disappearance of ringing in the ears is a sign of improvement in my hearing. That gave me new hope. I have no visitors and am very lonely, but I can rest well—besides, the ringing in my ears starts when I talk. I am lonely. I think of you and how lucky I am to be loved by you. I want to be a good husband to you.

I had x-rays yesterday. They give so many tests at Kyushu University Hospital, so many that I am exhausted. They took several x-rays of my chest and throat and jaws. Dr. Takahashi, who is in charge of x-rays, is another friend of Watanabe-sensei. They were together at the University of Michigan at the invitation of the Ford Foundation. Before he left for Hokkaido, Watanabe-sensei must have talked to Dr. Takahashi about me, and I was treated very nicely. He looks like Kawasaki-san who leads the choir of the Japanese Language Association—maybe he is a little bit more intellectual, but very polite. I gave him a razor. I still have a Gillette razor, which I'm going to give to Hiroyuki-san, and an old-fashioned razor which will be given to his girlfriend's father. I have the perfume for his girlfriend.

You worried about how I traveled from Tokyo to Fukuoka. It was very smooth, thanks to the many people who helped me. To get to Customs in Tokyo, I was able to get on a bus right from the plane. It was so easy. On the airplane I was given a special seat at the front so that I couldn't even wave at you.

Please send me the family photos. I don't know why I forgot to bring some photos of you and Yukiko. If I had them here, my loneliness may have been slightly less. I'm waiting for them anxiously.

I asked you to do so many things today. I think I have everything now, but I'm concerned very much about the printing for CYS. I might ask the nurse to help me make a phone call. Take care. I'll write to you again.

From KIYOKO, *July 25.*

THE LETTER YOU WROTE LAST Saturday, July 22, arrived today. I hope that by now you've received a couple of my letters. I am disappointed and so sorry because you had not received anything from me before Saturday. It takes longer for letters from here to Japan, doesn't it? There should be two letters to you in care of Prof. Watanabe.

Let me take care of the things to be done first—before I forget them. I asked the insurance company about the payments. They said that in cases of long term hospitalization, they pay each month upon receipt of a monthly payment request. I was advised to make copies of the blank form and use it to send the monthly request for payment, saving the original form to use at the time of your release from the hospital. Please ask Kyushu University Hospital if you can pay them monthly. They (the insurance company) say you can wire it, but I think sending it air mail is just fine. Or maybe you can use express mail. This is because the request for payment should be in their office within seven days. Perhaps, as we discussed before, we should fill in the date here—I'll talk to the agent.

Last night and tonight I finished shopping for things that you asked for: three pajamas (it was hard to find nice ones); five large packs of shaving blades; ink cartridges, black and blue, five each; two kinds of soap, 10 each. I'll add something you like because there is extra space in the carton.

Aren't you getting lonely being alone in that large room? Ask someone to get you some weekly magazines and *Bungei-shunjū*. How about subscribing to a newspaper also? I'm thinking of mailing you the *Hōji-shinbun*. Three months is a long time, yet it's short. By the time the sea mailing reaches you, one third of your stay will be gone. To people like Iwama-san and some others, it may be better to send postcards instead of writing long letters. It would be nicer than a letter if you affix interesting stamps.

Your daily letter is the favorite topic at our dinner table, and it makes your mother very happy. The fact that the ringing in your ears has decreased is a sign of hearing recovery. Please make up your mind to be grateful for each little improvement. In the next letter please tell me how you are treating your incision. I'll send you cotton balls and bags. Do you need paper bags too? I can guess about other things, but I'd like to know about the incision since you have not mentioned it. Impairment of your hearing certainly has been a blow to your spirit, but any physical damage affects your body. Do not put the cart before the horse. Before your departure you were more concerned about your hearing problem than your general health. Now your hearing is getting better—but if you don't take care of your body, you might lose everything. Enough lecturing for now! If you would like to have something to read from the States, please let me know.

I work every Saturday these days. Since you are not home, it's a good diversion for me. I'm used to this work, and it's better than adding a new job. Besides, the boss leaves everything to me and doesn't even show up. Fortunately Yukiko is a good helper around the house. She charges 50 cents for washing rice and turning on the switch on the cooker. This coming Sunday she plans to go on the annual excursion to the beach with Glen and his brothers. This weekend I'm going to put a reminder in the newspaper about the CYS Movie Night—I don't know which Sunday yet.

Please take it easy and be hopeful.

From KIYOSHI, *July 27.*

. . . YESTERDAY I HAD THE FIRST TEST after starting the treatment. It showed a slight improvement. The far left in the right ear went from from 55 to 50. The doctor was pleased too. I hoped this sign of improvement would stay. However, I couldn't sleep well the past few days because it was so hot, and today the ringing in my ears has worsened. I couldn't hear the whistling sound that comes through my nose just before starting the inhalation of carbonic acid gas. I'm afraid my condition regressed in spite of the bright hope I had yesterday. Or maybe it is caused by the massage on the eardrum done by using a motor to blow air on it. Yesterday I could hear the sound of my urination—but not today. I'm sad. . . . I'm going to ask Dr. Yasuda tonight because I'm scheduled to have another inhalation of carbonic acid gas. I'm sorry I cannot write the cheerful letter that I promised. I'm trying to be patient. I should be happy because yesterday's test showed some improvement on the eighth treatment. I'm waiting for your encouraging letter to arrive. You don't have to write a whole page—a half page will do. Please write to me.

· · ·

I took a nap for two hours in the morning and another two hours in the afternoon in an air-conditioned room. The ringing in my ears seemed to be reduced. I dreamed that Yukiko came back from summer school and quietly crawled up to my bed and slept by my side. And I let her go out to buy some fried noodles. It was a funny dream.

You must be busy. Yukiko is still too young to help you. Please don't get sick from overwork. You might get sick from cleaning the house from corner to corner, but you can't get sick from leaving the rooms untidy. I hope you rest as much as you can on Saturdays and Sundays. But this may not be possible.

Writing to you makes my mind peaceful. I'm full of tender love for you. Nobody can replace Kiyoko-san in my life. I am so lucky to be able to love you as my wife.

I'll write again. Please write to me when you can. I'm waiting for your letter more than anything else.

Say hello to Yukiko and Hisayo-san.

From KIYOKO, *July 27.*

TODAY I RECEIVED YOUR LETTER which says that your treatment started five days ago. I'm so sorry that you did not receive any letter from me till Sunday. I hoped to read in today's letter that you already had read some of mine. A letter from Nabeshima *[where Kiyoko's widowed mother was living with her oldest son and his wife]* arrived. Everybody there is in good health in spite of the heat. It would be so much better if their house had air conditioning. They are grateful to us for taking care of Hisayo for such a long time.

Also today I got a note from the repair shop telling that your hearing aid is ready to be picked up. I'll send it by air together with your ear medicine.

Yesterday I phoned Kasuya-san and Yanase-san at Japan Airlines. They said that the head of the branch, Mr. Tsuge, was not in, but the letter had arrived, and they would remind him of it themselves. I just said "Please." I didn't feel it appropriate to ask them to transport the packages so I didn't mention it.

I'm a little bit tired because it's been very warm since yesterday, and we had a baby shower for Yūko-san at lunch time. Everybody liked the cake from Aki Bakery. I brought home a piece for Yukiko.

After reading your letter, I checked the top of the dresser for the medicines and found both of them there. It would be better if you had prescriptions so I'll get them and mail them with the medicines. What else can I do for you? Please tell me freely. You know, of course, that I am the only one who is authorized to do things for you. Presently we are separated because you are being taken care of by the doctors in Japan. But anything else is left in my care. Please consider that we are going through this treatment together.

The other day I ran into Ozawa-san of Shūeidō. He sent his best wishes to you. His teenage son was in a terrible accident while driving a jeep in a mountainous area. He was pinned down under the chassis and got injured badly. I expressed our sympathy and a prayer for his quick recovery. . . .

Yukiko is taking a bath while I finish this letter. She wants to go somewhere in the car. So I promised her we'd go to the post office together— I'm too tired to go anywhere else. Tomorrow evening we'll go to a Japanese dance show. Lily and your sister will go with us. Lily has begun to show an interest in Japan so I suggested that she come along. The performers are leading dancers in Japan, and Mother is looking forward to the evening. Mitsuko-san doesn't want to go. She is not interested because she has seen Japanese dancing enough on television.

Maybe tomorrow I'll get a letter from you in response to mine. It's amazing that I can feel it. Something tells me whether your letter is on its way or not. And I become excited—and indeed your letter is waiting. But when I feel empty, there is no letter from you. Your letter is like a conduit that sends something to me. . . .

From KIYOSHI, *July 28.*

. . . NO CHANGE HERE. I'M LONELY but trying to take it as medicine to become well. I think it is good to be alone sometimes. I can reflect upon my past and try to correct it. Being so far away from you, I can see everything clearly and favorably so that I become filled with gratitude and yearning for you. I become grateful also to my mother and sister. I realize that I am a lucky guy.

It is July 28th, the 11th day of hospitalization and the 10th day of the treatment. Yesterday they started to give me an injection of a new medicine to stimulate breathing. Maybe because of it, the ringing in my ears decreased so much. I was surprised. Even now the ringing stays much less if I stay still. It comes back when I walk to the dining room or to the treatment room. This new medicine チトマック (*chitomakku*) is very expensive. I'm grateful for their effort to try everything. A few days ago, I had tests on the phlegm and the fluid from my chest. The result showed no tuberculosis bacteria in them. But a different bacterium was found so that a new injection to the chest was started today. They are thorough; they do everything; there is no comparison to our county hospital. A serious case cannot be treated in American hospitals and by their doctors. If you have a serious case, you'd better come to the Japanese university hospitals for treatment. First of all, the doctors' stance in research and treatment is different: they are more serious and scholastic. I'm so grateful to Kiyoko-san and Mother who suggested I come to Japan—particularly Kiyoko-san who seriously backed me up.

I am relieved to hear that TB bacteria were not found in my lung. I wasn't sure, to tell you the truth. It was such good news. I'm so grateful to Dr. Yasuda who is treating my chest also. Please send me some plastic bags as soon as possible. I have about 34 bags left, and I will need more if I stay here three to four months. I'm sorry I have to ask you to do so many things. If my hearing and lung can be healed at the same time, it would be a miracle —it's asking too much—but at least it gives me some hope! I think this is happening because of your devotion. Please take good care of yourself. Remember me to Yukiko and Hisayo-san.

From KIYOKO, *July 29.*

THIS IS SATURDAY. I RECEIVED YOUR letter saying that my letters finally reached you. Only yesterday I phoned my company's mailroom to question if they were neglecting the employees' mailboxes. They said, "Please be patient—soon you'll hear from him. We go to the post office four times a day and take care of the employees' boxes too." After that I felt a little more relieved.

Yesterday, July 28, I went to the county hospital. Since we had made an appointment for x-rays, I had no problem seeing Dr. Rowan and recording the information on their chart that you are temporarily at Kyushu University Hospital for hearing treatment. They gave me medicine but insisted that I should get the bags from the hospital in Japan. I went to the supply store in the hospital. They told me that we have to get that kind of bag directly from the distributor. So, if you can't get it in your hospital, we must write to the distributor printed on the box. Please make a note of the distributor's name and address right away, just in case. The doctor asked, "Was his hearing so bad?" The nurses were happy that you've gone for special treatment in Japan.

I couldn't reach your ear doctor because he is on vacation. So I'm going to send you some samples. The post office tells me that there is no restriction except on narcotics. The doctor will be back on Monday, the 31st, and I'll get the prescription from him then.

I finished packing the carton today. I put in four pairs of pajamas, including the ones you were wearing at home, and cotton balls—also, soap, razor blades, ink cartridges, a set of playing cards (I hope you haven't bought any yet), and the medicine I picked up from the doctor's. As we talked earlier, you can give PAS to the Japanese—it alone costs about $50. The man who put the stamps on was surprised at the $100 total for medicine. If you can think of someone to give the medicine to, I'll send two more bottles, dated April and May of this year. Maybe nowadays there are excellent medicines in Japan—we tend to think of Japan still as it was 10 years ago, unfortunately. . . .

What is the result of your comprehensive examination? Dr. Rowan said that perhaps the lung should be checked also. I told him that we are planning to do so. . . .

How are you taking care of your laundry? Does a laundry man come to the hospital? Pajamas or underwear may not be a problem, but shirts should be washed at a specific temperature for the fiber (shown on the collar). If the instructions are not followed correctly, the shirt will come out wrinkled up like a rag. You don't want to wear a shirt like that—please be careful.

Last night we went to San Francisco to see the Japanese dance. We were hungry for Chinese buns so we went to Chinatown. But the bun shop was closed. Because of that, we were 30 minutes late for the show. So stupid of us! We shouldn't have done that. We didn't have the sense of distance— from the corner of Geary St. and Powell we walked to Grant and turned left to Chinatown—it took half an hour. If we had driven, it would have been a cinch. I missed the leader who would tell us not to do such an unreasonable thing. It was Mother who suggested the buns and Sister who wanted to eat them (actually she wanted them for Lily), and it was I who miscalculated the distance. Both Yukiko and Lily enjoyed the dance very much, but for the grown-ups it was a mediocre performance.

From now on I can read your response to my letters. I am so relieved because we are finally connected. It takes two weeks to really communicate with each other, doesn't it?

From KIYOSHI, *July 29.*

KIYOKO-SAN, HOW ARE YOU? Hiroyuki-san made a surprise visit today. I was going to write a letter to him. I thought he was in Yokohama till next week. I was having the carbonic acid gas inhalation treatment, and Dr. Yasuda was here. He explained it to Hiroyuki-san.

I gave Hiroyuki-san the perfume you sent for his girlfriend. To him I gave the Gillette razor and a carton of Camels. We reminisced about the old days going back 15 years. We used pen and paper, but it was simply wonderful. I can see he's getting older—a big grown-up man now—and yet he hasn't changed much. We decided to go out tonight for a curry dinner. He went home, and I'm writing this to you.

This is going to be my first evening out, and Dr. Yasuda said, "Eat lots of curry, and get fat!" I'm always hungry—maybe because of the treatment for my lung. I nibble on salami all the time. Please send more salami in the next package. Hiroyuki-san said he will bring his girlfriend next time, maybe next Saturday or Sunday. Tonight, it will be only us.

I think my hearing is much better today. I could hear the sound of the air when the inhaler was placed on my nose. Today I heard the sound better than yesterday. I hope it will get better each time. I told Hiroyuki-san that I wanted to attend his wedding with my hearing back. I asked him to come and visit me once a week although he seemed to want to come more often. I don't want to become a burden to him, and I don't want to tire myself too much.

You take good care of yourself. I will stop here. Please tell Yukiko and Hisayo-san that I saw Hiroyuki-san. But maybe it's better not to tell Mother, and for that matter, maybe it would be better not to tell Yukiko either because she might tell Mother.

From KIYOSHI, *July 30 (morning).*

... LAST NIGHT HIROYUKI-SAN CAME back around seven o'clock, and we went out to have curry dinner. Curry rice was 120 yen—it tasted all right, but I was disappointed because there was not much meat in it. I guess that's why the price is so low—only 240 yen for two.

Walking around the town, we were still hungry. Then we saw a sign board saying, "Steak of beer-fed beef." We went in to check what it was. On the menu the most expensive steak was 1,500 yen ($4.00) so we ordered two to celebrate the occasion. It was a two-inch-thick filet mignon, but it didn't taste like it was worth $4.00. A $2.50 American rib-eye steak tastes much better. Hiroyuki-san was disappointed too. He said that the most expensive meat loses its taste because it is stored for too long since there are no orders for it. It was a first-class restaurant, and there were white people among the customers. The steak in America tastes much better—I won't repeat this mistake again.

Hiroyuki-san says he will take me to a Chinese restaurant. But I'm going to decline the invitation because walking around the crowded streets seems to be bad for me. Yesterday I felt good about my hearing, but when I came back last night about nine o'clock, the ringing in my ears became unbearable. I'm sorry, Kiyoko-san—I should not have gone to town. I must concentrate on the treatment only, so I won't go out anymore until I definitely get well. I'm happy when I stay in my room and write to you as if I'm talking to you.

Since this is summer break, there are many students who have come into the Department of Ear and Nose for treatment. Those who are not serious cases take evening walks. I saw them when I went out with Hiroyuki-san last night. There are a men's room and a women's room next to each other. Since the night air is so hot, they leave the doors open and sleep—I think this is Japan.

When Hiroyuki-san came back around seven o'clock, I asked him if he gave the perfume to his girlfriend. He said, "No. I'm going to give it to her in the office on Monday." I was impressed. If I were in that position, I would have run to Kiyoko-san and given her the present right away. This doesn't mean that Hiroyuki-san is ignoring his girlfriend, or the gift. They were talking about wedding plans. I think his manner is the manner of a Japanese man. I was delighted to observe this. Or maybe I'm more deeply in love with Kiyoko-san? I am more impatient than Hiroyuki-san, but maybe his manner is more attractive to women. Maybe I should act like him—no—it wouldn't last more than three days.

From KIYOSHI, *July 30.*

. . . (I WROTE YOU THIS MORNING TOO.) I got your letters, one in care of Watanabe-sensei, the other of the hospital—I'm so happy. . . .

I was so touched by Yukiko's letter. Thank you for enclosing it. She took a day off from summer school because of a stomachache—I hope she is all right now. . . .

Thank you for taking care of CYS. I think a donation of $12 was the right thing to do. I wrote thank-you notes to the people in Nikkō (Japan Airlines) and mailed them to the Sendai office in Miyagi Prefecture. If you would like to write also, please send a form letter to the eight people, plus the supervisor, Mr. Kōno, at Nikkō-ryō (dormitory), 8-16, North Nibanchō-dōri, Odawara, Sendai-shi, Miyagi-ken. They took care of me really well—especially Matsumura-san and Supervisor Kōno. . . .

I am glad to know that all my letters reached you. It makes me even happier than the days when I saw you every other night and called you every day. Regardless of the result, I'm going to do my best. Fortunately the treatment seems to be going on smoothly. After I went out for a walk with Hiroyuki-san yesterday, I was afraid that the symptoms were reversed because of the ringing in my ears. I'm relieved because it stopped today. I'll be more careful in the future.

Regarding the physician-in-charge, I was like a courtier, wasn't I? It made me laugh. From now on I'll come down to the level of a commoner and call him a doctor-in-charge. I'm amazed at my own words, ". . . since leaving Japan." I'm dumfounded to find I did it not only once but twice. Don't worry, from now on I'll say ". . . since leaving America." But I might have already written the other way to many people. . . .

From KIYOKO, *July 31.*

. . . I RECEIVED YOUR LETTERS DATED THE 27th and 28th. It seems to take a longer time for my letters to reach you. Is it because of the delivery system at the hospital? I'm anxiously waiting for your letter that acknowledges the receipt of mine. If you miss me so much, you must be really lonely. I worry about you. I wrote so many letters, but none has reached you yet—I am so sorry.

Today I had Hisayo mail your ear medicine by air, pajamas and other things by sea. These were sent to the hospital. I hope they reach you quickly.

I think it was fortunate that you went to Japan. When I heard Watanabe-sensei talk about the inhalation of carbonic acid practiced in Japan, I felt strongly that you should go to Japan. I never thought about the money. I just wanted to make this treatment possible for you. And thanks to your mother, your trip to Japan has materialized—it is like a dream. Everything about this trip was so smoothly arranged, thanks to the chain of unexpected opportunities. At the dinner table I relay your gratitude to your mother and share the news in your letters. Our apprehension was blown away all at once when we heard about the treatment for your lung. I must write to Dr. Yasuda and thank him. Everybody here has hope now. A hospital aide whose husband died of cancer said, ". . . so, lung disease, too, could be cured in Japan!" as though she was surprised at the superior medical programs in Japan.

There are all kinds of treatments over there, aren't there? If you get better in about eight days, you won't worry over a few days' setback, will you? Even if improvement is as slow as a snail's pace, you will get there sooner or later. Please be patient. You might get worn out if you look too far ahead. Be glad that every day you make some improvement. It's better not to worry much. Cure your ears and cure your lung; and also give time to curing your heart from worrying over other physical problems. Come home to me with a cured heart that is filled with happiness. I've said before that I've never felt this happy to send you to a hospital. Even Yukiko has an admirable attitude. Someone said to her; "You should have gone with your dad . . . you must be lonely." She replied; "I'm lonely, but I let him go because it's better that he gets well and comes back." I was surprised to hear her say this.

She had a tummy ache once, but that was all—she is fine. I told her to make something to show Daddy, but she is busy playing during the day. At night sometimes she doesn't want to go to sleep. Without paying attention to her, I stand up and start walking to her bedroom, saying to myself, "I must help Yukiko to go to bed." She runs ahead of me wanting to go to bed. It's so easy to lead her.

The other day when we went shopping, she took me to the notion counter to show me a watch and her $7.50. She was imploring. She knows if she gets A's she can have a watch, but getting an A isn't easy. Once she gets an A, she will learn the taste for it. I will encourage her more next term. She writes hiragana very nicely.

A few stoma bags were mailed to you a week after your departure. I think there are enough to last until we make another order. As I wrote earlier, please get the name and address of the manufacturer from the bag or from the container. Or maybe I should ask the hospital here just in case you can't find the info.

From KIYOSHI, *July 31.*

I WAS SO HAPPY TO READ YOUR LETTER with a photo airmailed on the 25th. Thank you for writing me so often in spite of your busy schedule. When your letter comes, I'm so excited that I can't sit still at all that day. I feel as though my whole body is surrounded with tingling warmth. Today I also received a letter from my sister. I've written a letter in English to Akira-san and Mitsuyo-san. . . .

I'm so glad that you sent me the photo. I'm keeping it on the lamp table by my bed. I wish the photo showed all of you. Someday have someone take a picture of you and Yukiko together and send it to me, please. I miss you so much. I wish you were here—just being by my side, just letting me touch your cheeks. I can't describe it exactly, but it's such a contented feeling. Here I am so far away from you, but my heart is filled with joy, thinking of your tender love, your everlasting love. As I am writing this, I feel very lucky to be alive, to love you and to be loved by you—I am so grateful.

I remember that Yukiko surprised me at how well she sang some songs from *The Sound of Music,* and one time in the car she sang "Swing Low" very nicely. I pray that someday I can hear her songs again. Now I feel that it is not impossible. I think my hearing is better today than yesterday.

I did not have the inhaler treatment yesterday or today because the carbonic acid has run out. But the injection of チトマック-P (*chitomakku*-P) seems to be working. The left side hasn't shown any changes yet, but I think that the right side is showing a gradual improvement. How far I can regain my hearing, I don't know. I hope all goes well. I tell myself that I must not give up hope even if I can't hear now.

I'm so glad to hear that Yukiko read 90% of my letter all by herself. Tell her that Daddy is waiting for her letter anxiously. Thank you for taking my mother to the folk dance show. I'm grateful for Hirose-san. I'll write to him soon. Regarding the insurance, I'll ask for Watanabe-sensei's help in the negotiation as soon as he returns. I'm sure he will help me. Thank you for pajamas, razor blades, and ink cartridges, etc. Soap is a good gift. Wash 'n Dri was new to everybody and was appreciated very much. After giving half of a box to Watanabe-sensei, I had a box and a half left—so it all went well. Please send me two more boxes. This is good for my hands too. Please send me more salami because it is a source of protein for me. I don't need cotton balls and gauze since the hospital supplies them, but I definitely need plastic bags. . . .

Coming to Japan, I had an urge to read in Japanese. But *Asahi-shinbun* is too difficult so I had to change to its English version. I can't explain why I feel more comfortable reading the English version since I was so anxious to read *Asahi-shinbun* in Japanese.

You say Yukiko started to cook rice?! Tell her that Daddy is so proud of her. Do you work on Saturdays too? Take care of your health for my sake—if something happens to you, I don't think I could live without you even with Yukiko there. . . .

You don't have to respond to all of my letters—I'll be content with two letters a week.

っちん、あんまりながくかかった

らめんな、とふ telephone かかってきました、よ！

な dress をこしらえました。

ゆそこ から。

ちゃんへ

M

Rich work Outfit

August

..

[*Month of Uncertainty*]

From KIYOSHI, *August 1.*

TODAY IS AUGUST FIRST, THE 14TH DAY OF my hearing treatment. I just finished breakfast. Meals are served at 8:10 a.m., 12:10 p.m., and five p.m. At six a.m. and two p.m. a nurse takes my temperature.

I look at your photo so many times. I'm content and grateful, having both the letter and the photo from you—I'm calling your name repeatedly in my heart. I miss you so much, it hurts.

• • •

I was hoping to receive your letter, and it did come this afternoon. It was written on July 27. You made me so happy. You say you were worried about me feeling depressed without hearing from you. Yes, I was, but now I am in seventh heaven—I'm so happy that I don't know what to do!

Thank you for calling Kasuya-san and Yanase-san. Thank you for the medicine. Thank you for saying that we are in this together. Nobody but you can say that—I'm a lucky man to have you as my wife.

Thank you for planning to take Lily and my sister to see the folk dance. They will love it, I'm sure. My mother will love it too. I don't know how to thank you. Please don't make yourself overly tired. . . .

Tomorrow I will write to you again, Kiyoko-san. Don't worry about me now—you've made me feel so contented. Send me a happy letter twice a week and give yourself more rest. Could you, please, send me two or three cans of Almond Roca if there is room left in the package? I'd like to give one can to Watanabe-sensei, one to the nurses, and keep one for me.

From KIYOKO, *August 2.*

I AM SO RELIEVED TO HEAR THAT YOU STARTED to receive my letters. I wrote to Hiroyuki only yesterday asking him to check at the hospital about the delay of the mail. I was worried that there may be a patients' mail box somewhere in the hospital. I thought you might not know that, and the letters could have piled up there. Anyway it takes more than one week from the States to Japan and less the other way around. The one you wrote on the 30th arrived yesterday. I was glad that Hiroyuki came to see you, but then I became concerned about the missing letters, so much so that I became constipated. I can't relax until I make sure that you receive my letters without a hitch.

Yesterday was the birthday of Cecilia's husband. She took him to a steak house and celebrated the occasion with delicious rib-eye steaks. When you come home, they want to take you there for a steak dinner. She said that they always go out for a Chinese dinner because of her, and that's why she chose to have his favorite steak dinner for his birthday. I think they are a wonderful couple. They told me they wrote a letter to you in Chinese—how was it? Why don't you write back in Chinese? It may be fun, don't you think so? Tsukiji-san has received a letter from you too. . . .

The month of July went so quickly; it's already two weeks since you left America. It's wonderful that you already feel some improvement. Reducing the tinnitus itself is a big help. There is no greater joy for us than discovering the level of Japanese medical science is so high. I read again *Bungei-shunjū*'s July edition. The article about Japan's free economy written by the former Director General of the Foreign Ministry was very interesting. He thinks that Japanese people should have more confidence in what they are doing. I fully agree with him. Unfortunately the Japanese are poor so they tend to lose confidence. You might have already discussed this with Dr. Yasuda, but it is hard to believe in your country's value unless you have lived outside of it, I think. I hope you can help them restore confidence in themselves.

You wrote in today's letter that there are no plastic bags in the hospital there, so I'll get some from the hospital here. My boss is away this week to attend a meeting in San Francisco. My partner seldom comes to work due to illness. I cannot take time off until this Friday afternoon at the earliest or Monday morning (August 7) at the latest. But I will get them and mail them right away, so don't you worry.

Regarding the medicine for your ears—will it be too late to send it after you try a sample and get your doctor's approval? By the time you receive this letter, the sample should reach you. After receiving a "go-ahead" from you, I can mail it quickly because I already have the prescription. This is my plan, and if it is different from what you thought, please forgive me.

I told Yukiko to write stories starting tomorrow and make a book. I think this is one way to encourage her to practice her writing skills. I will think of something similar for her mathematics too. Everybody here is fine. Hisayo is having exams now. She says thank you for thinking of her.

The rent is paid, and so is Sears. The interest was about $3.00. Starting this month, the tax is rising from 4% to 5%. Riots by African Americans are increasing. The Japanese jewelry store in East Palo Alto—remember that?—it was attacked, too.

It is reported that [U.S. Senator William] Fulbright is opposing the president [Lyndon Johnson] strongly and proposed a bill to control the rights of the president. He wants the voice of the Senate to be heard.

I'll write again.

From KIYOSHI, *August 2.*

... IN YESTERDAY'S LETTER YOU ASKED how I was taking care of my laundry. Please do not worry. There is an old laundry lady who comes around the ward every day. She charges 65 yen for a pair of pajamas, 30 yen for a T-shirt, and 40 yen for a regular shirt.

I am gradually getting used to life in the hospital. Among the patients, there was a man from Ōita Prefecture who lost his hearing in his childhood due to an inflammation in his middle ear. His name was Matsuda. After surgery his hearing was much better. He heard about me and came to see me just before going home. Using a pen and notepaper he told me how difficult his life was before the surgery. It took him three months of hospital stay also. He must be around 37 or 8 and has two sons, age 11 and nine. I wished him good luck in the future. He gave me his picture and also took a photo of me and said he will mail it to me. I gave him the razor which I intended to give to the father of Hiroyuki-san's girlfriend.

The nurses must be talking about me—everybody knows that I have a hearing problem and treats me so nicely. One of them—I don't know her name—she must be 22 or 3—came to see me with a pot of flowers. There is a girl of high school age across from my room—she brought me half of an opened can of Japanese tangerines along with an origami crane that she made. I didn't have any gifts left so I gave her a Kennedy coin.

It is generally thought that Japan has changed, but people are still very sympathetic and mindful of others, more so than Americans. Japanese women are graceful still. The high school student had a lovely manner, and she bowed to me so gracefully that I didn't know what to do! I thought it would be wonderful if Henry could find a girl like this for his wife. She looked cute in spite of her rather large build. I hope that the nice quality of Japanese women is preserved forever. I don't think this is just a selfish man's idea.

How is Yukiko doing? Tell her I am waiting for her letter. You said she can wash rice and switch on the cooker. She is growing up, isn't she! I pray that she grows up with good health and becomes a well-mannered daughter who will build a happy life for her husband and herself. She doesn't have to find a lawyer, a doctor, or an engineer for her husband. A truck driver is fine—if he is sincere and loves Yukiko and makes her happy. Since I know so well how wonderful it is to have a life filled with love, I can't help but wish the same for Yukiko. . . .

From KIYOKO, *August 3.*

. . . TODAY I MAILED BY SEA THE NEWSPAPERS FOR the month of July. They won't be current, but still they may be interesting—besides, air mail is costly. *Nihongo News* will be sent by air, and it costs only 25 cents. It will arrive about the same time as the bunch of newspapers or a little bit earlier. Surprisingly Hirose-san writes very well. It makes me laugh—you will enjoy it too. We haven't paid for *Nihongo News*, but they keep sending it. This is unusual for nickel-pinchers like the Santa Clara Branch of the Nihongo Society. Either they are waiting for us to initiate payment, or they are sending it as a favor.

Today I had a meeting with the person in charge of our insurance. He told me that the date you entered the hospital is the beginning date of the coverage. At the time when I talked with the person at the reception window, neither he nor I knew when you would arrive at the hospital.

I understand now what happened. Since my letters did not arrive soon enough, you went ahead and paid. We can send that receipt to the insurance company. Please talk with the hospital and from now on follow the policy of our insurance company. They say it's the fastest way to be approved and paid. The coverage is as follows: the first 21 days is 100%, the next 180 days is 50%; miscellaneous expenses are covered fully up to $300, and beyond that, 80%. This insurance is one we carry as everybody else does whether one works or not. On top of this we have Major Medical, an employee's insurance, and this covers 80% of that which the other insurance does not cover. The coverage by Major Medical may change slightly depending on the date of monthly application, but these two policies will cover most of your medical expenses. Another important thing is that the coverage differs depending on a private room or a ward. I think it would be better to obtain a note from the hospital saying that a semiprivate room is the only available room.

I also asked if the airfare could be included as a medical expense. They weren't sure and advised us to obtain a statement from the doctor in Stanford saying that the treatment cannot be done here. I don't know how much that will help, but I will try. I hope I covered most of the questions on the insurance policy. The rest depends on how much it actually is in dollars. Please do not worry—just concentrate on getting well.

From KIYOSHI, *August 3.*

. . . I SAID THAT I WOULD BE happy if you write to me twice a week. How-ever, I'm lonely because there were no letters yesterday and today. But maybe this is OK because I have something to look for with anticipation. Please don't overload your already full schedule—I'll be happy if I get a letter from you twice a week.

At the end of yesterday's letter I said that I would write again, but I couldn't. I went to bed instead because I had a headache. They gave me as-pirin last night, and the headache was gone.

Please don't worry about my meals. I can order out anything when I want. The rice curry special is 260 yen, but this was not so good—the one that Hiroyuki-san and I had tasted better at 120 yen. Yesterday I had chicken-rice (200 yen). It was very good. The best steak is 800 yen and is better than the one Hiroyuki-san and I had the other night and paid 1,500 yen apiece. But there is no comparison with the steaks in America. Anyway, please don't worry about meals here. . . .

I received a letter from Iwama-san today. She says the African violet began to bloom, the cornflower is large enough to eat, and the lady-in-moonlight is blooming in abundance. Please call and thank her . . . .

From KIYOSHI, *August 4.*

TODAY IS AUGUST 4, FRIDAY, a nice windy day. . . . It's been three weeks since I left America. It reminds me of your visit to Japan—it was three weeks also—I bet for you the time flew away too quickly to do anything. In my case, it is different because all I do is stay in my room. It is worth noting that for one like me who is afraid of loneliness, I have spent 18 days already alone in this room. But maybe by nature I'm able to adjust to a solitary situation if I am forced to. Think about the first two years when we were separated, the following six years when I was in the hospital, and another year after that—and the present—like a well-trained sheep, I seem to accept the loneliness. I cannot imagine myself going out to look for amusement or women to fill the loneliness. This is me and I'm satisfied with myself. For me, my family is the most important thing. If you and I and Yukiko, the three of us, can live a happy life together, nothing else will make me happier than that. A happy family life with warmth and our love will make Yukiko happy and help her to build a foundation for her own happy family life in the future. Observing the loving relationship of *Tō-chan* and Mommy, she will respect us and want to follow our footsteps.

I stopped here and waited for your letter, but it didn't come. I was disappointed—but don't worry. Instead, the medicine arrived by air mail. I will show it to the doctor this afternoon at the respirator session. If he decides to use this along with other medicine, please get some more from Dr. Childrey. . . .

I haven't written back to Iwama-san yet. I write one letter a day, but I have about 50 people to respond to. Iwama-san wrote back so promptly. Tell her that I was surprised to get such a quick reply. Tell her that I try not to use my brain. The doctor told me to slow down because the blood vessels are closely connected in the brain and ears. Actually, I don't want to write to her. All I want is a letter from Kiyoko-san. But I guess I have to write to others too. I'll write to you again tomorrow.

From KIYOKO, *August 5.*

. . . I'VE RECEIVED LETTERS FROM YOU, up to No. 4. Letters to the States arrive fast and without problems. But lately you also seem to be getting my letters without a hitch. I am relieved.

You say you cannot read the *Asahi-shinbun*. Have you become senile after living in America for so long? You can read *Bungei-shunjū*, can't you, since you were reading it here. However, I recall that I wasn't interested either in reading page after page of the *Nishi-Nihon-shinbun* like I used to do. Now you say that the English language paper is better for you—it's an interesting phenomenon, isn't it? You used to read the Japanese before reading the English in the *Hokubei-news* and *Nichibei-news*. That's why I took out the English section from the papers that I sent you yesterday.

Anyway I'm glad that everything is going smoothly there. I turn on the yellow light, and I have an illusion of seeing you lying down and looking towards me. Today I washed your coverlet which is made of new fibers. It came out nice and clean, and made me very happy. After that, I went to see *Dr. Zhivago* with Mitsuko-san and Yukiko. The movie was shown in Japan a few weeks before Mitsuko-san left the country. She wanted to see it, according to Yukiko, but thought it would be too much to ask for. She watches the house and takes care of Yukiko so I wanted to treat her to the movie as a way to express my gratitude. Yukiko didn't like the movie and says she needed something different to wipe off the sadness of the movie. So we went to Okida Hall to deliver a CYS donation and saw Takeda-san. We are now listening to a record of *The Sound of Music*. Tomorrow I will return the camera and radio to Iwama-san. Before returning them, I'll have the film and the batteries replaced at GEM. . . .

I tend to start writing without planning. That's why I run out of space every time. So I'm going to give you Fred Matsumoto's address now: 1625 Lundy Ave., S.J. If his father's name is Frank, this must be Fred's address. Also I was thinking that you might send a postcard to Mr. and Mrs. Eckford. They took Yukiko to a picnic, but I haven't thanked them. Their address is 493 N. Fifth. I think you wanted to have the address of Tao Tamotsu-san—it is 356 Third St., Watsonville. I'm sorry it took me so long to give you these addresses. To those who work at Japan Airlines, I plan to send a package containing soup plus something. . . .

It is a lonely night thinking of the movie and you. The onset of the Russian Revolution, its development, its influence on the life of the populace, a story of a conscientious doctor in the midst of the uproar—fate prevents him from meeting someone he wants to meet, and the story ends sadly. The plot of the story is similar to that of *Lawrence of Arabia*. *Flying Machine*, which we saw together, was much more entertaining. I was impressed by Mitsuko-san, for she said she enjoyed the movie, and she is only 16 years old. She also told Mother how much she enjoyed the movie, and Mother was so pleased. A spaghetti dinner was waiting for us, thanks to your mother.

Send me another happy letter. But watch out so you won't put your roots down in Japan where you meet so many nice people. Give them the candies in the package that I sent—I think there are plenty, and they are all wrapped individually. You say you found a candidate for Henry's wife. Too bad he isn't there.

From KIYOSHI, *August 5.*

. . . I'M SORRY YOU HAD TO GO to the county hospital for me. The problem is the bag. I can't find it here. Perhaps Dr. Rowan didn't want to sell it to us because it costs $5. But I really need it. I brought some loose ones in a paper bag, not the whole box. Therefore I don't have the address of the manufacturer. Can you talk to Dr. Rowan again and at least get the name of the manufacturer so that we can order it directly? It is not $5; it is 25 cents for one. Tell the doctor, "We bought them by paying 25 cents each because they told us this was cheap and you could pay us." Please try it again, because I really need it. Tell the doctor that "Karaya Seal" which is written on the bag is not Japanese.

The doctor said that he would first see how the present treatment comes along; then he would try the sample of medicine that you sent by air mail. Just in case you didn't take note of the name of the medicine, here it is—ARLIDRIN, brand name of NYLIDRIN HCL, 6 mg per tablet, 1,000 tablets in a bottle.

Thank you for the package. I'll tell the doctor that he could give the medicine to some of his patients for tuberculosis. I've told you about the general checkup so I won't repeat it.

I intend to write to Kawabata-san as soon as possible. He will be surprised. As I wrote earlier, an old woman comes to the ward to collect laundry. I have her take the better shirts to the dry cleaner's. So far, I have sent the suits (360 yen, which is a dollar) and silk shirts to the cleaner's. Hiroyuki-san said he would come every Saturday so I am going to ask him to take stuff to be dry-cleaned. Today is Saturday, and it is 3:40 p.m.—pretty soon he'll come. Visiting hours are from one p.m. to five p.m.

Starting today I am taking in carbonic acid gas for 20 minutes. I could hardly hear anything in my left ear, but I was so surprised yesterday when I heard the sound of the pump of the instrument in my eardrum. I couldn't believe it so I removed the instrument on the right side—I could still hear the sound in my left ear—I was so happy because before I could not hear anything on the left. But I'm telling myself not to be elated too soon—the least possible amount of rejoicing would guarantee a minimum disappointment. I'm going to rejoice when I am able to hear a human voice. In fact, I shouldn't think even that for now. About the lady of about 23 years of age—she had an operation on her right ear, but the operation was not successful and she was discharged today. I felt sorry for her. She wrote, "You have hope, that's good." I wrote back, "Whether my hearing comes back or not, I'm going to live happily." Also I wrote, "My wife said that we have to do our best in our life whether we can hear or not." . . .

From KIYOSHI, *August 6.*

. . . IT MUST BE THE MEMORIAL DAY of the atomic air raid here. The television in the dining room has been showing Hiroshima. I could not hear anything, but I saw millions of people were observing the Memorial. I think the mayor of Hiroshima was making his speech. I can hardly believe that it's been more than 20 years since that air raid. I pray the world will never again see an atomic bomb.

Hiroyuki-san didn't come yesterday. He might come today. Being alone in the room sometimes I feel so lonely. A few days ago I was reading a book, and in no time my head began to throb and the ringing in my ears became worse. So now I'm just looking outside through the window.

Writing letters to you is the happiest time for me. When your letter arrives, I feel even happier—and while I'm writing back to you, I am in seventh heaven! I miss you so much. Your letter is the only thing that rescues me from my loneliness. Sometimes I fantasize that three months pass like a flash and my hearing comes back like magic. Last night I had a dream—somebody was talking excitedly that he was able to hear his own voice, and in that dream clearly I heard someone talking. I am so depressed, and I need you. What sort of stages must I go through before my hearing comes back? I suppose it's not like peeling thin membranes from inside my ears, is it? I would be satisfied if I could restore my hearing gradually. It doesn't have to be hearing in both ears—I'd be more than happy with just one ear. As I wrote to you yesterday, I was startled when I heard the pumping noise in the left ear. I hoped I could hear it again, but it didn't happen today. I must not expect too much too soon. . . .

I thought the right ear might heal sooner, but it doesn't look like it. Anyhow it's a fact that exhaustion from traveling caught up with me right after I arrived here. It's annoying because the hearing aid does not work. I can't hear my voice. So I am not using the hearing aid any more. I wish I could hear my own voice at least—it would boost my mood. I'm concerned because since yesterday the ringing in my ears has gotten worse. I don't know what's going on. I thought the right ear was getting better—I could hear the sound when I urinated. But no more—maybe because of that, I am irritable now. I hope the left ear gets better soon.

Please write to me, Kiyoko-san. I can hardly wait for your letter, and when it comes, I feel so much better. I get so lonesome without hearing from you. I don't think it will come today. I feel so depressed today—I tell myself that I must get hold of myself, but it doesn't work. I am sorry, Kiyoko-san. I'll write again soon. Take good care of yourself. . . .

Anxiously awaiting your letter.

From KIYOSHI, *August 6.*

. . . I WAS SO DISCOURAGED AFTER writing the last letter, but I feel so much better now that your letter of July 31 came. I had given up because today is Sunday, but it came around four o'clock. I read it as if I was being resuscitated by it. . . .

It's strange that the sample medicine came before your letter did. The letter which came yesterday (written on last Saturday) said that you were going to send it by air mail. . . . It says you asked Hisayo-san to mail it. Maybe it is because of the difference in the location of the post offices, one in San Jose, the other in Mountain View—never mind! . . .

Watanabe-sensei might be coming back to Fukuoka very soon—maybe he might come see me tomorrow. Dr. Yasuda will be at a different hospital for two weeks starting tomorrow. I am disappointed. Dr. Shirabe is to take care of me during Dr. Yasuda's absence, and he is a far more senior doctor, according to Dr. Yasuda. I haven't met him yet. Today was the last day with Dr. Yasuda. With this and that, the ringing in my ears got worse since yesterday. . . .

What an admirable thought Yukiko had—she let her daddy go in spite of her loneliness because it's more important that Daddy gets better—I almost cried. I'm glad to hear that she is well as usual. I remember she didn't like to sleep alone by herself. And I can understand her wanting to have a watch. Tell her to wait because Daddy will bring one home for her.

When Watanabe-sensei comes tomorrow, I will consult with him about the insurance. . . .

From KIYOSHI, *August 6.*

. . . THIS IS THE THIRD ONE OF the same date. I had given up on Hiroyuki-san, but to my surprise he came about 6:30 p.m. with his girlfriend. So I'm writing again. . . .

Hiroyuki-san's girlfriend gave me a flower in a pot and a coaster which she knitted herself. I deeply appreciated her thoughtfulness. She has a cheerful personality. She reminds me of somebody, but I'm not sure who it could be; she is lean and tall and looks somewhat like Hiroko-san with a similar complexion—except her face is longer. Of course, she is much taller than Hiroko-san. She has rather large eyes with single-fold eyelids. Her mouth is large but looks nice because the lips are not thick. To some degree she reminds me of Miyazaki Shigeko-san in her high-school days. But Hiroyuki-san's girlfriend is 20 years old. She was so grateful for the perfume that you gave her and repeatedly said how happy she was. I think you gave her just the right gift.

Hiroyuki-san drove his company car today hoping that the three of us could go out somewhere, but unfortunately I had to decline because of the ringing in my ears and the exhaustion I might have after the drive. I restrained myself in case my condition should regress. Normally I would be the one who would suggest an outing, but I held back and told them I would show them around when I get well. Hiroyuki-san was hoping to take me out to a Chinese restaurant. I felt so bad that I couldn't go with them. I will invite them when I get well. The ringing in my ears, however, seems to be less; maybe because I feel encouraged since I received your letters. Because your letter gives me strength, this ear problem could become less and less bothersome.

I stopped here and went to bed last night. Today is Monday, August seventh—Sunday the sixth in the States. I wonder what you are planning to do today. Maybe you are taking Yukiko to the Watson Building. . . .

Please forgive me that all I do lately is ask you to do this and that. But I'm worried because my supply of bags will cover only 22 or 23 days. Sea mail might take more than a month. Please talk to Dr. Rowan and send me one box by air mail. It has to be American made—it says "Made in USA, Pat. Pending." Please tell that to Dr. Rowan. Tell him that we've bought this from him before. I'm really sorry that I have to ask you to do this sort of thing.

I'll write again after I see the new doctor and Watanabe-sensei. . . .

From KIYOKO, *August 7.*

. . . TODAY I CALLED THE HOSPITAL and arranged to pick up the bags in the morning. Watanabe-sensei called while I was out shopping with Mother. I guess the sample of the medicine arrived and Arlidrin is what the doctor decided to recommend. Tomorrow I'll pick it up too and send it together with the bags by air mail. I don't know what you meant by "no more bags"—I guess you meant "the bags are almost all gone." You wrote on July 28, "There are about 34 or 35 left." If you counted wrong or the package didn't arrive, you will have no bags for days so I'm sending by air about 20 bags, just in case. Tomorrow I'll mail by air 20 plastic bags and a bottle of 1,000 tablets of Arlidrin. Other items like salami, Almond Roca, Wash 'n Dri, etc. will be mailed right away by ship.

I was going to send the package today, but I couldn't get the bags because Dr. Rowan was busy, and Mrs. Miller, who usually takes care of these things, was on vacation. Later Dr. Rowan came out and told me that he would write a prescription so that I should come back to pick it up in the morning. But this evening he called to say that the medicine for your ears could be ordered at the same time. I'm happy that it worked out all right. . . .

Watanabe-sensei mentioned that you were disappointed because the condition has not improved as much as you hoped. Please don't get upset because change doesn't happen so easily. You are under a treatment that is so special that, aside from Japan, it is found only in Germany. At least we have a way to deal with the problem. We have to be patient. Kiyoshi-san, you have a rational mind; let's use it now and keep disappointment and impatience hidden away for now.

It will get cool in September so I'll put warmer pajamas in the next package. . . . I've been feeling a little bit dizzy since yesterday. Maybe the effect of Cecilia's medicine has run out. I must make that extract again. It is surprisingly effective. Since Yūko-san is on vacation, only Cecilia and I are left, like in the old days. Cecilia talks freely to me when nobody is around. . . .

I went swimming, Daddy! I eat so much, and get tummy ache.

Yukiko wanted some space to write to you. She is growing up and eats so much.

I expect your letter tomorrow. I forgot to tell you—Lily had a tonsil operation on July 31. If you have a chance, please send her a line. I'll write again. Please take care and don't lose patience.

From KIYOSHI, *August 7.*

IT'S STILL AUGUST SEVENTH. BUT this will be delivered a day later because I'm going to mail it tomorrow morning. I would like to report on the result of the examination by Dr. Shirabe and also the outcome of the meeting with Watanabe-sensei.

Dr. Shirabe is Dr. Yasuda's superior and also specializes in ear disease. Watanabe-sensei had a long talk with him. He will phone you this evening so I won't go into detail except to say that they will work together closely. The induction of carbonic acid gas is done only at the University of Hamburg in Germany and the University of Kyushu in Japan. Moreover, the machine that they are using on me is the only one in Japan. I have to get well because everybody is working hard to help me. From now on Dr. Shirabe will be the physician-in-charge and Dr. Yasuda will assist him.

About the insurance and the coverage for my hospital room—I have a private room here. The insurance says that it cannot cover above the average cost of a semiprivate room. But there is no similarity between an American semiprivate room and a Japanese one. The standard is entirely different. Watanabe-sensei pointed it out to Dr. Shirabe. But the hospital cannot change the description of the room I'm in because the rules for a national university hospital are rigid and different from a private hospital. Both doctors suggest that we should point out to the insurance company that a Japanese private room is poorly accommodated compared to even a semi-private room in America, and the food is very simple; that is the reason the hospital charges only $10 a day—it is cheaper than the cost of a semiprivate room in America. We can say that there is no bathroom in the private room here—but don't mention that there is a cooler in the room. Couldn't we point out that the semiprivate room in America is much quieter and more comfortable? In short, please tell the insurance company that a private room in Japan is far worse than a hospital ward in the States. Please try. After hearing from you, I will have the hospital complete the form and send it to you. . . .

I talked with Watanabe-sensei today, and I will give the Cognac Napoleon to Dr. Shirabe. I was supposed to give it to another doctor, but he seldom comes, and I can give him something else when I get well. Watanabe-sensei thought it would be better to give the same brand of whisky to Dr. Shirabe, but then I'll be left with this Cognac. When I get well I can make it up. We don't have time or money to buy another Parker fountain pen and mail it by air—besides, Napoleon isn't at all bad for a gift. If you have not finished the next package, will you please include a set of Gillette razors for shaving? I'd like to use some of them as gifts.

Forgive me for these requests. I will write you again tomorrow.

From KIYOKO, *August 8.*

I RECEIVED YOUR LETTERS NOS. 5, 6, AND 7 today, all in one delivery. I added soap to the shopping list right away. I decided to record in a notebook from the Sumitomo Bank what I did, when, and what you asked for in your letters. What I did will be entered on the lined page, and your requests in the letter on the plain page. So, today's page has 200 Arlidrin tablets and 15 stoma bags on one side, and 10 soaps on the opposite side.

I went straight to the hospital this morning to get the bags, then to the ear doctor and the pharmacy nearby for Arlidrin. I decided to get a three-months supply of Arlidrin because a bottle of 1,000 tablets costs so much, and we can have it refilled. The cost is $13.30 for 200 tablets. I was afraid that I wouldn't have enough left for the airmail cost so I got only 15 bags although I said I would mail 20 bags by air. I came home and read that letter again. I think 15 bags will do while you wait for the arrival of the package even if it is delayed a little bit.

The violet is growing beautifully at the ear doctor's office. The nurse said that a cleaning person knocked the plant to the floor yesterday; she was going to call me for advice so she was very glad to see me. And this is what she said about you: "What a nice person he is—always thinking of his family first—I don't understand why he has been dealt one bad blow after another." Also she said, "My mother told me, hardship befalls those who can stand against it, and I think she is right." I was impressed by her observation because she didn't just brush it away saying that God gives us pain, or something like that. My family is my treasure—so you wrote in your letter No. 6. I know how you feel, and I'm glad that the nurse could see it too.

We have not had a trip to the beach yet. After reading your letter, I decided to have an excursion this coming Saturday. Yukiko has written a card to Glen and the others. . . . I'm sure Dr. Takeda will be surprised because I haven't told him that you are now in Japan. We haven't had to work overtime lately because the company's sales index has gone down by 15%. To cut overtime isn't so bad compared to a reduction in work force. So, I'm going to enjoy the leisure while I can.

I was surprised to hear that you wrote to 50 people—whom did you write to? It's like spreading seeds—some might grow to be plants and write you back. Besides, it might save you from being bored. Be grateful, but respond to those letters only when you feel up to it. However, to me, to your wife, please keep writing like you have been doing. You've spoiled me, and I want to receive a letter every day—every other day may be OK—don't be bothered about the cost of postage. . . .

From KIYOSHI, *August 8.*

. . . I FEEL A LITTLE BIT TIRED TODAY, maybe because of the hot weather. Your letters came the day before yesterday and yesterday. So I may not receive any today although I'm longing for another. I'm thinking about your talk with Watanabe-sensei last night. Cecilia's letter has not come yet—maybe it will come tomorrow as you said in your letter. I plan to write back in Chinese and English mixed. I think I've asked you already all that I wanted to have sent here; so from now on you can relax, I hope. You told me not to hesitate—just ask anything—but still I felt bad to make you do so many things for me.

I get lonely because there's nothing to do. Reading books causes me a headache, and the ringing in my ears gets worse so I just stay still doing nothing. I don't have many visitors, which is good because the ringing gets worse after seeing them. I must get tense even though I don't talk much. I get so tired. I know this is selfish, but I wish you were here by my side reading a book in that chair. I miss you so much. . . .

From KIYOSHI, *August 9.*

. . . BREAKFAST WAS SERVED LATE this morning because a group of professors toured the ward in a stream—there seems to be many professors here, and the leader of today's group appears to be the dean. Dr. Harada, who treated me at the very beginning, came too and explained this and that to the group. The leading professor kept shaking his head. I am discouraged because he kept shaking his head from side to side as he was going out of the room. I felt so dejected since I couldn't hear anything. I guess the head professor thought my case was very hopeless; I can't help but suspect the worst. I'm going to ask Dr. Shirabe (he was in the group too and was talking about my case) when I see him today. Until then I'll try not to think about this. . . .

I just had a consultation with Dr. Shirabe. . . . I asked why one doctor was shaking his head. That doctor was criticizing the lack of attention to my ear problems while I was being treated for tuberculosis, said Dr. Shirabe, adding jokingly that he is always shaking his head. That doctor is an assistant professor and has just come back from Germany after two years of study there. But Kiyoko-san, that doesn't make me feel any better—I'm still depressed—lonely—I want to see you!

Writing the last line made me feel a little bit better. I'm going to keep fighting, don't worry. I must muster spiritual strength to fight this physical problem and improve my health instead of becoming disappointed, or getting lonely. I will put all of myself into getting better—that's what I tell myself.

I believe the plastic bags and medicine were already mailed; if not, please send them by air mail. Is Yukiko all right? Tell her, "Be good!" And this is what I must tell myself too. Please remember me to Hisayo-san. Give my love to Mother. . . .

From KIYOSHI, *August 9.*

. . . YOUR LETTER OF AUGUST 3 AND *Nichigo News* arrived a few minutes ago. Thank you so much. I can't say enough how much your letter means to me; I am so happy now. I read it many times—it makes me so happy—I miss you so much—love you so much—I don't know how to describe this feeling to you. I'm getting older, but I'm so lucky that I still have this burning feeling of love and yearning for you. There is nothing more precious than this love we have for each other. . . .

Regarding the insurance coverage—I will submit a document once a month. I checked into the hospital July 18; their accounting closing dates are the third and the 18th so I will ask them to put me in the 18th group. I've already paid $750 plus about $300 in Japanese yen. When the insurance company pays, that amount will be deposited in my account as a refund, and I will receive a receipt. I still have $670 left in my account.

Regarding the room that I'm in—I'll ask the hospital to write an explanatory note about it although the insurance company may not understand how to compare the living conditions in Japan given the complication of exchange rates. I'll write them also with carefully chosen words and explain the situation as best as I can. Please let me know if you have any ideas or suggestions. It might help if you could consult with the agent. It would be nice if they could cover my general expenses fully up to $300 and 80% of other expenses so that the airfare is paid. . . .

By the way, about the result of today's treatment—the left ear, which is worse than the right, seems to be getting better. The other day I wrote about hearing the sound of a pump in that ear. It was August 4 when I started to hear an even and continuous sound, and it lasted till yesterday. But today I thought I heard a faint sound with a high and low pitch. The left ear doesn't ring as much as the right side. I asked the doctor if it is possible that the more damaged side would get better first. "It's possible," he said. But it is too soon to be ecstatic—I'll save this good news for a day when I am discouraged. There is no change in my right ear. Also, I want to avoid disappointment when and if it is found to be a mistake. . . .

From KIYOSHI, *August 9.*

. . . I HAVE GOOD NEWS TO TELL. I thought my right ear was not doing well. So I was apprehensive at today's hearing test given by Dr. Shirabe. I went to the soundproof room at four p.m. with a heavy heart. To my surprise, the test result was 45. The first test was 55, the next one was 50 on July 26, and today it was down to 45. The doctor decided to continue the same treatment since it is showing improvement. I have not told you, but the plan was to start with a treatment for one month; if there was no improvement, we would change to another treatment. If that showed no improvement in one month, the treatment was to be stopped. I was so afraid of that. You must have sensed my anxiety in my letters. While the treatment is showing some improvement, it will be continued till I get well. So I almost cried with joy when Dr. Shirabe said, "Let's continue." . . .

I don't remember the result for the left ear because I was so excited about the right ear. I don't think Dr. Shirabe spent much time on the left side because we were talking about the right side mostly. I think it is getting better also because I heard the sound of the pump distinctly with its high and low pitch.

What a relief to hear the words "continue treatment." I'm sure you understand. But I'm going to remain cautious and try to be patient as you advised. Please continue to give me your advice. I need it. I'll rest more so that I can concentrate my energy solely on the ear treatment. I won't go out. You've told me that you are in this together with me. I remember your words; I hold them close to my chest, as if to hold you tight in my arms. I'll be patient and focused. Even the loneliness—I'll take it as my medicine. Together with Yukiko, keep sending me your support, "Hurrah—hurrah—Daddy!"

The loneliness and uncertainty of the past several days is now gone, and it is such a relief. The first two tests did not show any improvement; therefore I couldn't help but feel utterly depressed. But, of course, I am not cured yet. I have to be more patient. Be happy a little, and be sad a little—this is the way to go. Some sad event might be waiting for me so I must be prepared for that too.

Thank you so much, Kiyoko-san. I say this to you in total devotion and reverence with my hands together in prayer. I'll write to you again tomorrow. Share this news with my mother, but with some reserve. . . .

From Kiyoko, *August 10.*

Yesterday, August ninth, I received your letters of August sixth, Nos. 8, 9, 10, and August seventh, No. 11. I went to bed last night soon after taking care of the African violets because I felt a little bit tired. Forgive me for not writing right away.

Yukiko's reading ability [in Japanese] is still slow although she tries hard—I wish she would improve. The evening of the eighth we went to the cemetery. She read a story to me in the car from the house to the cemetery and finished it. That was the speed of her reading. Actually it is not too bad. After all she started to read only six months ago. I encouraged her to write a story, but she didn't stick to it. She was trying to write poems, so she said. I can help her with Japanese poems; but an English poem is too complicated with rhymes and such. She is growing up fast—physically.

Your mother says she feels lonely eating without us.* She's referring to the weekend when we eat separately. She has some company, which is better than eating alone, but still it is not like having all of us together.

Changing the subject: Hisayo has received a notice from the Immigration Office about a public hearing. She is confused and worried and went to see the lawyer, Nakahara, today. She was supposed to renew her permit every year, which she didn't; she just kept working. It may be settled by her lack of awareness of the regulation.

I'm so busy and fed up with my work. The supervisor didn't even show up today. To add to my misery, a letter from Stanford stated that the doctor cannot write a note on your behalf because it was your choice to go to Japan for treatment. The insurance office promised to phone me if they find a better way to cover the cost. Maybe we should be satisfied that at least the hospital cost is fully covered. As for Stanford University Hospital, they cannot back you up because it may suggest their incompetence and hurts their pride. I wonder if you cannot find something to prove that the treatment of your particular symptom is done only in Japan and Germany. Anyhow, please don't worry too much. The ringing in your ears might have increased because of your concern about the bags, don't you think so? Start using the 15 bags that I sent by air, and if you don't receive the first package by sea by that time, let me know; I'll send some more by air. . . .

At the rate of one bag a day, we have enough to cover September, October, and November. If you have to stay there after November, I'll send some more at the end of September or early October. So please do not worry.

Yoshimitsu-san caught a lot of squid and gave me some. I ate too much. Do you have the name of Hiroyuki's girlfriend? Get her name next time, please. It would be easier to use her name instead of just speaking of her as "his girlfriend." I'll pack two sets of Gillette razors. Let's not be discouraged; let's live with hope! Please return to my normal jovial Kiyoshi-san. This is the reply to your letters 8, 9, and 10. It appears that both coasts of the Pacific Ocean had a bad week. Let's look at it this way—for every downward moment there is an uplifting, joyous moment—that's the way we should look at our life. Take care, I'll write again.

*During this period, Kiyoshi's mother had rented the house next door to her house on Fifth Street in Japantown and was living there with her niece, Mitsuko, and Kiyoko's sister Hisayo.

From KIYOSHI, *August 10.*

. . . TODAY I WENT TO MEI-NO-HAMA to the Laboratory of Thoracopathy (Chest Disease), a branch of Kyushu University Hospital. I feel a bit tired. To examine me, they took many stratigrams with the x-ray that I've never seen before. Aiming at my chest, the camera moved from down to up while changing its angle. Japan is so advanced, I think, in the treatment of tuberculosis. Dr. Yoshida examined me thoroughly. According to him, it can be cured completely, but it will take three to five years. One method is to cut the chest open wide, fill it with gauze, change it often, then at some point implant muscle. Alternatively the left lung would be completely extracted. A horrible way to explain it—it makes one faint—and three to five years!? But according to the doctor, I can live a normal life span if the right side is well taken care of and the left side is kept clean.

It made me think—three to five years of medical treatment may not be bad for a young person. However, suppose I live 20 years more, it is a quarter of my life; and if it is 10 years, I'd have to spend half of it away from you and Yukiko. Should we sacrifice our precious life together and be separated for medical treatment? Or, should we live together the rest of our life with me in my present condition? The hospital stay costs about $150 a month, and the room is very nicely accommodated. But I can't say yes. Besides, the recovery rate is only 60 to 70%. I told the doctor that I would like to concentrate on my hearing problem first, and I want to discuss the rest with my wife before making a decision. If I can live with you the rest of my life happily, I would rather maintain my present condition. When I returned to the Nose and Ear Department, everybody congratulated me on the possibility of a successful recovery. I didn't know what to say to them. There may be an improvement in medicine in the future—the treatment with hormones may advance greatly so that a new medicine could be introduced that would restore the muscles. I thought it unwise to sign up now for a three-to-five-year treatment. What do you think? . . .

Dr. Yoshida will give me advice from now on. He is very helpful. He consulted with another doctor in the Surgery Department. If you have not yet sealed up the package, will you please add another razor with extra blades? I think this is the last present for the doctors. . . .

Please take care of yourself, Kiyoko-san. I'm anxiously waiting for your letter. Please write when you find time. . . .

To my precious Kiyoko-*sama*, from your Kiyoshi.

From KIYOKO, *August 11.*

. . . YOU SOUND SO DESPERATELY LONELY—I don't know what to do. You say that Watanabe-sensei should have called here Monday morning, but he did not. I may be a late riser, but I would get up to answer a phone. Monday morning I was awake from 4:30 a.m. on. I don't think I missed any calls. Sensei might have thought that it is better not to call so early. . . .

Each time that you have been hospitalized I have told myself that it is better to send you to a hospital than to send you to a war. Compared to sending one with perfect health to the front and possible death, in hospitals they try to cure patients—two opposing acts of us human beings. The latter is so much more humane. I am lonely, but I'm so grateful that you are in a hospital and hopeful for our future. If you were sent to the front, that loneliness plus my rage would make me utterly restless. To go through a war and perhaps lose sons and daughters, or become a widow—as many have—and yet to keep on living would be so hard. I think that our life is firmly rooted and should be revered. I cannot accept the type of life driven simply by force of habit. To live is to do something worthwhile; we will make our life worthwhile and help others to do the same.

I followed your example of philosophizing, Kiyoshi-san, and have used up so much space to do that!

This morning I mailed the package out to you. It contains a box of 30 plastic bags, three cans of Almond Roca, two Wash 'n Dri, two Wash-ups, two sticks of salami, one can of cashew nuts, two sets of Gillette razors with spare blades, 20 soap bars, and three sets of flannel pajamas plus Yukiko's drawing and construction work. I left the price stickers on in case of a Customs check. Please remember to take them off when you use them for gifts. This applies also to the contents of the package I sent earlier. I declared the price conservatively, but it was over $20. You may have to pay a tax so please be prepared for that.

I couldn't write to you last night because I spent time making the package. After taking it to the post office today, we went to the beach. Glen and the other children are old enough now to select the beach themselves. After some discussion, we went to Rio del Mar near Santa Cruz. Akira-san and his wife joined us too. We left the beach at five p.m. and got home at 5:45 p.m. After supper, I washed the car and wrote this letter. I told your mother that the tension of my body seemed to have gone away after sitting on the warm sand. Next time she might come with us too. Rio Del Mar is a bleak and dreary beach, but Yukiko had fun playing in the waves. I wish you had been with us. I will send some pictures. . . .

I am glad to be your beloved wife.

From KIYOSHI, *August 11.*

. . . MY HEARING HAS NOT BEEN good for the past few days. According to my diary, when I don't have the carbonic acid inhalation, it gets worse. I might have mentioned it before, but the last few days I didn't get the treatment due to a malfunction of the machine. Since it is a test machine, it goes down often. Sometimes I go without the treatment for two to four days in a row. At first, I thought the intense heat was the cause of my hearing loss. However, my diary shows that the hearing loss coincides with the skips in carbonic acid inhalation.

Today I'm going to show Dr. Shirabe the excerpt of my diary from the day I started the treatment, July 18, to the present to see if he can help me with this problem. My diary shows the agreement of the dates between my difficulty in hearing and the skips in carbonic acid inhalation. This will prove that carbonic acid stimulates blood circulation to the brain. I wrote earlier about the close connection of blood vessels to the brain and to the ear. I'm going to ask Dr. Shirabe to make sure the machine is in operating condition at all times.

I hope the medicine that I asked you to mail arrives soon. I believe the doctor is interested in it for its ability to stimulate blood circulation in the inner ear. I'm anxiously waiting for that medicine, more so than the doctor. I want to supply blood vigorously to the ear before its cells weaken or die.

I'll continue after reading today's letter from you.

It is 2:30 p.m.. Your letter of Saturday, August fifth, arrived. As always your letter gives me back my life. A lump came up into my throat when I read your line, "I am so lonely tonight thinking of Kiyoshi-san." I am blessed to have your warm and tender and boundless love—I want to lean on you—I bow to you sincerely with my deep gratitude.

I showed the excerpt from my diary to Dr. Shirabe and had a long talk with him. He assured me they will have one inhaler machine set aside for me so that I will not skip the carbonic acid treatment. He also told me about the additional prescriptions of medicine. He says histamine helps to expand blood vessels and vitamin E is good for hearing difficulty. I told him that I brought vitamin E from the U.S.—the bottle that my mother gave me. The doctor wants to see it. I'm grateful to Dr. Shirabe for his attention and keen interest in my case. He is a cheerful man and looks like Nozaki-san in San Jose. He explains very carefully. I thanked him, and he said, with a smile, "An extra machine will be ready for you—I've already ordered it." So tomorrow the carbonic acid treatment resumes; I don't have to skip it anymore. Regarding vitamin E, please ask my mother to get a large bottle, will you? It is "E. 100 int. units" and the distributor is Radiance Products Co. I've been taking it, and now half a bottle is left which should cover me for about 20 days. . . .

This is my last sheet of air letter. Hiroyuki-san is supposed to bring 50 sheets tomorrow. In a separate package I'll send you some photos.

I'm so happy today because I got your letter. I'll write you again tomorrow. . . .

From KIYOSHI, *August 12.*

. . . IT LOOKS LIKE WE ARE GOING to have a hot day. No wind—it is only nine o'clock, but I have to use *uchiwa* in this room. . . .

In spite of this heat, I have not lost weight. Every Tuesday I get weighed. I was 58 kg last time, which was 58 x 2.2=127 lb—almost the same as I was when I was home. I drink two bottles of milk three times a day plus a bottle of orange juice twice a day. In the evening I order chicken-rice or fried rice from the caterers. I try to eat regularly even when I don't have an appetite so as not to lose my strength. Physical stamina may help me restore my health. . . .

I think a lot about the work you have to do for me. It must be so hard doing everything all by yourself. I owe you so much, Kiyoko-san.

I was exhausted day before yesterday when I went to Mei-no-hama Laboratory. But today I feel much better. The nurses and the aides are very kind and sympathetic.

The high school girl across the hall is also nice. The other day she brought chrysanthemums to me in an empty can decorated with paper and ribbon. Nowadays we don't see such thoughtfulness in young girls. One day she brought me her English homework and asked me to teach her. She said, *"Oji-san,* please teach me," and bashfully bowed—what an unspoiled girl she is. She asked, *"Oji-san,* do you like Japanese *umeboshi?"* I said, "Yes, I like it," without thinking much further. Later she gave me a jar, saying, "This is just some homemade *umeboshi."* I was so touched. Imagine, I can take the jar to the dining hall and let my fellow patients see how much I enjoy *umeboshi!* I guess it is good for one's health. I think she would be a good wife for Henry. I think she was born in Yame-gun, Fukuoka. There is no hint of arrogance about her. She gives me the impression of an unsophisticated but utterly honest person. She looks so innocent and bows like a grade-school child. And she is pretty. I really think she is the right one for Henry. But she is going home next week.

I wanted to find a wife for Yotsuo-san too. But I have to get my hearing back first. I'm encouraged because it is getting better—55 at the time I checked in to the hospital, 50 on July 26, and down to 45 on August ninth. I may start to hear a little when it goes down to 30. If it goes down five points every two weeks, in six weeks I should get down to 30; I hope I get to that point in two months. In any case, I'll work hard toward that goal. I need encouragement from you too.

Kiyoko-san, your letter gives me the very encouragement I need. Nothing makes me happier than reading a letter from you and soaking in your love. I am such a lucky man. Sometimes I fancy myself holding you tight and repeating "I love you." I am so fortunate to have somebody like you to love. When I was alone last night I was thinking how glad I am to be born in this world and to be married to you. That was the best thing that happened to me. There is nothing greater in my life than marrying you whom I love with all my heart, with all my body, with everything that I can think of. I love you so much. I don't think others can understand this feeling. Kiyoko-san, *arigatō!* I am over 40—yet I can't help but want to write to you every day—I am so lucky! Another man might let a week or a month go by without writing to his wife. He may have excuses, he may have passionate love—but I don't understand—I don't think he is talking about real love between a man and wife. If it is a real relationship, he can't let days go by without picking up a pen.

I don't care if I'm laughed at—I love you, Kiyoko-san—I love you so much my heart hurts. . . .

From KIYOKO, *August 13.*

AFTER FINISHING THE LAST LETTER, I realized that I forgot to tell you about the insurance. Our policy covers only up to a semiprivate room. If you are in a private room, we have to pay the difference. If a semiprivate room costs $7 and private room costs $10, we pay the difference of $3. The quality of a Japanese hospital room is none of their concern. I think it is better not to pursue this issue. We should be glad that at least $7 is covered. Miscellaneous expenses related to the treatment are covered up to $300. So let's be satisfied with that. Hospital regulations are rigid and insurance policies are firm, but most of our expenses are covered—I think this is good. Please don't feel disappointed and worsen the ringing in your ears. Please think of our dreams and my hopes and get sustenance from these.

Regarding Hisayo: She is relieved a little bit because her lawyer is working on the case of her immigration status. Her adviser at school is also helpful.

Your mother is complaining that Mitsuko-san wants to sleep on the mattress without sheets and a pillow case and takes a bath only once every 10 days; she is worse than Matsuji-san. But since you told your mother, "Don't say anything to them that they don't like," she just let it go. I can't do anything either because I'm an outsider. If I'm asked, I'll try to help them. For now, I'm just observing. . . .

It's getting late—I'll stop here. I can hear your sigh tonight, Kiyoshi-san. . . .

From KIYOSHI, *August 13.*

I WROTE THIS MORNING USING regular letter paper. This aerogram which I asked Hiroyuki-san to get for me is a continuation of it. He also brought a package that arrived at the residence of Watanabe-sensei. To my surprise, a package airmailed on August eighth arrived today also. I was amazed because it was mailed on August ninth Japan time and arrived here on the 12th—so fast, faster than letters! Thank you so much. All of a sudden, I feel that a burden has been removed from my shoulders—no more worry about bags and medicine.

This medicine is so expensive, isn't it? The price of a bottle containing 100 pills is $7.50 or 7.5 cents (27 yen) per pill. The doctor's prescription says "two pills per day," but the sample that I have says, "three to four per day," which means a day's dosage costs 30 cents. It costs as much as a pack of cigarettes. I'll follow whatever Dr. Shirabe recommends.

Today I started a new treatment with a hypodermic injection. I'll start on a new prescription this evening. Also the inhalation of carbonic acid resumed this afternoon. I feel so much better after the inhalation—the ringing in my ears reduces noticeably—this treatment really works. I pray there are no more machine breakdowns. But the movement of the pointer is not steady; instead of moving up and stopping, it hangs up at the bottom moving to and fro. Just looking at it, I become anxious and pray that it will keep moving at least for 20 minutes [while I'm on it]. I know I can't do anything—the doctors are all trying hard—this is the only machine in Japan, and it is still in the experimental stage.

I couldn't help but open the package while Hiroyuki-san was here. I gave him about $1/3$ of the contents. Perhaps I gave him too much, but I felt it was the right thing to do. After all, he and Watanabe-sensei are my closest contacts here, and they are like my second family. I still have some left to give to others, but unfortunately Watanabe-sensei's portion has been reduced a little bit. I may need Hiroyuki-san's help more and more from now on. You may say that he could have waited, but I wanted to thank him now because he really takes care of me like his own family. Please understand.

Regarding Arlidrin, the medicine that just arrived—can you get ready to ship another bottle? If I have to take four pills a day, it will be gone in 25 days. I wonder if it might come down to $60, or even to $50, if we buy 1,000 pills. I'm sorry to bother you so often.

How is Yukiko? . . . How about you, Kiyoko-san? Are you all right? Are you still working every Saturday? Please take care of yourself.

I wrote to Iwama-san the other day. I hope she will not write back again. I told her that her letter reached me as quick as a telegram and that I was sorry for my delayed response because I had more than a dozen letters to reply to ahead of hers. I think I said it nicely. I warned her that in the future my reply might take time for the same reason, and also for medical reasons because the doctor told me to avoid too much mental stress. . . .

From KIYOSHI, *August 13.*

TODAY IS THE FIRST DAY OF Obon in Japan. I didn't know it, but the high school student across the hall wrote a note explaining it to me. Her family is of a samurai clan, and she wrote about the custom of Obon in her family— for instance, they prepare a chariot made of eggplant for the departed soul of the ancestors to ride on. It was so interesting.

She wrote at the end that she hopes my hearing gets better soon so that I can visit her family. She is really an unassuming and graceful young lady. She adores me and calls me *oji-san*. I gave her some of those coffee candies, and she was delighted. A few days ago, a group of young women came to see me and asked me to talk about America. I didn't know what to do! I told them about my hearing problem; they said they would write their questions on paper. So I ended up talking about the life of students and Japanese people in America. It was tiring to keep talking when I couldn't hear so I taught them how to play dominoes. They were delighted to learn the game, so much so that they played again yesterday in the room across the hall. The high school girl, after losing round after round, said laughingly that she was not smart like others, but she could learn to play better if she had more time—she goes home next week though. I think her family line is too high, and she is too beautiful to marry Henry; her family may not let her come to the States. She has an older sister. If the parents had more daughters, they may not mind letting one of them marry a foreigner—but just two daughters—I doubt it. Anyway I'm going to ask for their address. By the way, have you mentioned this girl to Sister? What would she say, I wonder, about us talking of Henry's future wife.

I'm looking forward to a letter from you today because none came yesterday. I'm glad that mail is delivered even on Sunday in Japan. I'm going to continue this letter after reading yours this afternoon.

· · ·

No letter from you—I feel lonely. But, it will come tomorrow. I'm waiting. Cecilia's letter never reached me—I wonder why. You can't ask her, can you? It was not lost, I hope.

This afternoon the high school student across the hall came to see me together with her sister who made *botamochi* for Obon; they gave some to me. The sister is shorter and more slender—quite a different type from her younger sister. But she has large eyes just like the ones Nakahara Jun'ichi paints in his portraits, and very pretty. She has darker skin than her sister's. I think she is one or two years older.

Today's letter is all about the student across the hall. Without your letter, I don't know what else to write. Please forgive me.

From KIYOSHI, *August 14.*

No letter yet—what's going on?

I don't know what to do. The end.

Madam, what are you going to do?

From your anxious hubby,
August 14, 1967

From KIYOKO, *August 15.*

I'M SO GLAD TO HEAR GOOD NEWS FOR A change. I think I can understand how you felt when Dr. Shirabe told you that—you almost cried—and now your hope is back! I was worried because you seemed to be discouraged unnecessarily. I feel relieved because you now have something to look forward to. We should always wait for the results of tests before getting discouraged or relieved. Your blood must have rushed up to your head because of that worry. It was not fair to your body, which is trying so hard to get better. You were preventing your recovery by your own worry. It was not necessary. In the same way, excessive worry about a marriage can destroy a marriage. I myself experienced panic once or twice when I lost confidence in my own health—I was very frightened. Looking back, there was no basis for that. But it was very hard to shake off that panic. So I can understand how you felt. I admire you, and I am so grateful to you, Kiyoshi-san, for listening to my advice and trying to control your panic—I can't continue . . . I'm overcome with emotion . . . and about to cry.

I am now brewing the herbal medicine that Cecilia bought for me this weekend. Since I over-boiled it last time, I'm using a timer now. Yukiko is eating cereal for a snack after her dinner. We are appreciating an evening breeze coming through the window since it's been so hot for the last few days.

Please keep your spirit up and keep fighting against this illness. We've come this far together, and I want to win this together. Normally I am not greedy, but this time I want to succeed in this fight so badly. That's why I want you to hold out firmly. It's all right if your hearing is gone or the use of your limbs is gone. The purpose of our life is not hinged upon these exterior things. Let's not forget that.

We know that the treatment will continue—that means we have hope.

However, suppose we are told that there is no more treatment left to try, and your condition has not improved. We don't have to give up, because this is the age of electronic medicine, and we haven't explored that yet. Time moves only forward improving our life and our environment. Remember, this was your belief. I think it is better not to be swept away by the immediate problems. This may be a healthy person talking, but it has merit, I think. . . .

I try, but it is so hard to express all of my feelings on paper. I hope you can understand my intention.

Yukiko went shopping today with Mother and Mitsuko-san to get some sewing material. She has a great plan to sew something by herself. It will be wonderful when and if it is done. But she is too occupied by this project and delays writing to you. I tell her that you wouldn't like it, but she doesn't believe me. I'll try a different approach next time. . . .

From KIYOSHI, *August 15.*

. . . THE LAST DAY OF OBON. Most of the patients are going to a nearby park to see the folk dance. I was invited too but decided not to go because of my hearing. If I get tired, the ringing gets worse. . . .

Dr. Shirabe was astonished to hear that the doctor in America did not specifically recommend taking vitamin E and B, and Arlidrin for my ear problem. I told him that I brought E to enhance the health of my peripheral nervous system. He said it is used to help my hearing too. So, I started to take all of them. If I stop moving around, the ringing subsides; if I walk fast or strain myself in talking (because I can't hear), it increases. The ringing definitely decreases when I keep still. At times the left ear hardly rings. I think the left side is getting a little bit better, but not the right side. Please ask my mother to get a large bottle of vitamin E. Arlidrin is so expensive, but please get it—I start with two pills for three days, three pills for the next three days, and four pills after that.

The last part of your letter that came today moved me so much. You too wait for my letters impatiently. I was so happy to hear that. . . .

Please rest well after working overtime. I might have said that I still have to send replies to about 50 people—of course, it was an excuse to Yamada-san. The other day I asked Hiroyuki-san to get 70 air letters. The post office was so surprised and asked Hiroyuki-san, "Are you going to write this many letters?"

Today the sister of the girl across the hall brought branches of persimmon and chestnut trees from her garden, and said, "Please feel autumn in Japan although it is a little too early." Also she gave me tempura of *shiso*, *myōga*, flowers of pumpkin, and other vegetables. I couldn't help but marvel

On a picnic at Rio del Mar, *Aptos, California, August 11, 1967; from left: Mitsuyo Shibata Tao, Paul Tao, Alan Tao, Yukiko Tokutomi, Kiyoko Tokutomi, Mitsuko Haraguchi, and Glen Tao. Photo by Akira Tao, courtesy of Yukiko Tokutomi Northon.*

at how exceptionally well brought up these two sisters are. They certainly carry the grace of a good family background. I gave her some candy that you sent—she was very happy.

Please tell me, Kiyoko-san, that you miss me, you long for me—I want to hear it. I want to hold you so tight—till I crush your body—I love you, I love you!

I'll write you again. Say "Hi" to Yukiko and Hisayo-san.

From KIYOKO, *August 15.*

... YOUR AIR LETTERS OF August 10, 11, and 12, and a regular letter with a photo all came today. Your numbering is off by one, so I corrected it. As I was going to note the change in my diary, which I carry in my bag, I found that I forgot to mail my last letter. I had brewed an herb drink last night and felt so relaxed that I didn't discover this till now. I was thinking all this time that the letter was on its way to you.

The Japanese are very advanced in the treatment of tuberculosis, aren't they? I wish we could go back to Japan as a family and treat you there. But there is a possibility of being healed naturally here in the States if you can hold on to yourself in spite of the scar on your lung. What do you say? Of course there is always a possibility of regression. But a healthy diet will prevent that, I think. And, of course, the best way is to become totally cured. The doctor said that it'll take three to five years to completely heal, but that couldn't be the duration of the hospital stay. Why don't you find out more about it from the doctor? In any case, we don't have to decide it right away. ...

It is interesting that carbonic acid gas treatment is so effective. Dr. Childrey was surprised when I told him that you were taking a treatment using some kind of gas in order to stimulate blood circulation. Perhaps doctors in this area are not familiar with that treatment. Dr. Childrey might be searching for information on carbonic acid gas treatment right now. It was so kind of Dr. Shirabe to have arranged for the availability of the machine so that you will not miss the treatment. The note in your diary did help you a great deal, didn't it?

I am so glad to see your photo—you have not changed at all. Judging from the penmanship, Matsuda-san must be an honest person. If you have something left, please give it to him and tell him that the photo made your family so happy. Letters can tell me a lot about how you are, but photos can show me more. Soon I'll send you mine. What is the machinelike thing behind the bed? I see a bottle that looks like a shoyu server and another like a thermos. I'm glad to see you dressed neatly in a bathrobe and that the bed sheets are smoothed nicely. A hospital aide here once complained that it was hard to keep the sheets in place so I commend you for taking care of that. I'm so happy to note that you have not lost weight. Please continue taking good care of yourself.

The letters that you wrote around early August were disturbing—they made me so worried. But I received an encouraging one yesterday. Tonight I'm going to the post office to mail this and the one I forgot to mail. Yukiko went to Mother's place with letter paper intending to write to you there while watching TV. She started with "Daddy" but came home without continuing it. I hope she will finish it someday. Cecilia is practicing driving. There is a letter for you from Takagi-san; he recommends you to come to Japan in autumn. Hisayo's immigration case has been well taken care of by Lawyer Nakahara.

Insects are singing—I'm going to take this and the other letter to the post office—it might reach you a little bit faster. Shall I send you American air letters? Please let me know. I'll write you again.

From KIYOSHI, *August 16.*

THEY SAY THAT AFTER OBON IT COOLS DOWN, but it's not so—it is still very hot. . . .

How was the beach? I bet Yukiko enjoyed it. I wonder if I can go to the beach next year and have a good time with my family.

In yesterday's letter you said that I would make excellent connections if I kept writing to many people. But I am not really writing to 50 people, Kiyoko-san, only to a few and only when it is necessary—I don't have the energy to write to 50 people. I want to hear from you and Yukiko—most of all from you, Kiyoko-san. . . .

Regarding the letter to Stanford University, I don't care any more. I will ask Dr. Shirabe about the treatment that only Japan and Germany are practicing. I'll let you know later.

The name of Hiroyuki-san's girlfriend is Kuroki Noriko-san. The other day the three of us went to a Chinese restaurant called Fukuju Hanten. I needed to get some change for dollars so that I can pay cash in yen for newspapers, milk, cleaners, etc. It was a Chinese restaurant that Mitsuyo-san liked, and I had the best food for the first time since I came here. Maybe I have the blood of the Chinese in me—I like Chinese food. It didn't cost much—only about $10 for 3 people, and it was a special order. Noriko-san enjoyed it too and asked many things about her future sister-in-law. She was deeply impressed when I said that we are writing to each other every day. . . .

P.S. I haven't received a letter from Cecilia. Remember me to her and tell her that I had delicious Chinese food that she would enjoy.

From KIYOKO, *August 17.*

. . . LAST NIGHT I WAS TELLING Lily about you in the hospital. I had intended to casually mention something about Henry's future wife and about the girl across the hall, but I missed the chance because another guest joined us. I'll try again some other time. I'll tell her that a Japanese girl would make a good wife for Henry. Your mother said laughingly that Henry should finish school and get a good job first. Frankie is growing his hair long too. Lily looked good. In the freezer I had Chinese buns that I had asked Cecilia to get. I took them to Lily, and they were just right for her because she has started to eat solids since last weekend.

Yukiko finished the one-piece dress last Tuesday. This is her first dress that she made. She is so proud of it though Mitsuko-san did 80% of the work.

Cecilia asked me today how to write "Kiyoshi" in Japanese—that means she has not written to you yet. She has been very busy taking care of her friend's child. It not only makes her exhausted but also makes her wonder how her best friend raised her child. Her friend is an exceptional individual but a poor parent, so much so that their friendship may become shaky. I have to watch out so that Yukiko does not become like that youngster.

You must have the quality that attracts people. You will have more people like those. How about showing them the *Nihongo News* and other periodicals? I'll send it to you if I find some suitable teaching material. Maps are good too—but you may have to spend a lot of time on them. It is nice that they like you, but at the same time, it may become bothersome for you. How about cards? I put cards in the first or second package—I can't remember now.

Last evening I went to San-ni-biru and then couldn't sleep well. We are having record heat in San Jose, and then it drops down at night so drastically that many people are suffering with colds. As usual my work is slow in summer. Since the project I've been working on will be completed soon, I'm thinking of taking time off for a week at the end of this month or the beginning of next month. It will be good for Yukiko too because we can prepare for her new school year. September first is Yukiko's birthday and also Hisayo's graduation day. Yukiko and I will attend that. Since she didn't get very good grades, it wouldn't be proper to invite guests—besides attendees are limited to three per student.

I will write again. I'm writing every other day. I'll send some more newspapers. The serial novel, *The Freezing Point* {氷点 (*Hyōten*)}, is continuing, and I'm still reading it and getting mad at it.

From KIYOSHI, *August 17.*

... THERE IS NO CHANGE HERE. Today marks one month since I checked into this hospital. I can't tell if I'm getting better or not. I wish I could tell myself that I'm getting better. Although the left ear can hear the sound of the pump, I wish I could hear it more clearly. There is no further improvement. Since yesterday I take the inhaler treatment in the recovery room next to the operation room. I could . . . see a patient who had difficulty breathing; sometimes patients die there—I felt a chill all over me. My temperature went up after that, and I wished I didn't have to go back there. They say I have to use the inhaler in that room until a new machine comes. I couldn't help but imagine a dead patient using that inhaler—with an oxygen tank attached. I almost fainted. I want to get well—but I don't have the nerve to look at the inhaler—I don't know what to do. I'm so anxious to have the new machine. It is a larger machine and will cost 500 yen for 20 minutes of use.

Iwama-san must have written to her cousin who wants to pay me a visit—I don't know what to do. She must have good intentions, but it's annoying. I can't hear anything—I'll get exhausted. I must send her a polite letter. Forgive me for this gloomy letter. I'll write again after reading yours.

From KIYOSHI, *August 17.*

. . . YOUR LETTER CAME — I'M very happy. . . . This is going to be a quick note so that you will receive this together with the previous one.

I'm all right now. I'm sorry to have you worry. Thank you for sending another package. You say there is an extra shaving set—it will help me a great deal. I'll ask Hiroyuki-san to take it to Dr. Yoshida at the Mei-no-hama Lab. The other one is for Dr. Shirabe.

Regarding Mitsuko, I think it is better to leave her alone—maybe just put clean sheets on her bed and not discuss her habits. Some people do not like to be told to clean their rooms or to wash their shirts. If they don't mind dirty rooms or soiled shirts, that's their choice. Nobody should pry into another's life—otherwise it just creates discord among us. When Mitsuko reaches a marriageable age and has visitors in her room, she will change her way. Tell my mother that she should not say anything to the girl because sooner or later she will grow out of it—it won't be long. Tell her that it is better to be remembered as a nice lady. . . .

From KIYOKO, *August 19.*

. . . I'M ENCLOSING THE PHOTOS. Yesterday I received your curt message —like a telegram—only 29 characters. This morning I sent by sea mail the newspapers up to August 17. I'll continue sending the papers till one month before you come home so that you won't have to read a bunch of old editions all at once. . . .

I slept better last night. It was cooler too. Thursday night I was tired and sleepy but couldn't sleep. I felt you all around me. Neither plum wine nor Anacin helped me to sleep. . . [but] holding on to you in my mind— that ecstatic sensation came back to me at last. I think I can be ready for you any time. Lately I was so tense and tired because of the worries that I've been through. In spite of that, my body still [is aroused by] you.

I was restless that night with my yearning heart, with my burning body. I hardly slept. Friday I went to work, and your letter of 29 characters was waiting when I came home. I am sorry! You wrote it a week ago on a weekend so I think you've received some letters by now. We receive a letter written the week before, and it takes another week to send a response. So it takes two weeks to exchange our thoughts in writing. I cannot blame you, Kiyoshi-san. I take your scolding without challenging it.

Last night I went to Fourth Street to get the photos. Most of them came out nicely, especially Yukiko's Bon dancing. Some of them were taken the day of your departure. There are two shots that Yukiko took. She is very proud to see her first photos even though they are blurred. The overexposure must have happened when the film was taken out of the camera, but these are especially nice. The Mrs. looks so plain as usual. Don't show this to others. The Rio del Mar excursion didn't produce any interesting shots because they were taken by Akira-san with his two cameras. Besides, Yukiko was having so much fun that she wouldn't come close enough to the camera. Although they are taken from a distance, I enclosed 10 of them. The rest are the full length shot of Alan and Yukiko in *yukata*, which came out too dark—I'll show them to you when you come home. . . .

Today was washing day. I went to Macy's because I found that my underwear was worn out. Now I'm writing this. Yukiko is outside cutting the lawn, so she tells me. She has not finished the letter to you. She wanted me to take her out somewhere—I told her that I was too tired—she pounded on my back and said, "Do you feel better?" After that she gave up asking to go somewhere and went out to cut the lawn.

I'm going to take a week off. . . . I have about 18 days vacation time, and I'll lose it unless I use it before the 20th. I'll save the remaining days for the time you come home. During the vacation, I'll spend one day going to Watsonville to get strawberries. I want to give some to Kanemoto-san, Cecilia, and Tatsuno-san.

Even if you don't get my letter every day, Kiyoshi-san, please keep writing me tender, loving notes. It is better that way because you are gentle and affectionate by nature. I will try to write at least every other day. Take care.

From KIYOSHI, *August 19.*

MADAM, HOW HAVE YOU BEEN? I DID NOT HEAR *from you yesterday or today—for two days. I am deeply concerned about you.*

How does it read? Is it better than the letter of a crestfallen man? It may be better than a crybaby's letter. And, how about this version?

Hey, what's up? Are you OK?

This is terrible—I'll go back to my normal way. I'm sorry.

I wonder what Yukiko is doing. I wrote her yesterday. I'm wondering if she read it without help.

I was feeling unsteady because of the histamine that I was taking—two pills after meals, since Saturday last week. My appetite was gone, and my hearing was worse. I told that to the doctor, and he stopped it. This morning I feel much better and my hearing is better too. I'm still taking the carbonic acid inhalation treatment in that big operating room. I still don't like that room. When there is an operation, the nurses wear green uniforms, aprons, masks, and tight head-coverings—all ready for the big moment—just looking at them, I want to run away like a frightened horse. Just the operation room sign makes me want to turn away from there. . . .

From KIYOSHI, *August 20.*

. . . LAST NIGHT THERE WAS A display of fireworks over the Bay of Hakata —it was so beautiful—far more beautiful than the fireworks at our State College. Here they shoot up five or six at once, or seven or eight, and sometimes more than 10 are shot up continuously—it is spectacular to view. I was very impressed by this display. Hakata or Fukuoka City must be hosting this event.

Have you asked Mother to get more vitamins? They are about to run out. Please send them along with Arlidrin by air mail. . . . I lose my appetite when it is so hot, but I'm trying to eat something. Sometimes I buy ice cream, or order chicken-rice from an outside restaurant. I drink orange juice as often as I can as a vitamin C supplement.

I have not heard from Cecilia. I'm looking forward to seeing the photos of the beach trip. I'll write again today if I get your letter—if not, this is all. Take care. . . .

From KIYOKO, *August 21.*

. . . I'M WRITING THIS IN THE OFFICE hoping that maybe your letter is waiting at home. The weather turned cold, and it is like autumn. At night the heater comes on. I added a coverlet just like in wintertime. This weekend I felt so tired and thought I was catching cold. I'm feeling a little better now because I had a relaxed weekend. Since I decided to take a vacation, somehow my strength is gone, and it is an effort to come to work. Getting up in the morning is very difficult, as always. Acronyms like VCE(Sat), VBE(Sat) that I use at work came up in my dream this morning. It is so disgusting—I'm so tired of work. Things are slow in the office—this may be the other cause of my laziness.

In Japan autumn steals in after Obon, but I guess the daytime is still very hot. I mailed the photos last Saturday. I'm holding the letter from Takakise and the air letters because I decided to wait for your instruction.

Yesterday Mr. Eckford came to the house. He received a letter from you, and he was so happy. I'm glad too. I hear that Tsukiji-san's food service is very successful, better than their gift corner, and that the store has been remodeled. Dobashi was closed after 12:00 noon yesterday, and I thought I'd try something from Tsukiji-san's. So I sent Yukiko to get dumplings for three people. It cost $3.00! The bean-curd shop didn't have anything left; steak is too heavy so I thought dumplings would be just right. But $3.00! This is the first and the last time I buy food there. . . . . .

Yukiko's birthday is approaching. The long summer vacation is about to end. To my surprise she doesn't even bring up the name of Disneyland. Compared to a Japanese kid, she has so much freedom to play. I try not to restrain her because having freedom is not a bad thing. This weekend she was playing with her doll trying her own dresses on it. When Hisayo-san said she would never marry, Yukiko said she wouldn't either. If she has to marry, she says, she would find a Salvadoran. She is completely taken by the Salvadorans.

At this point I'm writing from home, standing. Friday and Saturday I didn't receive any letters, but today four letters came all at once. Maybe because of that I had a bowel movement with lots of rabbitlike turds—I feel so much lighter. This morning I couldn't fasten my skirt because I was so bloated.

Yukiko wants me to take her to GEM to prepare for her birthday. I'll stop here and will write in response to the four letters tomorrow.

From KIYOSHI, *August 21.*

. . . AS I WAS WONDERING IF I would get your letter today, two letters came while Hiroyuki-san and his fiancée were here. . . . I showed [them] the one written on the 14th. Noriko-san was much moved. I'm sure she made a silent vow to herself to emulate you. . . .

Today Watanabe-sensei came; we talked about the insurance at the office. If my stay exceeds two months, I must submit an application with three photos to City Hall. So Watanabe-sensei took my picture. With this and that, I couldn't start writing until now—I don't think I can finish in time for the mail pickup.

I am overwhelmed by what you wrote in the letter. "I admire you and I am so grateful to you, Kiyoshi-san, for listening to my advice to try to control your panic. . . . I can't continue—I'm overcome with emotion and about to cry." I'm about to cry, too, Kiyoko-san. Also you wrote: "It's all right if one loses one's hearing or the use of one's limbs. The purpose of our life is not hinged upon these exterior things. Let's not forget that." I'm so moved that I don't know what to say. And you continued, "This may be a healthy person talking, but it has its own merit, I think. I bow to your sincere effort to accept the opinion of others instead of fencing yourself in the cocoon of a sick bed." Kiyoko-san, thank you! I will try hard to become worthy of being your husband—worthy of your respect—and, quite apart from restoring my hearing, to become a better man.

Thank you so much for this letter. I am a lucky man to have you as my wife. . . .

From KIYOSHI, *August 22.*

. . . TODAY IS WEIGHING DAY. I lost one kilogram. I was afraid that I might have lost more because I didn't eat much last week due to the adverse effects of the histamine pills. I'll eat more and rest well so that I gain weight.

Yesterday Watanabe-sensei came, and we discussed my insurance before talking to the office here. I'm charged 2,000 yen a day for the room I'm in. A "semiprivate room" costs 1,000 yen in this hospital. Therefore I'm paying 1,000 yen extra (about $3.00) for this room. According to our insurance policy, for the first 21 days the company pays the entire amount of a "semi-private room" plus medical costs. I figure that the out-of-pocket expense for the first month is about $530 including the cost of the room. For the ensuing 180 days, the medical coverage will be reduced by 50%. If the coverage of the room is also reduced by 50%, I will pay 1,500 yen a day out of my pocket. In other words, I will pay about $4.00 per day for the room plus 50% of the medical costs. The estimate of my medical costs is about $350 a month so 50% of it is $175. Therefore, after 21 days, my out-of-pocket expense will be $175 for medical and $120 for the room, nearly $300 a month. Does your insurance from work cover me too? I have enough money with me now to take care of my expenses for roughly one more month.

In any case, I'll fill out the insurance papers and mail them to you in a few days together with the hospital receipts. I wonder if the insurance company will pay the amount of coverage to you since I've been paying all the charges directly to the hospital here. If they do, can you send me the coverage amount? . . . There is no way to negotiate the difference between a semi-private room in an American hospital and a Japanese hospital. Here they have "special class A, B," "first class A, B," "second class A, B." The second class A is equivalent to an American semiprivate room, and second class B is the ward. I am in a first class A—that means the third from the top and two classes above a Japanese semiprivate room. In the classification of their "special," "first class," and "second class," their first class is equivalent to our semiprivate room. I'm going to write a note saying that the first class here is equivalent to the American semiprivate—though I'm not sure if they would accept it.

The form will be mailed in a few days. The amount on the receipts from the hospital has been converted to dollars—one of the patients helped me using her abacus. I'm going to stop here and start working on the insurance papers. . . .

From KIYOKO, *August 22.*

YESTERDAY WE WENT TO GEM TO SEE WHAT Yukiko wanted to get. When we got home, Hisayo told me, "Yukiko was so naughty this afternoon." Then, Yukiko wanted to see how hard she could hit me as she followed me around. She got too excited and tore up my brand new hose. I slapped her cheek. So, last night we all went to bed without making a peace treaty. She has reached the age in which retreat is not easy.

When your four letters arrived all at once the day before yesterday, I opened them, arranged them by the dates, and started to read them. I feel autumn in Japan in your letters. Please tell the lady who brought the twigs of persimmons and chestnuts that I wish I could have seen them too. I'm glad you found a good Chinese restaurant. Chinese food in Japan is so tasty, but I didn't have a chance to have it the last time I was home for three weeks. In spite of the excessive heat and mosquitoes, I miss Japan. I wanted to go home with you and Yukiko. Now you are there alone—I wish I were with you right this moment. But let me stop grumbling!

When I came home from work, Yukiko was waiting for me. She said she was so sorry about last night, and she will buy new hose for me. I said, "You don't have to—just don't do that again." I wanted you to know the end of the story. Mitsuko-san tells me that Yukiko stalks her even if she is told not to. I told her not to disturb Mitsuko-san, but she doesn't seem to understand. I have given up. . . .

Nobody can get used to an operating room—it is like an earthquake to Japanese people. Maybe you would feel better if you imagined a happy patient after the operation, or if you thought of what a great success modern medical science was. Suppose you have a terrible toothache—you would hurry to the dentist and have the tooth pulled out—wouldn't you feel better after that? Maybe you shouldn't think so hard. The husband of Kiyoko-san has got to be more relaxed and rise above those gory stories in the operating room. Revulsion and fear get worse unless they are stopped early on. I don't want my precious husband to be in that situation. . . .

This is all for today. Give my love to Hiroyuki and Noriko-san. Tell them I like her name. To my Kiyoshi-san, I hope this letter will save you from the fear of going near the operating room.

From KIYOSHI, *August 23.*

. . . I'VE FINISHED THE INSURANCE form and got Dr. Shirabe's signature, but the office has not signed it yet.

By the way, about the cost of airfare—if Stanford does not help, how about asking Dr. Childrey? He might write for me that the carbonic acid gas inhalation is not practiced in the States. If he would, please tell Dr. Childrey that I'll get detailed information on the treatment, and how they are giving it to me here. If he could certify that carbon dioxide inhalation treatment is not practiced in the States, it might work—what do you say?

I received a card from Cecilia today. I think I understood her Japanese. She says my letter written on July 25 arrived; she is glad that the treatment is working, and she's looking forward to talking with me as in the old days. Please tell her that I'll write back soon and that she should be careful when she practices driving.

I feel tired from working on the insurance form.

How is Yukiko preparing for the new school year? Tell her to do her best in school. . . .

From KIYOKO, *August 23.*

. . . I HAD A COLD—SPENT ALL day in bed soaked in sweat. I'd not been feeling quite up to par for a couple of weeks, and I finally got hit by a fever. I don't have extra pajamas so I borrowed yours. I thought I might get a letter from you today, but didn't. Yukiko took care of me this morning by making soup and bringing water, but when somebody is around, she's too busy with her toys to take care of me.

I was exhausted last night and crawled into bed still in my day clothes. Then Mr. Haruta called. He didn't know the purpose of your trip to Japan until somebody told him, and he wanted to write to you. I gave him your address. He wants to work there like he used to using his bilingual ability. He asked me if I wanted to do the same. I wanted to say, "My English is not good enough," but just said, "I'll think about it." I didn't want to be overly modest. But if you want to work in Japan, I'll go any time. . . .

Did my last letter pep you up a little? I had Yukiko mail it this morning. I planned to mail it myself last night, but I went to bed because I felt so miserable. This morning my neck and back are as hard as a wood board. I wish you were here to give me a massage. Maybe I should do exercises, something like go-go dancing, but I can't move my body, my head aches so. It seems the more I perspire the better I feel. I should be back to normal by the time you read this. So please do not worry. . . .

I wrote this in bed lying on my belly—hope you can read it.

To my Kiyoshi-san, I miss you!

From KIYOSHI, *August 24.*

. . . THIS IS A HASTY NOTE SO that I can post it today. I was delighted to have your letter written on the 17th; I'll respond to it later.

I finished the paper for the insurance company. The hospital agreed to call the classification of my room "first class-2," and their signature is on the paper. This will help. (I'm in the room which they call "first class-1.") "First class-2" costs 1,500 yen, which is $4.67. The difference between "first class-1" and "first class-2" is 500 yen, about $1.42. If the hospital classifies my room as "second class-1," the difference would be 700 yen. We asked, "Which is equivalent to an American semiprivate room, first class-2 or second class-1?" After listening to our explanation, they decided on first class-2. I am so relieved.

Dr. Shirabe has already signed the paper. The translation of the receipt is done. I'll need Mr. Ishibashi's signature for the hospital side. Having the English translation of the receipt and the signatures of the doctor and the hospital, the insurance company can't do much other than accept this statement. I'm glad that I translated the receipt. Mr. Ishibashi will sign the paper tomorrow afternoon, and I'll have Hiroyuki-san send this by special delivery.

How about coverage of the airfare? Do you think Dr. Childrey could possibly write a letter for me?

I'll post this now and start writing a reply to your letter that came today.

From KIYOKO, *August 24.*

. . . I WANTED TO WRITE A THANK-YOU note to Watanabe-sensei but have been unable to do that because writing to you precedes everything else. He wrote to me once and said "no need to reply." I took those words literally and so far I've sent only one thank-you note to him. I'm going to write to him when I feel much better. . . .

I wonder if you could ask one of the doctors about the following. The palm of my left hand is numb, and I can't feel anything with it. I slept on it about a week ago as I remember. But the numbness doesn't go away. If you have a chance, please ask one of the doctors around you. If this is a sign of aging, I should look for proper treatment as soon as possible.

Cecilia tells me that one of her friends, a Chinese lady, lost her hearing after taking some strong medicine to treat a problem in her brain. Because of the difficulty in hearing and the ringing in her ears, she quit her job in the Data Processing Lab at Stanford University. She has enough money and wants to go to Japan to get treatment. But according to Cecilia, it's been some time since this lady lost her hearing. I recommended taking some medicine to stimulate the blood circulation in the head. Apparently there are many people who have lost their hearing because of taking medicine and ended up suffering unnecessarily. Is it possible to find the procedure that enables a foreigner to receive treatments in your hospital? How about having Hiroyuki assist you in this?

Hisayo's lawyer, Mr. Nakahara, filed an application for an extension of her visitor's status, but she has not heard anything from him yet. It seems that my application for citizenship is shelved also. Yesterday's paper reported that there are an increasing number of immigrants but not many naturalized citizens. Maybe this is a good time to take the exams at the Immigration Office.

I'll stop here and give the remaining space to Yukiko. I'll write to you soon—take care.

Daddy, I'm sorry I've not written to you for some time now.
Carol called! I made a dress like this with a quilted patchwork
  of the letter M.   I love you.
    From Yukiko to Daddy.

[Yukiko's drawing of the dress and the sign of a heart pierced with an arrow (page 62) are part of her letter.]

From KIYOSHI, *August 24.*

THANK YOU FOR THE LETTERS, ESPECIALLY THE PHOTOS. I stared at your face for a long time and read your letter a thousand times. I'm so happy and homesick—I don't know how to describe this feeling.

[Part of the letter has been cut off.]

I received a letter from Mitsuko. She said that Yukiko showed her one of my letters to copy the address. I was surprised. Some time ago Yukiko said that Mitsuko was reading a letter of mine to Takagi. They are at an age where they are full of curiosity—please be careful and put my letters away somewhere where they can't be reached. Be sure to tell Yukiko that she must not show Daddy and Mommy's letters to others.

I'll continue this tomorrow.

From KIYOSHI, *August 25.*

. . . I HAVE MAILED THE INSURANCE papers. You will see one side of the envelope opened and resealed. Please don't be alarmed because I was the one who did it. After sealing the envelope, I realized that I could send it together with the air letter that I wrote yesterday.

How are you, Kiyoko-san? I've got my strength back after seeing these photos and reading your letters. I want to get well and come home to you. I read your letters repeatedly, calling your name many times in my heart. You can understand how much I miss you and want you.

• • •

I wrote this far yesterday before Hiroyuki-san and his fiancée came. I had asked the nurse to call him because I wanted to have him send the insurance papers by special mail. But the day before yesterday he was still in Sasebo working. Yesterday I found someone to mail it as he was going to the post office. When Hiroyuki-san came in the evening, it was all done. I showed the photos to him and his fiancée. Noriko-san looked at your photo for a long time. She must have been thinking of the perfume that you sent to her. She was so appreciative of your thoughtfulness. Maybe you want to write to her. Her address is: Noriko Kuroki, 34 Myōken-chō, Fukuoka-shi.

Nothing has made me happier than receiving these photos of you. I keep looking at them and feel you next to me all the time. How is Yukiko? Is she swimming every day? I like the photo of you that she took. It is slightly out of focus, but I like it. There are a few nice shots of Yukiko Bon dancing. You are getting better with the camera. But sometimes you forget to include the feet—next time try to include the sky and the ground—it would look much better. . . .

From KIYOKO, *August 26.*

. . . YOUR LETTER WRITTEN ON TUESDAY, the 22nd, came today. You calculated only the basic insurance which pays 50% of all medical costs. We also have other insurance which covers 80% of the remaining medical cost. We must pay the balance of the room rent and 20% of the remaining medical cost. Suppose the medical cost is $350. The second insurance payment is $350 minus $140 ($350 x 50% x 80% = $140); in other words, our payment is $350 minus ($175 + $140) = $350 − $315 = $35. So, we pay 10% of the total medical cost. According to your calculation, we have to pay about $300. But actually we pay about $155 out of pocket, that is, $35 for medical cost plus $120 for the room.

If the insurance company sends their coverage here, I'll forward it to you. If their payment is delayed, I'll borrow from the credit union and send it to you so that you can pay the bill. Please do not worry. Just let me know. I can have it sent by cable.

Today I sent a package of Arlidrin, 200 tablets, and vitamin E, 150 tablets, by air mail. Please transfer the vitamin E into a glass jar. The pharmacy kept the prescription slip so I could get the medicine for your ears without a problem. Taking four pills daily, you have a 50-day supply for your ears. Please don't be alarmed at the price I put down on the mailing slip—it was just an approximate price. You said in an earlier letter that you received 100 tablets of Arlidrin, but I thought I sent another 200 tablets last time. Please check it out, and let me know.

Last night I dreamed about you coming home. You were saying, "I should have stayed in the hospital for another month and a half, but I came home—I've got to go back there." In dreams we can go anywhere—isn't it wonderful?

Yukiko's birthday is approaching. She wants me to write invitation cards, order a cake, buy this and that—she keeps me busy. I told her that unless I finish this letter, we won't go to GEM. So she is waiting patiently.

I always thought histamine didn't agree with you—and it was so again. But you'll get back to your normal weight if you eat well and rest well. A strange flu is breaking out here. The temperature drops suddenly, and I run around closing windows or putting on sweaters. . . . The outside temperature goes up and down, and I get awfully sleepy—maybe I should take vitamins. . . .

From KIYOSHI, *August 26.*

. . . THANK YOU VERY MUCH FOR your letter dated August 21 and written mostly at your work. You say you received four letters all at once. I'm disappointed because I write every day hoping that you would hear from me every day. I often get two letters on the same day, and sometimes they skip a couple of days. I don't think we can change this pattern—rather we just have to be patient.

Today I also received the package. Everything is in it—thank you so much. Pajamas are greatly appreciated. The ones I've been wearing are getting tattered from daily washing because it's so hot here. . . .

You sound awfully tired—please take care. I'm glad you are going to take a one-week vacation. Take it easy; don't tire yourself doing housework. Relax and rest.

So, Yukiko doesn't mention going to Disneyland anymore?! She must be thinking about my ear problem and trying not to be selfish. Poor child! It touched my heart when I read her note, "Daddy, don't worry about your ears—Yukiko is with you." I must get well so that I can take her to Disneyland. She is a good child. I want her to be healthy and grow up to be a happy person.

You paid $3.00 for three servings of gyoza! You didn't want to spend too much for dinner, but you ended up paying a lot. Once in a while, it is all right—it is for the support of the store. It sounds like the store is now a food store, not a gift shop. How is the man who owns the store, I wonder. . . .

From KIYOKO, *August 26.*

KONBANWA, KIYOSHI-SAN. . . . I JUST CAME HOME FROM visiting Iwama-san. They went fishing today. They caught a lot and wanted to share some with us.

Akira-san and Mitsuyo stopped by after doing shopping for the new school year. I treated them to Sapporo beer with pickled cucumber. They didn't stay for dinner because in the evening they had to go to the Buddhist Association in Watsonville to take photos. We made jokes because it appears that Akira-san has become the Association's "kept photographer." Yukiko was not pleased because their three boys had gone to Monterey to be with their grandparents instead of coming to see her. We made plans for them to visit us in San Jose during my vacation and stay here overnight. Tomorrow they will bring the boys home. When we get together, we'll take the children to Mission San Jose. It will be a memorable experience for all of us.

Yesterday Nagasaki-san called to say that a baby girl was born. He said Yūko-san wanted us to be first to have the good news. She may have calculated that letting us know of the good news might reduce our ill feeling toward them. Nonetheless I went to the hospital to congratulate the couple. I know how you feel about Nagasaki-san, but I cannot treat Yūko-san coldly. I'm trying to be neutral. They will eventually leave us alone. I think it is your loss to stay infuriated at somebody who knowingly ignores the rift. Nagasaki-san has a clever wife so that we are still connected. If you had exploded like Takeuchi-san, it would have become uncomfortable to go to the Sumitomo Bank after all these years of doing business there. How about keeping your distance from him in your heart while you remain unchanged publicly? Will this work? I think this is a wiser approach to the problem. What do you say? I cannot forget how terribly annoyed you were at that time. But let time take care of the situation. Cecilia has put some distance between the Nagasakis and herself after she heard about your experience. I'm sorry I didn't get back at them as you might have wanted, but I couldn't do that. Forgive me please.

How is your hearing? You've mentioned taking a different treatment. How is it coming along? As I ask these questions, I still can't believe that you've lost your hearing. We must be grateful though for having your eyesight intact so that you can still read letters. Please eat well and rest well and take care of yourself for both of us.

Hisayo has been invited by her math teacher and his wife to have dinner at a French restaurant and just went out. She has not heard anything from the Immigration Office. Mitsuyo remembers the Chinese restaurant that you wrote about, and Akira-san has eaten there from time to time.

It must be still day time in Japan. I wonder what you are doing now— maybe you are writing to me at this moment.

From KIYOSHI, *August 27.*

. . . I'VE NOT WRITTEN BACK TO Cecilia, but I plan to write her soon. I hope everything is all right there; over here nothing has changed. Yesterday was the first day of the world athletic competition of university students. But the students from the Communist bloc are missing, and their reason is not satisfactory to the Japanese. As an outsider I think it is rather childish to argue over it. . . .

From KIYOSHI, *August 27.*

THIS IS STILL SUNDAY, AUGUST 27. I'M FEELING so much better since your letter arrived after four o'clock today.

You sound put out with Yukiko because of her naughty attitude. But please think this way—it is a blessing compared to her being sick. Today I heard from Mitsuko too, and she also has some problems with Yukiko. By the way, Mitsuko was complaining about her chronic headache (nothing to do with Yukiko)—maybe you should give her Anacin.

Although I found a good Chinese restaurant, I can't go there often. Not only is it expensive, but also it tires me out and the ringing in my ears gets worse. In my present condition, it is better to stay here and rest quietly.

About your comment on the approaching of autumn and the branches of persimmons and chestnuts—I showed your letter to the high school student who is still here. It made her very happy. She was supposed to go home about a week ago, but that plan was changed because she came down with tonsillitis. She will be here for another week. Yesterday her father came and thanked me for the candies that I gave them for Obon. We talked using pen and paper. Evidently he is a descendant of a daimyo and the 17th head of the

Tachibana clan. His family history goes back 700 years to the Shogunate era. The daimyo in Kyushu district in the Shogunate era (1600–1867) were Kuroda, Nabeshima, Ogasawara, Arima, Tachibana, Hosokawa, Shimazu— there were altogether seven lords. He invited me to come see him before I go home. I said I'll do that if my hearing gets better. No wonder his daughters are elegant and graceful. But intellectually they are ordinary girls. . . .

I'm glad that you are getting my letters regularly. But I get concerned if three or four letters reach you all at once and then no letter for a while after that. I wish they could ration the delivery so that you get a letter every day. The delivery here is the same; sometimes I get two or three one day, and nothing next day—then I get depressed. I should separate one special letter to read over and over so that I feel warm and happy all the time. I am looking forward to your reply to mine sent together with the insurance paper. Now I'm so anxious for your reply to that letter!* From time to time write to me that way—it would make me so happy. . . .

*Kiyoshi is referring to letter No. 31, his second letter of August 24, a large part of which is missing. We surmise that Kiyoko cut parts of the letter off for the sake of privacy.

From KIYOKO, August 29.

. . . WE ARE IN FRONTIER VILLAGE. I'm writing this in the shade while everybody is enjoying the rides. Today I received your letters 31, 32, and 33. The insurance form and another letter came yesterday. I took the insurance form to the company myself. After they read and approved it, I added my signature and made a copy for us to keep. They said they will process it.

Now I have one of your letters put on a clip which I leave on the desk at all times so that anybody can copy your address. Your letters addressed to me are kept in the file cabinet—nobody knows about it. The one you sent with the insurance form is in my bag, and I carry it with me always.

I brought Glen and his brothers here and distributed strawberries to Yoshimitsu-san, your sister, and Cecilia. It was a lot of work but an enjoyable task, and Yukiko was literally mad with joy. I'm grateful that we could close this summer vacation on such a happy note. When they grow older, they may not play together with such an open joy—for now, they are enjoying each other guilelessly. Tomorrow Hisayo will take all of them to the movie, *The Sound of Music*. I'm afraid it will be a big handful for Hisayo, but for the children it will be a memorable event.

Hisayo has not heard anything from the Immigration Bureau. She took this as a favorable sign and is still going to NB every day with plans to continue with school.

Kiyoshi-san, my heart throbs with longing whenever I think of you. I'm going to keep this yearning in my heart. And when you come home, we are going to start a happy new life. As I read your letter, I feel your skin so close to me. I can't help but get excited just remembering that beautiful sensation of being tightly squeezed. . . . It would be so wonderful to cling tight to your body and touch you. . . . If a husband and wife are not in love with each other, there isn't much physical joy and excitement like this. I feel sorry for such a couple. Kiyoshi-san, you are the one who guided me and taught me how wonderful it is to love someone. Somebody wrote that behind a good wife there is a good husband and his leadership. I do agree. I bow to you for your great effort. Please teach Hiroyuki how to become a perfect man. It is a challenge for a young couple to start living together and manage a home. But it is a most important time in order to build the foundation of a solid family; it's the time to shape one's philosophy or belief in family life. Tell him that now is the time to be thinking about his future family life which he will build with support from his fiancée. The secret of our successful marriage rests on measuring each step against a far-reaching and mutual objective and together making decisions to adopt it or drop it. When you talk to Hiroyuki and his fiancée, please add my advice to yours.

It's so difficult to open a Japanese air letter. It is suitable for writing a secret message in it. I tested the American counterpart—one can read everything through the hole. People might become curious about our letters because there are so many of them coming and going. So important matters must be sent inside a [standard envelope].

In five minutes Frontier Village will close. The kids are playing with the ducks, feeding them popcorn. I will stop at the post office and mail this. I must hurry—sorry for this poor handwriting; it's so bad that it looks like somebody else's writing, not mine!

From KIYOSHI, *August 29.*

. . . YESTERDAY FOR THE FIRST TIME I did not write to you. In the morning I mailed one which was written the day before so the letters have been going out without skipping a date.

Yesterday Mr. and Mrs. Ōshima came to see me all the way from Saitama Prefecture. I just received a postcard from them a few days ago. I thought they might come after their trip to the States, but they came by before flying out tomorrow—I was overwhelmed! Mrs. Ōshima thanked me for assisting and standing by her husband and asked me to relay her gratitude to you too. They gave me a pot of beautiful flowers and a can of rice-cake cubes. They arrived in Fukuoka around nine o'clock, came to the hospital around 10, and went home by an afternoon plane. They asked if I had some message or something to take to you. But I didn't have any. If you see them, please thank them for their constant care and consideration. I really owe so much to Japan Airlines. They are going to stay in Oakland for about a month. They said they were going to get a Hakata doll from this area to give to Yukiko.

After Mr. and Mrs. Ōshima left, Watanabe-sensei came with my photos. I had my treatment done quickly and went to the City Hall with Watanabe-sensei to apply for an extension of my temporary stay. Before going there, I stopped at the bank and exchanged dollars to get about 220,000 yen. I had deposited 250,000 yen earlier and spent about $500 (180,000 yen) in a month, leaving the balance of 70,000 yen. This morning I deposited 200,000 yen of the 220,000 yen, leaving 20,000 yen for spending money. This should cover the payments on the third and 18th of next month, but it is not enough to cover the first payment in October. Maybe the insurance coverage will start to work by then. If not, could you please send five or six hundred dollars by sometime between September 10 and 14 or 15? Could you please ask my mother to loan us this amount if the payment from the insurance does not start. I'm sorry to bother you this way. It would help us so much if the airfare was covered.

Please forgive me for writing a hasty letter like this. I hope I get another letter from you today because none came yesterday. I'll take more time to write then. . . .

From KIYOSHI, *August 29.*

IT IS STILL AUGUST 29. SINCE I DIDN'T GET your letter yesterday, I hoped to get one today, and it came. I was so touched when I read toward the end of your letter, "I am your only and beloved wife . . ." and at the closing, "To my Kiyoshi-san, I miss you!" I can't say enough how much I was moved by these words of yours. I am a deaf and beaten-up man and my self-esteem is at its lowest—yet you say you love me—I don't deserve it—I can't thank you enough! Maybe it's misleading to say that one must live only for love, but it is the most beautiful thing in man's life, isn't it? I can't think of anything better in life than the love between couples. There is nothing better than a happy and rewarding life born out of such love. I can't understand why I am so blessed with a wife like you and have been given a life of such happiness and love. I think our kind of love is the strongest and the most revered. There couldn't be many other couples who are in love with each other like us. Our love is so different from just satisfying sexual desire. We want each other because we are each a part of each other. We are so lucky to be able to love each other this way. Kiyoko-san, I can't describe enough my joy when I read "your only and beloved . . ." at the end of your letter. I can't help but pray that this happiness will last forever. I am a deaf man, and a weak man who becomes discouraged easily. Your word, your tender loving word, is the best medicine for me.

My hearing has not improved because my medicine has been changed since a week before last. I have had a headache, no appetite, and besides have come down with a fever at night. I couldn't be worse! Even if my circulation is restored, there is no way to supply nourishment to my ears if I don't have an appetite. . . . They will change my medicine starting today. I'll try to get my appetite back. I'm so disappointed that the indicator has gone from 45 back to 55 or more. I wish it would get to 30 quickly; then a hearing aid might help with the rest. I'm so grateful for your encouraging words.

So you had a cold? The post office stamp on this letter is Mountain View so I think you must be OK now. Between San Jose and Mountain View there is a day's difference in delivery. Please take care of yourself. . . .

From Kiyoshi, *August 30.*

. . . The nurse just brought me your letter of August 24. I read it while having a massage of my eardrums. When Dr. Shirabe was here to change the pad on my chest, I showed him part of your letter. He said that your case does not sound serious, but he could be wrong. Why don't you consult with Higuchi-san just to make sure? (This is my opinion. Don't forget that you are my very precious Kiyoko-san.)

Now about the friend of Cecilia—I took notes, so I'll copy it here. Dr. Shirabe wants to know the following: 1. type of infection; 2. the medicine she took, its description and the length of time she used it; 3. subjective symptoms, meaning degree of hearing, and one ear or both; 4. completely deaf or partially deaf, and whether she lost her hearing suddenly or gradually; 5. relation to fever, etc. Also he wants to know if the hearing difficulty was caused by the medicine or the infection. This may be difficult for her to tell, but the doctor says that if she lost her hearing because of an infection caused by meningitis or encephalitis, it is very hard to cure. And, even mumps and measles could cause loss of hearing. In conclusion, it is necessary to get more information. It is important to take a lot of vitamin B_1, B_6, B_{12}, and similar pills like Arlidrin, in order to stimulate the metabolism of the nerves. Take 25 mg of B_1, 25 mg of B_6, 250 mg of B_{12} three times a day. (The doctor said she could double the amount, but definitely that is the limit. But maybe you can skip this part.) . . .

From Kiyoshi, *August 31.*

This is the last day of August, and my 45th day in the hospital. Tomorrow is Yukiko's birthday.

Are you all right, Kiyoko-san? Is the numbness of your hand still there? I'm worried. Please take care!

The month of August is about to end, but the heat lingers on. Only the morning air is a little bit cooler. Sooner or later the heat will go away.

My hearing is not good since I started to take histamine and *karikurein* two weeks ago. At first I was getting better, but I am back to my starting condition now. I even inhaled opium. Something has to work. I'm taking a different kind of injection now. I'm starting all over now and trying to get back to the level I reached once. Nothing moves in a straight line, or so you said to me on many occasions, and I'm trying not to be discouraged. . . .

There are a couple of patients here who suffer from tinnitus, and everybody says that exhaustion makes the ear ringing worse. Me too—when I get tired it gets worse. Since I can't hear well, I tend to talk loud, and then the tinnitus gets louder—so I try to keep quiet. It seems Arlidrin is working. Also I'm taking an injection of an antidote to neutralize the poison in my body. I didn't know that I had a residue of poison in my body. . . .

はじめに ここを おる

〜〜の字を〜つい新年・
〜を乱しました。
もありませんか？おわびしますが
〜れば、〜〜ふやすえ〜〜〜
すかくとうは婦様に
〜〜〜〜〜〜新々

September

..

[*The Moon is East, the Sun is West*]

From KIYOSHI, *September 1.*

YUKIKO'S BIRTHDAY. I JUST WROTE A LETTER TO HER. How are you, Kiyoko-san? I'm just about the same.

Yesterday I went to City Hall with Watanabe-sensei and signed the papers for foreigners. It felt strange to come back to Japan and register as a foreigner. But, now I can stay here till January. I owe so much to Dr. Watanabe.

This is the 46th day in the hospital—it's been about 50 days since I left you. Sometimes I fancy that the doctor might tell me that I can go home since the rest can be taken care of at home. I miss you so much. But I have to be patient.

Thank you very much for the medicine. I'm relieved now that I have this. It came yesterday just before I went out with Watanabe-sensei—that's why I opened the seal of my air letter and wrote that line. I am not taking histamine and *karikurein* so that I'm slowly recovering.

Anything new over there? Here, Smith of San Jose State University won second in the 100-meter final, which surprised everybody. . . .

From KIYOKO, *September 1.*

I'M SORRY I HAVE NOT WRITTEN TO YOU SINCE the trip to Frontier Village. I was thinking of all sorts of things to write about but didn't have time. I got in bed but couldn't sleep. . . . It was almost three o'clock. I . . . whisper your name—*Tō-chan!* I still couldn't sleep, Kiyoshi-san.

When you are lying down by my side, I don't get this wild. It was like this when you were in the hospital here. But I had no problem sleeping after you came home in April. Also this sleeplessness may have something to do with my menstruation cycle. Finally I took out the old sleep machine that electrically induces sleep—and it worked.

Yesterday Hisayo took four children to the movies. I went to my office intending to work for a half day, but it lasted till three o'clock. Then I went to pick up the children from the theater. To my surprise, Yukiko came out with her eyes red from crying. She has seen the movie before, but this time she could understand the story better and, I suppose, with more empathy. Glen and the other boys didn't understand why she was crying. I thought this was a surprising development in Yukiko.

Another anecdote on Yukiko. She didn't know the English for *kusaru* meaning "to spoil." So when she was talking to Glen and the boys, she kept saying "*kusaru* milk" for spoiled milk, mixing Japanese and English. It was so funny. Is this a sign of her physical growth preventing her mental acuity, I wonder. Anyway her English vocabulary is quite good. She wishes she were Japanese rather than American. The other day Glen and the boys were talking about Communism. Paul said that the Russians and the Chinese were not human; then Yukiko protested saying that the Chinese were our friends. The boys simply regard all Chinese and all Russians to be Communists; they hate Communism so they don't like Chinese and Russians. What can I say! They are still very young. But our Yukiko is different. She is accepting of all people based on her own judgment. I believe our way is correct. I think it is better for grownups to refrain from hasty judgment in front of the children until they are grown and able to understand world affairs. If we had a boy, I would still think the same way. I was thinking about this while driving Glen and the boys to their home.

Last night Mr. Ōshima called. Saturday is Yukiko's party. On Sunday I plan to prepare a box lunch, and we'll go to Hayward. Tomorrow is Hisayo's graduation ceremony. I'm going to take some photos—this time I'll focus better so that I won't cut off the heads or the legs! . . .

From KIYOSHI, *September 1.*

... THE DOCTOR WAS TELLING ME today that there was a case where someone's hearing was restored by drinking a lot of soda. Do you remember that I used to drink Coke and soda because they seemed to help my hearing? They contain a great amount of CO_2. Starting tomorrow I'm going to drink a lot of soda. The adverse effect of histamine on my left ear is fading away, and I feel slightly better today because I can hear sound faintly. The right ear is also better. Taking care of my health this way, I'm going to improve my hearing bit by bit so that I can start using a hearing aid. I shall not lose hope; I shall be patient—thank you, Kiyoko-san.

As to the case of Nagasaki-san, you took a better and more correct attitude. Now I thank you and respect you more for that. I'm not bothered by it any more—I'm not going to waste my energy on such a travesty. I'm going to concentrate on restoring my health. Please don't apologize—I was so emotional and didn't listen to you. I am sorry.

I have to stop here. Tokuda Yaeko-san wrote me. Please give my regards to Iwama-san by telephone.

From KIYOKO, *September 2.*

... I WAS BUSY YESTERDAY WITH Hisayo's graduation ceremony. So, we had Yukiko's birthday party today instead of yesterday. Penny and Peggy were here but three other girls couldn't make it. We invited Mother and Mitsuko-san and cut the cake. It was a huge cake—so big that it was scary to light all 10 candles. . . .

I'll ask Cecilia about her friend when I go to the office. I'll tell her about the vitamins. She'll be happy to hear it. The numbness of my palm is almost gone. If it happens again, I'll see Higuchi-san.

It is very humid today—like in the rainy season. People are complaining about having headaches. Mine started yesterday. I took two Anacin capsules and slept for about two hours till I was wakened by the telephone. I'm writing this since I feel a little bit better after the nap. . . .

In early September I will borrow some money from the credit union and send it to you. I think it is better than to keep borrowing from your mother. When the insurance company starts paying, we will pay her back.

Regarding the coverage on the airfare, I'll try to talk to Dr. Childrey again. I'm going to start saying that I now have a clear description of the treatment that you are getting. Maybe he'll write a letter this time.

Please do not worry about money. I will take care of it.

You have a thank-you note from my mother for the $15 for the Obon festival. Shall I send you four or five sheets of air-letter paper? If you return the written sheets to me, I'll write the address and send it to my mother. Some time ago I asked you if you wanted to send some airmail letters, but you have not told me one way or the other. Please let me know.

Akizuki-san sent us $25 for Obon. Maybe for *Hokubei* you could write about Obon in Japan and how the house of Tachibana celebrates it. If it is not too much of a burden, I thought, you might write just one article a month for the paper.

Hisayo is taking it easy for a change and says she will write to you on this Labor Day weekend. She is translating the Pan-American announcement for Okumura-san.

There must be more things to tell you, but I can't think well because my head is still hazy.

The telephone that woke me up was from Kamiya Kyōko-san. She said that Mrs. Suzuki told her about you. Also she told me that Mr. Suzuki was suffering from cancer of the red blood cells, and his family has known about it for more than a year.

I took a box of strawberries to the Kanemotos. Mr. Kanemoto was not home but I had a good visit for about two hours with Mrs. Kanemoto and the children. They send their best regards to you. Mrs. Kanemoto has mellowed and is very friendly.

Please don't lose your courage. When you brace yourself up, your body tends to become strong too. . . .

From KIYOSHI, *September 2.*

. . . I'M SURPRISED AND DELIGHTED because since sometime middle of the night my ear-ringing has been drastically reduced. I could hear sounds this morning. It is noon now and still it is utterly quiet. I was hungry so I sent for lunch from outside. I've never felt this hungry. I'm so happy! I have never felt hunger since I came here so this must be a good sign. After lunch the nurse came with my medicine. While I was talking with her, the ringing in my ear started a little. In any case, the ringing has never disappeared before. I think the antidotal injection is working. I reported that to Dr. Shirabe, and he was very pleased. The disappearance of the ringing in my ears means that there is a possibility of restoring my hearing—this is an important thing—I shall not forget it. I feel a chill creep all over me when I think of my condition for the past weeks. I want to get well, drinking Japanese soda and eating a lot of Japanese food. I have hope now! However, I shall not forget what you said—"Be modest in rejoicing as well as in grieving." Kiyoko-san, you encourage me, comfort me, teach me, and help me to live like a man. I am not exaggerating when I say that you make me grow. I don't know what to say beyond that, but you make me a happy man.

You said you dreamed of me coming home. I had a dream of me coming home too—I was talking with you and Akizuki-san and someone else. Then I remembered that I left my stuff in the hospital and started to think what I should do about it. It was a dream full of hope. I was so happy to be with you in the dream. It is the only place where I can be with you.

I'm a bit worried about the case of Hisayo-san. How about asking Mr. Nakahara once more? There are people who find it easy to say nice things, but only few of them really try to help you. Why don't you talk to him? I hope all goes well with Hisayo-san. Please tell her that I am thinking of her.

I'll write again tomorrow. I put my pen down now hoping that tomorrow I can write even a better report on my hearing. . . .

From KIYOKO, *September 3.*

. . . YUKIKO'S BIRTHDAY CELEBRATION IS over. The preparation for her new semester is done because she had presents from everybody. Now it's time to get ready for work. I had made a plan to clean the whole house before going back to work, but it doesn't look like I'll make it. Instead I'm going to follow your advice and take it easy for the rest of my vacation— I'll not drive myself to exhaustion doing housework. . . .

Last night I had a dream. I was about to die within a year. I took that announcement calmly. But it was just a dream. If it were a reality, like in the case of Suzuki-san, it would be very difficult to remain calm. Suzuki-san himself was not informed of it and did not lose hope till his last day. His wife and his father-in-law took very good care of him.

Starting the first part of August, I've been sending the newspapers to you every 15 days. The first package was the July papers—have you received it? The serial novel, *The Freezing Point* {氷点 *(Hyōten)*}, seems to have reached its climax. In front of her boyfriend, Kitahara, Yōko was told that her father was arrested for the murder of one of his daughters. Kitahara is a friend of Tōru and doesn't believe the accusation. I'm anxiously waiting for this coming Tuesday to find out which way the story develops. Novels in the newspaper have a wonderful effect on the reader—they make the subscriber look forward to the next issue. I could go to a bookstore and get the book, but somehow I'd rather follow the progression of the story day by day in the newspaper. . . .

Today Yoshimitsu-san gave us one of his catches, a bass about 17 or 18 lbs. Tomorrow I'll make sashimi and *onigiri* and take them to the Japan Airlines office in Hayward. Tomorrow is Labor Day. So, I'm going to the post office by 10 o'clock tonight to mail this letter so that you'll get it without delay. . . .

From KIYOSHI, *September 3.*

. . . IT SHOULD BE MUCH COOLER, BUT the indoor temperature is already 30° C in the morning. It's slightly windy, but until it gets higher than 30° the air cooler won't kick in. So I must wait.

I'm eating more since the day before yesterday, and I feel much better. Even my hearing seems to be better this morning. If this condition lasts till this evening, it would be stupendous. I wrote down in my diary today that I must rest as much as possible. Last night the nurse who took care of me when I first came here returned to night duty and came to see me. She said that resting is so important to reduce the ringing in my ears. For example, if I jump out of the bed in the morning, I get knocked out by the ringing in my ears. Therefore, I first move my head to and fro while still in bed to let my ears get used to movement; then I get up. If I am overcome by the ear-ringing in the morning, it never goes away the whole day. . . .

How is Yukiko these days? I haven't seen her for more than a month and a half—she must be so big by now. She will grow up without us realizing it; she will grow out of our hands soon enough. In about 10 years she may not need our care. I pray that then she has a happy life of her own—loving her husband, being loved by him, and living together happily. That's the best way to live. . . .

From KIYOSHI, *September 4.*

. . . THE RINGING IN MY EARS HAS been reduced considerably, maybe because I rested well. Two-thirds (or slightly more) of the symptom has gone away. I wish my hearing had improved also. But maybe I shouldn't be so greedy.

Unexpectedly Hiroyuki-san came around four o'clock yesterday. He was dressed in a suit and tie. He was on his way home to Saga for his engagement ceremony. He wanted to find out if I would meet Masayuki-san who is to come to this area next Sunday. I asked him to keep my presence here to himself for a while since meeting someone might make me too tired until I get well enough to use a hearing aid. He understood my sentiment and agreed with me. I'll meet Masayuki-san when I get better. Hiroyuki-san didn't stay long because it was close to the lunch hour. I wished him a happy marriage. I think it will go well because Noriko-san seems to be a gentle person who can follow Hiroyuki-san. . . .

I went to bed earlier than usual last night. I had a wonderful dream! You and I were bathing together, and I was washing your back. To my surprise, my hearing was back. It was such a happy dream. I'll tell you more about it in a separate letter. . . .

There couldn't be any better asset like this in a man's life—no other happiness surpasses this happiness. I have a wife whom not only I but also others respect highly. As time goes on, my respect for you increases; my yearning for you becomes stronger. What a lucky man I am! I thank you, Kiyoko-san. . . .

From KIYOKO, *September 5.*

. . . I WENT BACK TO WORK TODAY. I felt a little bit tired after eight days of vacation. But your three letters with good news perked me up. It appears that you will be cured for sure. But let's not be now glad, now sad with each day's little symptoms. Let's be patient.

I just came home from the Safeway. I saw a white man get caught stealing three cartons of cigarettes; his arms were being twisted by security —it made me upset. The cost of cigarettes is higher now, but it has not doubled—what a meaningless act to walk out without paying.

Yesterday I cooked rice twice; the first for *onigiri*, the second for *donburi*. I took them to Japan Airlines together with sashimi, pickled cucumbers, and honeydew melon. Everybody enjoyed the food. They are a new group of people, but all nice. One of them is from Karatsu in Saga Prefecture and his name is Nishimura-san. He seems to be the leader. Somebody gave Yukiko a large *kokeshi* doll, which Matsumura-san sent for her. It is 12 inches high. Yukiko is in seventh heaven! I'm impressed by the courtesy Matsumura-san expresses. I must write him a thank-you note. Ōshima-san gave Yukiko a doll dressed like a character from a nursery song and a small mirror in a case woven Hakata-style.

We stayed there for three hours and came home around four o'clock. I'll send you some photos. Ōshima-san is going back to Japan on September 23. I invited the group to our house before he leaves. It may be less work to invite them to a restaurant, but somehow it seems tasteless. It may cost money to serve the group at the house, but it is not impossible. Please let me know what you think about this. Ōshima-san didn't accept the invitation right away. Maybe he was hesitating because he didn't want to put a burden on the family while you are in the hospital. The group is around 14 people—the largest group we have ever had at our house. If you have a good idea, please let me hear it. Maybe the group could be divided into seven and seven; but that means we have to hustle and bustle twice, and it is not fair to Mother and Hisayo.

Regarding Hisayo, her immigration case seems to be OK. Evidently Mr. Nakahara told her that there is no reason for her application to be denied; and if that ever happens, he will take the case to the court at his own expense. So Hisayo is not worried about the delay, but she is worried about how much Mr. Nakahara will charge for his service. She is working hard on the translation for Okumura-san.

Yesterday I prepared to make *saba-zushi* before I went to Hayward because your sister and her family were coming with birthday gifts for Yukiko and Mitsuko-san and a graduation gift for Hisayo. I asked Hisayo to tidy up the house, etc. She says she has not had time to write to you yet. Your sister and her husband enjoyed the *saba-zushi*. We still have the fish from Iwama-san to make more sashimi.

Regarding Nagasaki-san—thank you for agreeing with me. We don't have to be as close to each other as we were—just courteous friends. . . .

Like you, I am at peace when I write to you. I look forward to having another letter from you tomorrow. Yukiko seemed to be having a difficult time writing Japanese, but I was so happy to note that she used a lot of kanji. She wants to go to the Japanese Language School. . . .

From KIYOSHI, *September 5.*

. . . I HOPE YOU ARE ALL RIGHT. Working in the office all day, coming home and tidying up the house—I know it must be tiring. Please take good care of yourself. When you feel tired, please go to bed. Don't worry about me. . . .

Lately the ringing in my ears has been reduced noticeably maybe due to the shots and extra rest. My appetite has improved too. It is not because of the autumn weather. Today's paper reported that this heat will last for a week more. The daytime temperature is over 35° which is very unusual according to the Fukuoka Weather Bureau. Anyway it is still very hot.

I drink a lot of milk. I spend $14 to $15 monthly for milk and orange juice. Sometimes I order out for chicken-rice or curried rice (not often) or fried rice. Since it's so hot, I change my pajamas every day. It costs 65 yen per month for laundry. I bought a cooler for 500 yen. Every day I pay 15 cents (50 yen) for ice and cool drinks in it all day. It's small, 40 cm x 30 cm x 25 cm, with a lid—very convenient. I buy a newspaper every day. These are my fixed daily expenses. . . .

From KIYOSHI, *September 5.*

. . . THERE WERE NO LETTERS FROM YOU last Saturday, Sunday and Monday. I should receive one today! But don't worry—I won't get depressed even if it doesn't come today.

It may be a bit early, but I'm going to write about the payment scheduled for October 3. We have deposited about 27,000 yen in the hospital. As of September 3, the expense sums up to $250 or $300; therefore about 9,000 to 10,800 yen has to be subtracted from the deposited amount in the hospital, which leaves a balance of about 16 to 17,000 yen in the hospital account. After the September 18 payment, the balance will become 6 to 7,000 yen—which means we are 3 to 4,000 yen short for the payment on October 3. Could you send about $600 of which $100 would be for my daily spending and 10,000 yen for the wedding of Hiroyuki-san. If you can send it through the Sumitomo Bank and by air mail on September 15, it should arrive in time for the October 3 payment. Later than that date, it'll be iffy. That is why I am writing this letter today. . . .

From KIYOSHI, *September 5.*

. . . I ASK THE NURSES ABOUT THE mail so often that they were teasing me this afternoon. But about 15 minutes later, one of them came in smiling hiding your letters behind her. I was so happy! . . .

From KIYOSHI, *September 6.*

THIS MORNING THE ASSISTANT PROFESSOR MADE HIS rounds. He said that I was doing fine so far. The ringing in my ears has been reduced quite a bit, and last night it completely disappeared at 1:12 a.m. I was so surprised, and I looked at my watch—that's why I know the time. I told this to the assistant professor. All the doctors are beginning to feel optimistic about my recovery. . . .

It was a great improvement, but it's too soon to exult about it. I have to be cautious. I remember what you've told me—I should not be mad with joy over such a slight improvement. Even if my hearing comes back a little, I should exercise caution. Pears are in the market now. I'm going to eat one every day for a supply of vitamin C. The hospital food is so bad that I often order meals out. Hope you don't mind. Hiroyuki-san took a look at it and said that it wasn't fit even for healthy people. . . .

From KIYOKO, *September 7.*

. . . I OVERSLEPT, AND IT WAS 9:30 A.M. when I signed in at the office. I felt so bad. But I was told I could finish the day as usual because I had been working hard. There was an earthquake early this morning. I remember vaguely that the heater had the pilot light on. I remember thinking that it was a potential fire danger. Also I was thinking that the tremors might break the Hakata doll. But I evidently went back to sleep. . . .

I received your letters of September 4 and 5. Regarding the money, tomorrow we should get approval of the loan from the credit union. I'll send $100 separately because the loan amount is $500. There should be a payment from the insurance company soon.

In yesterday's letter, you wrote "two steps, or one-and-half steps until I get better." I don't understand what you mean. Will you please explain? You seem to have picked the number five to represent the worst stage and against that you mention two steps or one-and-half steps—of what? Anyhow, isn't it wonderful that your appetite is good in spite of the hot weather? I'm glad that you found an icebox of just the right size. We might find a similar carrier which we can use for a picnic. By the way, the Japanese-made ice shaver named "Ice Pet" is becoming popular here. Glen's family has it, and Yukiko wants it too. I wonder if it's not cheaper to buy it in Japan. Here the deluxe model costs $7.90. Will you please look into it? It may be about the same if the shipping cost is added. . . .

There was an announcement on the bulletin board in my company about the austerity program. It will be enforced for three or four months, and already it has become harder to get supplies. It has not affected our salaries yet, but some layoffs may be unavoidable. One may be laid off if his performance is not up to par with one's salary.

Thanks to my colleague who knows English well, my English is improving. But when I don't have enough sleep, I get confused and falter. I'm amazed that most people understand me in spite of that. This morning was a little different because I overslept. I was so tired last night and didn't even write to you. I washed dishes and watched television with Yukiko for a while, but then I went to bed because it was such a silly program. It was 10 o'clock. It's amazing that Yukiko can sit in front of TV for long hours. When school starts, I'm going to select the programs for her. Summer vacation will be over next week. She has stopped over-eating. She likes to play rather than study. She was so happy to have a new binder and told me that she wrote something in it very carefully. But it was only one line! She has forgotten already that Daddy told her to listen well to her mommy and get a lot of A's. Perhaps you can write about multiplication. When school starts, please teach her in that way.

I'll write again. I feel your kiss on my forehead. I'd like to kiss you!

From KIYOSHI, *September 8.*

. . . YESTERDAY FOR THE FIRST TIME I could not write a letter. I had a cold with a severe headache. Since I was getting so much better, this setback is such a blow to me. I have to be extremely careful in the future. I feel slightly better this morning so I decided to write a few lines to you.

Yesterday I received a letter from Matsumura-san of Japan Airlines. Right after returning home he began to prepare for the National Examination because the date of the test had been moved up. He studied every night until very late, and passed the test with high marks. He says for the first time since he returned home, he is having a relaxing Sunday and is writing a letter to me. He is an exceptional man. . . .

The high school girl across the hall went home yesterday. Her father came to say good-bye to me. His name card indicates that he is a part-time instructor at a junior college.

Forgive me for this hasty note. I'll write again later when I feel better. Give my love to Yukiko and Hisayo-san. . . .

From KIYOSHI, *September 9.*

. . . I AM EXHAUSTED FROM THIS COLD. I had a temperature close to 40 degrees. Yesterday was the worst. Things were looking up lately, and then this happens. I am so discouraged. I am tired out with two injections plus pills. I perspired so much last night that I used up all five pajamas. The fever seems to be going down, but I am completely worn out. Your letter is the only thing that holds me up in this condition, but none has come for three days—Wednesday, Thursday, and Friday. I felt so lonely. Maybe I'll get one today—I'm waiting.

The ringing in my ears was decreasing considerably, and now this happens. What a disappointment! I can't help but become pessimistic about everything. I need a letter from you to pep me up! . . .

From KIYOKO, *September 10.*

SUNDAY, 8:30 P.M. YOU MUST HAVE BEEN WAITING for this letter so anxiously. The last one was written on Thursday. I'm sorry I could not write sooner. You must be about to faint—please breathe easy. Friday I had the Sumitomo Bank send $500 by cable. $100 will be sent on the 15th or, at the latest, by the 22nd.

Employees at the insurance office were not familiar with the exchange rate so that I had to be called in and help them with the calculations. I was more than happy to help them with the arithmetic since I wanted them to pay me the amount I computed. But I couldn't believe the lack of professional capability on their part. This happened on Friday. . . .

I'm so glad to hear that the ringing in your ears is markedly reduced. But this is the time when both doctors and patients have to stay calm and not get excited prematurely. They might be tempted to increase or change the dose of medicine. But rushing on to the next phase too soon might cause a reverse effect. Please be cautious. I was so happy to hear that the ringing stopped even just for a second. I could feel your excitement. . . .

Hospital food tends to be very poor. Shall I send you something—maybe cereal for breakfast? I've been shopping around for things, including salami, to put in the next package. It will help if you tell me what you would like to have. I know you want Kiyoko-san first and her daily letters next. And if possible, take a short break away from the hospital and come home, or I will come to see you. Such luxury being impossible, at least I would like you to enjoy the contents of a package.

We celebrated Mitsuko-san's birthday today, a week early, before school starts. We had just sushi, fishcake and soup—not enough if you were home—nonetheless we thought they were so delicious. Yesterday I bought an umbrella as a gift for her. It is white, slender and stylish and cost $7.50. She liked it. Your mother was pleased that I got it from Macy's. I couldn't find anything at GEM or White Front.

Yesterday after shopping, Yukiko wanted to go to the fall festival at the Methodist Church. She thought your mother's group might be at the bazaar. I gave her a dollar and let her go while I was packing the car. She didn't buy anything to eat but played one game. I told her that I would take her to Spivey's anniversary celebration. On the invitation it said that food less than $1.00 for children was free, and there would be presents for them too. Yukiko was so elated. She had a cheeseburger and milkshake there. She came home contented. Because of these events, I could not write to you. I began to ache on one side of my body just thinking of skipping writing to you—even now it aches as I am just about to finish this letter.

Tomorrow Yukiko's school starts. We all will follow a schedule. She should start going to bed regularly at a set time. I don't know how it will go, but I would like to succeed in this plan.

From KIYOSHI, *September 10.*

. . . I HAVE NOT HEARD FROM YOU for four days now. I am lonely. I know I must hold on tight and be patient, but I can't. Kiyoko-san, are you there? Are you all right? Without your letter, I cannot bear this isolation, this loneliness—particularly when I am so exhausted. Forgive me for this selfishness. . . .

How does the insurance situation stand? The other day I wrote about the deposit in the hospital account. Have you sent it? You should receive this letter on or about the 15h of September. If you have not sent the money yet, please send it immediately. I hate myself for asking this way—it makes me feel doubly lonely. Maybe the exhaustion from the cold and the anxiety for any news from you causes my loneliness. Please forgive me.

I will write again in a better frame of mind if I get your letter today. I'll put down my pen now praying ardently that I hear from you today. Please take good care of yourself. Give my love to Yukiko and Hisayo-san.

From KIYOKO, *September 11.*

. . . YUKIKO'S SCHOOL STARTED. YOUR LETTER came today. It was written on September 8. I hope your cold is gone by now. You might have skipped writing on account of the cold, but I received one from you both on Saturday and on Monday.

I'm writing every other day, and that's the best I can do. Last weekend I could not write for three days. I am so sorry that it made you worried about me on top of your own discomfort from a cold. Luckily your appetite returned before that cold, so you will get better quickly. Don't get discouraged! Be careful so as not to catch cold again. I don't know how you got it this time, but colds seem to catch us when we are not on guard. The papers predict that flu will be rampant this year too. Here summer is definitely gone. In the morning the heater kicks in, and in the evening we need a sweater when we go out.

As I wrote yesterday, I started to put restrictions on Yukiko's TV time. She is complaining. Today she took a long time to turn off the TV and finally left to take a bath but came back just to complain again.

I had been trying to reach Yoshimitsu-san on the phone to talk about registration for the school. The line was busy for a long time. So after dinner, I decided to catch him at the house of Shiroki-san. I talked to Jane Tokutomi, too. Her son, Kenny, is in kindergarten now. "Kenny isn't a baby anymore," I commented. She said it was like losing something of her life.

It was a busy day at work. As I was driving home, I was writing a letter to you in my head. . . . I want you, Kiyoshi-san! I can't wait till you come home. This mommy needs a hormone injection! If I could have . . . [you] now, I would feel so much better. . . .

In spite of his busy schedule, Matsumura-san spent time to buy a *kokeshi* doll for Yukiko and had it delivered to her. I am so grateful. We invited him for dinner only once, and he returns his appreciation this way—a very rare person he is. It is wonderful to meet a person like him.

The high school student across the hall went home, and maybe another patient will come in. You make friends easily. Write me about them. I enjoyed reading about the high school student. You went to Japan, registered there as a foreigner, and you are a model patient in the hospital—by the way, I'm sure you will find true Japanese qualities in the nurses there. Kiyoshi-san, you may be lonely but I'm right behind you—don't forget that. . . .

From KIYOSHI, *September 11.*

. . . I THOUGHT FOR SURE YOUR LETTER would come yesterday. But it didn't. The last one came on Tuesday last week—now it is Monday. I have not heard from you for six days. Has something happened to you?! I am not feeling well—besides no letter from you for so long—it drives me to indescribable sadness and loneliness. Why can't you write? I've waited for your letter day after day, and this is the seventh day. But I'm still waiting. I don't know what I'll do if I don't get any letter today. I can't help but feel so left out. I hope nothing has happened to you.

How is Yukiko? How is her new teacher? I hope she likes the teacher and studies hard this semester. It is still around 92°[F] in Fukuoka. It is hot. But it goes down to about 75° in the evening.

Take care, Kiyoko-san. I'm praying that today your letter will come. . . .

From KIYOSHI, *September 11.*

. . . THIS MORNING I WROTE A desperate letter, but still I had hoped to hear from you today. And indeed your letters of September second and third came together with one from Yukiko. Now I am totally exhausted and have some fever and headache. But I am so happy. I am relieved to hear that you are all right. You wrote, "You must be a little bit anxious. . . ." Well, it was not "a little bit." I was just about down for the count. I'm OK now. Autumn is just around the corner. As the saying goes, "It's the time when the sky is clear blue and the horses are fat." Me too, I'm going to get well in this beautiful weather. . . .

Re: U.S. air letters—please send some to me in an envelope. I'll write on one and send it back to you, also in an envelope, so that you can send it with the U.S. postmark.

I think Cecilia's friend should try Arlidrin in addition to vitamins. It seems to work for me. Start with one pill twice a day and continue it for two or three days. If it doesn't work, take one pill four times a day—after breakfast, lunch, dinner, and about 10 o'clock just before going to bed. She has to rest in complete silence. Particularly talking seems to have an adverse effect. Sometimes the ringing in the ears increases between half to one hour after taking the pill, but she should not worry. Sometimes the ringing disappears an hour and half to two or three hours after taking the pill. Two hours or so after taking the pill, tap her head lightly. She should feel something flowing out of her head leaving her in total silence without the ringing noise. She should not talk or move then. She should close her eyes and be still as long as she can.

When you talk to Cecilia read this letter to her so her friend can follow exactly what I recommend. When I first took this medicine, the ringing increased so that I thought this would not work. She should not worry if she feels some sensation in the limbs and the ringing increases one-half hour to one hour after taking the pill. In two or three hours that sensation will go away—sometimes totally. She should not forget to take vitamins B_1, B_6, and B_{12} to help the function of the peripheral nervous system.

If Cecilia's friend is an older person, there is a chance of cholesterol clogging up her veins and preventing the flow of blood. In Japan there is a new medicine called Arturo-gold. It is especially effective in the case of high blood pressure. It cleans the blood and blood vessels. I think it would be good for her and for you also. It is recommended for high blood pressure, constipation, dizziness, ear ringing, numbness of the limbs, and short breath. It is sold over the counter. Shall I send it to you?

Take the friend of Cecilia to Dr. Childrey. He would gladly write a prescription for Arlidrin. *[Continued in next letter.]*

From KIYOSHI, *September 11.*

[BY REFERRING CECILIA'S FRIEND TO Dr. Childrey] we can express our gratitude for his help to us too.

I am under complete rest. With the doctor's approval, I take meals in the room. It certainly makes a big difference. Tell Cecilia's friend to avoid talking. At least she can experiment with it and see the result. When the ringing is reduced, I feel so much better. On the other hand, I would go mad if it increased. I have been trying very hard to keep it under control. And now this cold—the fever and coughing do not help! I have to be really careful because, in my case, the restoration of hearing is hinged upon the reduction of ringing in the ears. This is the reason I am now under absolute rest in the room. Reading a book is not good either. Tell Cecilia's friend that it's not easy to put restrictions on oneself, but it's an indescribable relief and joy to get rid of the ringing in one's ears.

. . . Once a week the doctor, who is also an assistant professor, makes rounds to check the patients. He treats me very well and leaves instructions to Dr. Shirabe. Please include a razor by Gillette with a few blades and a can of Almond Roca candy in the package. I'd like to give these to the professor. . . .

Tell Yukiko that Daddy was so happy to have received a letter from her, and he will send his reply in a few days.

From Kiyoshi, *September 11.*

. . . Yesterday I received two letters from you. I didn't expect any today but two more came! They were written on September fifth and seventh. I was surprised and happy all at once—also with a bit of anxiety that I'll not hear from you for a long time after this. But THANK YOU! Thank you, Kiyoko-san, especially for describing your lips—a rush of tingles runs through my body when I read it.

. . . It must have been quite a trip to Hayward to see the people of Japan Airlines. I am glad you went to see them though. And I am touched by Matsumura-san's kindness to send a doll for Yukiko. He was so helpful to me then and so thoughtful now even to Yukiko. I can't express my gratitude enough. For Christmas we will send presents to their daughters, Mayumi-*chan* and Kumi-*chan*, who are now in Fukuoka with their mother visiting the grandparents. I'll get their address later.

About an invitation to the employees of Japan Airlines—it may be better to invite them out to a place where they can eat and relax at the same time. Once I was taken by Akizuki-san to a buffet lunch in a special room large enough for about 25 guests. At $1.50 per person—$22.50 for 15 people—adding Yukiko, you, and Ōshima-san, it would be around $25.00, plus beer and soda. It will be easier to carry on a conversation in a separate room. If we invite them to the house, it will cost around $50.00. If we invite them out, it will be less, and you don't have to clean the dishes either. You can get the address from Akizuki-san or Okumura-san and reserve the room at least a couple of days in advance. . . .

About "one step and a step and half"—it's about the ringing in my ears. Suppose I give five to the worst stage of ringing—sometimes it's so close to disappearing, there remains only "one-step" or "a-step-and-a-half" until it goes away completely. When I'm still, I get to the "one step" or "a step and a half" stage before there's complete silence. I've experienced complete silence during the night. Because of a severe cold, I was thrown back to stage five, and now I'm slowly coming back to stage one or one and half since I'm under the regimen of absolute rest. I hope I get better soon now that fall is finally here, and my appetite may come back too. By the way, if I can find the cooler that I described, I'll bring it home. . . .

From KIYOKO, *September 12.*

. . . IT WAS UNCOMFORTABLY WARM TODAY. At 10 o'clock at night the indoor temperature was still about 80 degrees. I received your *[September ninth]* letter telling me that you were sick with a high fever. You must have felt so lonely—being separated from family and being sick with fever on top of it. I am praying that it will go away by the time you read this letter.

I didn't feel well either last night. After posting a letter to you, I realized that my throat was getting irritated. I took two Anacin tablets and went to bed without taking a bath. I felt better in the morning. I think the cold I caught a few weeks ago is still with me and surfaces from time to time.

You didn't get any letters on the sixth, seventh, and eighth of September. I didn't write on the eighth and ninth, so there will be another spell of disappointment. I am really sorry.

After work, on my way home, I return to myself and start thinking about you. I want to be close to you—I want to be held tight in your arms. . . . I think about this every day while I drive home. In the car, I have the world of only you and me. I want you to get well and come home to me. I want to writhe in the ecstasy of love together with you. I'm sure you feel the same way. Come home to me!

This is the second day of school. I told Yukiko to work on multiplication instead of watching TV. She still has a problem with her 8's and 9's multiplications. After she did her homework, we took a present to Nagasaki-san for their newborn baby. Mr. Nagasaki excused himself and went out somewhere. Later he phoned me and apologized that he stepped next door for a moment because he thought we would stay longer. It was apparent that his wife was prompting him to call me and apologize. I think we won this tussle. Poor Hiroko-san—she is trying hard to mend the gap her husband created. Someday we will be free of them. I gave $15 for the birth and baby shower of their newborn. It should cover amply the $10 that they gave you as a parting gift.

I'm making an appointment for a tune-up of our car for this Saturday. It has had over 6,000 miles since the last tune-up, winter is approaching, and it's an old car. It needs to be taken care of. . . .

I was so relieved to hear that you were getting better, and so I skipped writing one day. Then I received your lamenting note saying, "If only I could hear from Kiyoko-san, I would feel much better." It hit me like a whip—I felt punished and can't forget what I've done to you. Please forgive me.

It is now 11:20 p.m. I'll post this in the morning. Please don't feel defeated! Our bodies may suffer illness, but it should not invade our soul too. That was our philosophy, wasn't it? Let's take care of our bodies as well as our souls. . . .

From KIYOSHI, *September 12.*

. . . I'M BACK TO LIFE SINCE I received two letters from you and one from Yukiko. For one whole week I felt completely beaten up, but this morning I'm writing in a totally different mood.

In yesterday's letter you wrote about *The Freezing Point {*氷点 *(Hyōten)}.* One day when I was reading it in the newspaper, another patient came by. He was very much interested in a Japanese newspaper published in America. He had the book version of *Hyōten* and lent it to me. I finished reading it two weeks ago. The ending after the passage on the will is written so superbly, isn't it? It captures the reader's heart—I couldn't stop crying. I think it is very well written from the development of its plot to its ending. It is rare even among first-class novelists to write perfect fiction like this. What do you think, Kiyoko-san? The ugliness of the woman's nature is described well; so is the shameful nature hidden in a seemingly honest man.

We must seriously think about the true meaning of happiness. We must stop chasing after superficial happiness. We must seek happiness that stands firmly on the earth—happiness like fresh air, not like perfume. Particularly for an aging couple—it's not just disgraceful, it's pitiful to lose themselves chasing after the scent of perfume. We are lucky. We are plodding step by step toward the real happiness of a couple. I am a lucky man to have a woman like you for my wife. . . .

From KIYOSHI, *September 12.*

. . . I'LL CONTINUE ANSWERING YOUR INQUIRY. Yes, the package of news-papers had arrived. I'm sorry I didn't tell you that earlier.

I'll ask Hiroyuki-san to check on the cooler "Ice Pet," and I'll bring home a deluxe model. Or, I'll ask him to ship it now if it is not too troublesome.

. . . I imagine that not only your company but also many others are enforcing the austerity program. Have they curbed new employment? It sounds like the government has grown tired of the war [in Vietnam]. I thought that Governor Romney's speech was rather bold and daring. That one statement might spread like a fire in an open field. It's a big headache for President Johnson, isn't it? It is reported here too that America is searching desperately for a way to end the war honorably. . . .

The following is the address of Mrs. Matsumura:

Kyōko Matsumura-*sama*

c/o Mr. Yasunosuke Kuroyanagi

4-824, Sumiyoshi,

Fukuoka-shi, Japan

Their daughters are Mayumi-*chan* (one year and 11 months) and Kumi-*chan* (five months). For now just send a thank-you note to Mrs. Matsumura. She and her husband will be happy to hear from you. . . .

I'm going to close today's letter. Typhoon No. 22 is approaching Japan, and the sky has a strange glow here in Kyushu. . . .

From KIYOKO, *September 13.*

. . . IT MAY BE TOO SOON TO TELL, but Yukiko seems to realize that she should study more. I hope the new teacher is a good one. Yukiko says that she is married and has children. Evidently the teacher told the class, "The introduction is over and study begins tomorrow." "So there is homework," says Yukiko. But now she is cutting paper and making a boat and a man with oars.

Everybody is busier since school is open. Mitsuko-san likes her 11th grade class. Your mother is all right with her chronic head-shaking. Chan-nel 9 has started to show *The Tale of Genji* in English. The narrator speaks English beautifully, and I'm learning from her a great deal. This broadcast is for the general English-speaking audience and is not targeted for the Japanese in this country. Therefore, it is far different from your plan. Your mother viewed the broadcast but said she didn't understand it very well. In yesterday's paper there was a column reporting on Mr. Kataoka of Aki Travel Company and one other travel service being cited by the Minister of Transportation in Japan. I thought it was appropriate because they were so helpful when you left for Japan.

As I wrote in the last letter, I'm going to send you another $100 this Friday. You should have received $500 by now. I sent it in two drafts, and I wonder if it was the best way. How did you receive the money? Did you have to go to the office twice to receive two drafts? If so, I'm sorry for the inconvenience. By the way, we should get a check from the insurance company very soon.

I'm writing this with your letter in front of me describing how discouraged you are because you have not received any from me for some time. I am disturbed too, so much so that I cannot write a sensible letter today. Forgive me. I had been writing every other day, but you have not received any from me for six days—it makes my heart sink!

I'll stop here and mail this in the morning. I hope I get a happier letter from you tomorrow. . . .

With a sunken heart, Kiyoko.

From KIYOSHI, *September 13.*

. . . AT LAST WE CAN FEEL COOL autumn air here in Japan, or to be precise, in Fukuoka. But it is cloudy because Typhoon No. 22 is approaching. And more is to follow since September is the typhoon season here. But I'm relieved from the discomfort now that the heat is gone. . . .

I read a story on Robert Schumann yesterday. It moved me so deeply. He fell in love with the daughter of his piano teacher, who vehemently opposed their marriage though he knew very well of Schumann's great talent. His reasoning was that both the father and the brother of Schumann had a mental disorder. Schumann himself lost the use of one of his hands due to his relentless practice on the piano and so had to become a composer instead of a concert pianist. But the daughter, Clara, was in love with Schumann. He composed a piece for her and called it "My Heart Cries for Clara." She played it at a concert and received an enthusiastic ovation from the public. For Clara, it was a declaration of independence from her father, and she left him for Schumann.

Schumann composed many songs for Clara; for example, the *Myrthen* series which were dedicated to her, and popularly acclaimed songs like *"Frauenliebe und Leben," "Dichterliebe,"* and *"Du bist wie eine Blume."*

After one year of their marriage, Schumann began to suffer from insomnia, a speech impediment, [and] hallucinations and was institutionalized like his father and brother. On July 29, 1854, he put Clara's finger to his lips, whispered "I know this is my Clara," and died. One hundred fifty years after his death, a statue of the couple was built in Leipzig. It is called "Eternal Love." A part of his love letter to Clara is engraved on the statue: "A rose bud is about to open in my heart. I feel the most noble and pure love for you. If I were a smile, I would dance on your lips; if I were a tear drop, I would float in your eyes."

From KIYOKO, *September 14.*

... I GOT A SPEEDING TICKET this morning. It makes me sick. I was going on Fourth Street as usual. Just before reaching the point where 30 mph changes to 40 mph, I felt I was accelerating a little bit; at the same time I saw a police car, and its red light started to flick. This happened in a flash. I'm so annoyed! I phoned the police office to find out about the fine, but I was told to wait till Monday.

This weekend will be an unpleasant one without knowing how much I have to pay. I guess police cars have better radar equipment nowadays. The officer handed me the ticket and his pen, which had Sumitomo Bank's name on it. I know I was speeding so I will pay the fine. Asking someone to void this ticket will not help me wipe off my annoyance. I have muscle pains here and there lately; after this incident, my right hip joint started to hurt. It went away after taking one Anacin. Maybe I should try the pill you mentioned in today's letter—what do you say? It may be good for the numbness of my hand too.

Tomorrow I'll send an additional $100 to add to your pocket money. Soon I'll get another package ready to mail. Let me know if you need anything, particularly for the cooler weather. You will have three winter pajamas in the next package. You took a sweater with you. Shall I send you a wool bathrobe? I'll hold this package until you tell me what you need. . . .

When I started this letter, I was so upset. I'm all right now. I'll go to bed early and get up early and drive carefully. I don't know what else I can say!

From KIYOSHI, *September 14.*

. . . I RECEIVED A WATSONVILLE newspaper yesterday. A photograph of Akira-san is in it. Did you send it? The address looks like your handwriting. That was all yesterday; I hope I get a letter from you today.

Yukiko must have started school. How is she doing? I hope she has a good, young teacher this year.

I wrote about Robert and Clara Schumann yesterday. I'm sure you were moved by their unbreakable, loving bonds. Things born out of superb love— be it art, or academic achievement, or farmer's work—all these are the fruits of love—there is nothing more noble and precious than steadfast love. I think we get strength to create from being nurtured by sound love.

Today I read an article written by an American psychologist, in which he said that love is "short-lived," and "adultery helps to keep family life going." I was flabbergasted by this statement. It may be a rational and academic observation of our society, but it overlooks the families who are bound to each other and try to go forward together. This psychologist expounded on his finding that love between couples lasts for about five years; everybody wishes for someone else to be his wife or her husband—any other way is abnormal. I suppose it is true between the couples who have nothing to share with each other. What a sad family life if they cannot maintain peace in the family unless they betray each other. I don't need a family life like that. It is so different from ours. Here we are, a couple over 40, loving each other more than ever and writing letters every day—we are lucky! Yes, I have physical problems, but my body is too clean to be touched by anybody else but you; my lips seek only yours; my love for you is sacred. The deduction of academic research on married couples does not apply in our case. I'm sure you agree with me. No one else but we two knows how our love has deepened as we have gotten older. How lucky I am to love you so much and to be loved so much. I know you understand. . . .

From KIYOSHI, *September 15.*

... TYPHOON NO. 22 CHANGED course and missed making landfall. It's a beautiful autumn morning although a bit too warm to call this autumn. How are you, Kiyoko-san? I feel much better and hope it stays this way. However, the ringing in my ears remains the same. I can't help but be anxious to get rid of this ringing, but I should try to stay calm and wait and see.

How is Yukiko doing? I didn't hear from you day before yesterday and yesterday. I hope your letter comes today. Every day around 2:30 in the afternoon, I begin to wait for the mail delivery. ...

· · ·

I didn't get a letter today. I shouldn't expect it, but I can't help it! I wait and wait; none comes. I get lonely; I can't help it! I can take the loneliness for two days, but it gets worse on the third and fourth day. I know you are busy, but I can't help but want to hear from you every day. Forgive me!

By the way, you haven't said anything about the pansies that Yoshimitsu gave us. Are they all right?

Today is Seniors' Day in Japan. I think it's a national holiday. According to the news, an increase in the subsidy to seniors has been proposed. We will soon be seniors if the retirement age is 60. It won't be long! Yukiko will be about 30—middle-aged! By that time, man will travel back and forth to the moon.

I couldn't write well today. Forgive me. Tomorrow your letter will come. I'm looking forward to it. ...

From KIYOKO, *September 16.*

... THREE LETTERS CAME YESTERDAY. I'm so happy to hear that you are recovering. Also a check of $494.82 came yesterday from the insurance company—this will help us! I'm sure you are pleased too. Less monetary pressure might hasten your recovery too. In the next insurance application, we'll convert the yen to dollars so that it may speed up the process. They are very sympathetic women, but they have only elementary school knowledge on conversion and regard mathematics to be as mysterious as an occult art in Japan.

I'm at European Motors now to have our car repaired. Bob, the fat one, was amazed at the growth of Yukiko and even mentioned it to another customer whom I didn't know. I'm writing this in the lounge while the car is being repaired. This area is changing; construction vehicles to build an overpass are all over from Noda-san's nurseries all the way to the judge's house. Our world changes fast and grows up just like a child, doesn't it? Even the uneven road around here is now paved.

Yukiko is not attending the Japanese Language School today. It seems difficult to find someone who can teach Japanese after Hiroko-san left. I'll ask Tsukiji-san about this.

I called Okumura-san to discuss inviting the Japan Airlines employees to dinner, but he was at a board meeting of the Japanese Language School. I couldn't talk about this with Akizuki-san so I asked Okumura-san to call me tonight. Akizuki-san kindly sent us $25 when you left for Japan, but I hesitate to discuss with him things like my dinner invitation plan.

I called Tsukiji-san to ask about the Japanese Language School, but he also was at the board meeting, and his wife was out to see a Japanese movie. It's nice that she's able to find time to relax in her busy life. . . .

The newspaper series, *The Freezing Point* [氷点 *(Hyōten)*], is at the passage in which Kitahara and Takagi arrive to tell about their parents. Since you've read the book, please tell me if I should continue sending the newspaper. I've sent the second package of Arlidrin and vitamin E. A bundle of the newspapers was sent on the same day, but I'm afraid they'll all be outdated.

I'll send Matsumura-san something he can enjoy.

I almost forgot to mention—yesterday I sent you an additional $100 by cable. The next item is the fine for my traffic violation, the amount of which I will find out the day after tomorrow, a Monday. I'll subtract the fine from the insurance coverage which will be deposited in the credit union. I was really vexed at my traffic violation, but now I try to think that the fine is like an injection bracing me for daily life.

The bulldozer is making a horrible noise, and there's not much writing space left to continue either. I'll write again tomorrow evening. Usually I write every other day. Please remember that. Also please remember that I may have to delay another day on some weekends and holidays. Let's be prepared for these situations so that you won't get upset. . . .

From KIYOSHI, *September 16.*

. . . I WROTE TO CECILIA THIS MORNING. As you suggested, I wrote it in Chinese. Please ask her if it is readable. I didn't know how to address a couple in Chinese so I used the Japanese, 御夫妻様, for that. Please tell her that it means Mr. and Mrs. I said, 秋波訪而 涼風快適 (Autumn is here; comfortable cool breeze) but maybe I should have used 爽快 (refreshing), referring to "cool wind" instead of 快適 which is appropriate for a situation like "riding in a car." Please ask her if this is correct. I'm sure there are some more questionable words. So at the end, I wrote, 乞容赦 拙文乱筆 (Excuse me for my poor expression and terrible writing). Tell her that I worked hard on this, and ask her if she was able to understand my poor Chinese.

• • •

I stopped to leave space to write when I received your letter today. And, as I hoped, two letters came; one was written on Sunday, the day before Yukiko started school, and the other on September 11th, after the start of school. They made me so happy!

My cold is almost gone. From now on, I'm going to be very careful not to catch it again. . . .

I'm glad to know that you are receiving my letters without a hitch. You don't need to send me food because I can order out from time to time; but I appreciate your concern. Now that Yukiko is back in school, be sure she does her homework. Find out at the dinner table if she has homework; if she does, have her finish it before watching TV. It's better if you can train her to start on her homework as soon as she comes home from school. Be sure to go over the finished homework to see that she didn't skip anything. I'm sorry you have to do all this, but it's important. . . .

The nurses here are all kind to me. The high school girl across the hall has written me saying that she might come see me today or tomorrow. She thanked me for my help on her homework during summer break. . . .

From KIYOKO, *September 17.*

. . . WHEN I CAME HOME FROM European Motors and was entering the door, I felt a sharp pain in my back and couldn't breathe. I thought it was a sign of a cold, and I lay down in bed early in the evening. Yukiko cooked rice, went to the store, and got a filet of tuna. She brought Mother here to ask her to make sashimi. By that time I felt a little better, and Mother went home. I removed the skin from the fish, and then Yukiko wanted to slice it. She sliced it so thick that we had a luxurious sashimi dinner!

I had rested well the day before yesterday after taking two tablets of Anacin at night. This backache has something to do with my nerves—after all, the traffic violation is still bothering me so much, and I can't complain about it to anyone.

Your letter to Yukiko came yesterday. After dinner we practiced reading it aloud until she could pronounce all the words correctly. Since she knows some words, she seems to understand what you are saying in these scripts. Although you wrote the letter carefully, there are some mistakes like "*chōtai,*" instead of "*chōdai.*" She questioned why you wrote that way. I told her that you made a mistake because you were in a hurry. Also I suggest you write the assimilated* sound smaller so that it's easier to read. It's a trivial point but it may help.

I was very touched by the story of Schumann. I think he was a happy man to be in love with his wife till his last moment of life. I am not sure, though, if Clara was that constant. Guessing from the monument and the inscription, however, she must have loved her husband tenderly. It is a moving episode, and one that echoes your own sentiment.

I had Hisayo mail the newspaper with Akira-san's photo on the eighth of September. It made Akira-san very happy but Tamotsu-san is afraid that the publicity might invite the visits of bill collectors, according to Mitsuyo. Akira-san himself is delighted and collecting the papers to give to his friends, while his brother is discouraging it. Is it a difference of opinion, or jealousy? I don't know. By the way, it was my handwriting—your wife's handwriting. Didn't you recognize it?!

Your mother is in the mood to buy a house again. She is suggesting that I buy a property that the daughter of her friend is putting on the market. I told her that we won't be able to do that because even the deposit money has to be borrowed. But she wouldn't rest until at least I took a look at the property. Your brother and his wife also came. They will be attending church with their children starting this fall. I brought up the subject of a future wife for Henry. Your brother said that he would appreciate if we would keep looking for a candidate, be it Tachibana-san or any others. Regarding the house, he said to Mother that he didn't have any money left since he bought a piece of land. Your mother was disappointed because nobody is rich enough to buy a house. I don't know why, but she seems to want a three-bedroom house. Perhaps she wants "her own house"—the idea everyone dreams of in his lifetime. Please don't mention this to anybody. I don't know yet if you are going to be included in this discussion.

*Assimilated sound (促音) is a sound using staccato. Example: 赤 (red) is pronounced *aka*, but まっか (very red) is pronounced *makka*. Kiyoko is advising Kiyoshi to write assimilated sound small, as in まっか, because if he writes it in the same value, as in まつか, it is pronounced *matsuka* and has no meaning.

From Kiyoshi, *September 17.*

. . . Summer heat lingers on in Fukuoka. How are you, Kiyoko-san? I received two letters from you yesterday. Thank you so much. My strength returns, and even my appetite is better when I receive your affectionate letters. It would be wonderful if I could eat a lot and get my energy back so that I can't sit still any more. I wish I could kick and move around fast like the sparkles of fireworks at a judo match. Little Paul used to do that. I can't be that quick, but I wish I could feel the urge to jump up and down like him!

Yesterday the girl across the hall came to see me, bringing some flowers and cookies that she made. She said she brought some "biscuits" so I told her that they are called cookies in America; then she said softly, "Cookies." Also she gave me some pottery. There is a message baked into it: "Get well soon!" She is really a nice girl from a respectable family. She is big-boned but still a gentle and guileless child. She looks much younger than Mitsuko. . . .

Last Sunday was the day Hiroyuki-san exchanged betrothal gifts with his fiancée. Masayuki-san was to come see me in place of Hiroyuki-san, but he didn't come either. Maybe Hiroyuki-san and Noriko-san will come today. If they do, I'm going to mention "the mental disposition" of marriage that you talked about. First, I'm going to tell them that you said, "A couple may argue, but never think of leaving each other." I want to talk about what you and I have been practicing as a couple—that is, each of us individually grows to become a respectable person, and together we build a profound love for each other.

It must be quite a job to oversee Yukiko's homework every day, but please do that until I come home. . . .

From KIYOKO, *September 18.*

. . . THIS MORNING I WAS GOING TO mail yesterday's letter in San Jose, but I forgot to do it although the letter was right next to my bag! So I mailed it from Mountain View instead. It might reach you together with this letter.

Before lunch time, I called the Office of Traffic Violations to find out about the fine. I was speeding just a little bit, but the fine is $36—I feel so miserable! I hope I don't get any tickets in the future—at least for five years! I feel better now, however, that I know how much I have to pay.

At lunch time, I deposited $400 at the credit union. $96.82 will be used for incidentals.

Cecilia and her husband will leave for New York this weekend and travel on the East Coast for two weeks. She says that her savings are almost gone because of this trip. She has a friend whose husband works at the U.N., but he is about to retire and might move to another city. She, the friend, invited Cecilia and her husband to come east while they are still in New York City.

Your letter didn't come today—this is rare. I bet a bunch of letters will be delivered tomorrow. I'm spoiled because I'm used to receiving at least one every day. I feel like I'm missing something today.

Lately Yukiko does not spend so much time in front of the TV. I told her that she ought to study without my help. She doesn't bother Mitsuko-san anymore. Today she cooked rice by herself because all the grownups were late coming home. But she didn't know what to do with the side dishes, and she was just staring at the hamburger meat and beans when I came home. She can chop lettuce nicely too. You would be very proud of her.

I asked her what she studied at school today; she said she studied multiplication of one unit and two units. She is practicing it now. She is not quite sure about 9 x 8 and 9 x 9, but she can do all the others. However, she hates writing. We just had an argument over her copying the questions. All that good food at dinner time began to boil up in my stomach—I'd better drink soda right away to settle it down.

The weather is unsettled here too. The leaves of the elm tree keep falling, and I keep sweeping. I felt good all day because I slept half a day on Saturday. The other day you wrote about an article by Governor Romney, and I saw a sticker "Save Lives, Not Face" on a car. I memorized it to tell you about this. I think it says it all about the Vietnam War and the sacrifice that we are paying in order to save the face of the nation. I don't know the content of the Governor's speech since I didn't read the newspaper.

As I was writing this letter, Yukiko started to challenge me over my spelling, and we ended up in a verbal fight—she told me to spell "source," and I said, "Can you say BILE in Japanese?" I barely maintained my parental authority, but it is getting difficult!

The car is running nicely without any trouble. This week I'll work on the invitation to the people of Japan Airlines, and I'll prepare another package to send to you.

May you feel happy remembering us being together! I'm always with you. . . .

From KIYOSHI, *September 18.*

. . . HEAVY SMOG HAS ENVELOPED this area, and I can't see the Tsukushi Mountains. Maybe the temperature will go up again. According to the paper, it was 79.52 degrees yesterday at the highest—the first time it stayed lower than 80 degrees—and the lowest was 68.72 degrees.

How are you, Kiyoko-san? I start on a new treatment today since the antidotal injection was over yesterday. I'll tell you about it later.

Today the compilation of the hospital receipts of my payments was supposed to be ready at the office. I went there at nine o'clock, but it wasn't ready. They asked me to wait for a couple of days so I'll go back on the 21st.
. . .

I'm guessing that in about two more months we will know whether the treatment is successful or not—or I may have to stay till December 18th. The new treatment which starts today will tell us. The doctors are trying everything they can. This morning the head of the team was conferring with Dr. Shirabe. The head professor and the assistant professor come to check on me twice a week. It makes me so frustrated not being able to hear. Most probably they are talking about the ringing in my ears. The other day I asked you to mail a set of razors for the assistant professor. Could you please make it two sets so that I can give one also to the head professor?

Yesterday Hiroyuki-san came around 4:20 p.m. He was alone. I talked to him about our marriage: your unchanging love and respect for me in spite of my condition; our love for each other being nurtured tenderly for a long time. He seemed to be very inspired. I told him that, like any newborn being, love at the beginning is frail, but it grows strong and beautiful by being carefully nursed. In case of a dire situation like we are in now, our love is giving us inspiration and assistance. One should not get married only for sex. To live as a pair helping each other with deep love is the most important purpose of life. Fame, social position, and wealth do not have anything to do with such love. If those are the objectives of one's life, a woman becomes only an object of sexual pleasure, and changing partners one after another takes away any real happiness. Our toil for earnings and our work toward recognition are means helping us achieve a clear and happy married life, and so on. Anyway, it was a good talk although Noriko-san was not with him. There will be a chance to talk to her some other time. . . .

From KIYOSHI, *September 19.*

. . . THE MOUNTAINS ARE COVERED with smog until about noon when the wind clears it away.

I started a new treatment yesterday evening with an injection of vitamins; this evening I will start a cellular therapy with a tablet called ATP together with Arlidrin.

The ringing in my ears can be controlled as long as I don't move, but it gets bad if I move around, for example, going downstairs to the office and trying to talk to the employees there. However, as long as I stay still, it is bearable, and this is an improvement. I'm waiting for the day when my head gets clear, my appetite increases, and I begin to feel the urge to hustle around —it'll be a great day! Since that cold, I've been afraid to open the window for fresh air because I might get a fever; if I keep the windows closed, I'm afraid I'll get a headache because the air is stuffy. But this condition won't last much longer. Maybe I should get an ice bag to cool my head. . . .

I had the nurse call the Fukuoka Branch of Sumitomo Bank; the money is in my account. Thank you so much. It was sent by regular mail, according to the nurse. But I think it was cabled to the main bank in Tokyo and transferred to Fukuoka by regular mail; otherwise it was too quick. I was supposed to go there with my seal, but I had the check mailed here instead. . . .

I started to subscribe to the newspaper called the *Nishi-Nihon*. I'm reading three papers; the English and Japanese versions of the *Nishi-Nihon* and the *Mainichi*, which I trade for the *Nishi-Nihon*. I want to learn more about the state of business in Japan, particularly about small business. Compared to the U.S., its scale and profit must be smaller; I wonder how they make money. Studying this now may help later when my hearing gets better. I was thinking of correspondence school in mathematics. Wouldn't it be a big hit if I were to do it here in Japan? A company like Ōbunsha is doing well in various academic subjects. Small printing companies are making money by handling advertising for stores. Also, I'm surprised to find that there are so many people who want to go to America. Here in this hospital, there is a doctor who just graduated from a school of dentistry; he yearns to go to the States. An employment agency would be a good possibility in this case. In fact, not only people in the field of electronics but also in many other fields are very eager to go to the States. I think it would be so meaningful if I could assist them; I can serve them with honesty and sincerity and make them happy. But, most importantly, I must restore my hearing first!

I'm sure I'll hear from you today. I'll write again then. Take care. Please remember me to Yukiko, Hisayo-san, Mother and Mitsuko.

From KIYOSHI, *September 20.*

. . . THIS IS TRUE! A BUNDLE OF four letters was delivered to me today! The post office didn't understand how much I was fretting over your silence, did they! They held your letters Sunday, Monday, and Tuesday, and made me out of my mind! . . .

You may still have a virus so please be cautious with your cold. I feel much better now; I'm getting over the hump—my head is clearer and my appetite is back. I will be very careful from now on.

I'm thrilled to hear that you think of me while driving home after work. I'll write my reaction and send it to your mail box at your office. Together with it, I'll send the receipts with yen converted to dollars and the insurance paper with the necessary signature from an official of the hospital. So, be prepared! . . .

I'm glad to hear that Mother and Mitsuko are in good shape. I wish I could have seen *The Tale of Genji* with you. I read the article in the local paper here about the citation on Yasunaka Travel Bureau. They serve their customers with sincerity and excellence; they really deserve this honor. Here again, I'm so glad that I followed your suggestion. . . .

About the traffic ticket: think of it positively—it's better than not being caught, and ending up killing people or getting yourself seriously injured in an accident. Don't forget that you are my very precious wife. Think this way—the fine is to warn you to be more cautious as you drive. You should have said to the officer, "You are a Sumitomo customer, aren't you? The director, Kimura, is a good friend of mine."

I'll ask Hiroyuki-san to send you the medicine for high blood pressure together with the one for hemorrhoids for Mother. I'd like you to add two sets of Gillette shavers in the package—also some coffee candies and the wool bathrobe. I'll need a couple of dress shirts when I come home. Pretty soon I'll need winter underwear. . . .

I'm so glad that the insurance paid us $494.82; I feel as though a burden is removed from my shoulders. With the next refund application, I'll change yen to dollars on the receipt before sending it to the insurance company. I'm happy to hear that you decided to invite the employees of Japan Airlines to the restaurant, not to our house. The Japanese Language School would be overjoyed if you would teach there. If that happens, I'll prepare a syllabus for you. Re: the local Japanese papers, please continue sending them to me.

Lastly, the package arrived. But it was difficult to claim it this time. They didn't deliver it to the hospital so that I had to ask somebody to go pick it up. It cost me about 2,000 yen for the taxi ride and incidentals plus the import tax on the package. I don't understand why it is so complicated this time. I had the nurse phone them to explain my situation, but it didn't work; they insisted that I had to come to receive the package. After some arguing, it was settled that I could send a proxy. . . .

From KIYOKO, *September 21.*

THIS IS GOING TO BE a very short letter.

I was going to invite the Japan Airlines people to a restaurant, but I was told that there were not many who could attend. So I decided to bring something to their office.

Tuesday evening, I did the shopping for the ingredients; Wednesday I roasted beef, delivered it to Hayward, and served it along with soft drinks. I couldn't find time to write to you—I'm sorry. But they were so happy, and they ate everything! Ōshima-san said that he would see you again and be happy to deliver a package to you. Since he urged me to prepare a package for you, I'm going to accept his offer.

I'll send the plastic bags by air mail; the rest will come by sea. Cecilia was happy to read your letter; she said your Chinese was good and she understood everything. I want to give her something too, so I'm going out now to shop although the sky is threatening.

By the way, the day before yesterday Tokunaga-san came to see me, and I decided to teach temporarily at the Japanese Language School until they find a qualified teacher.

From KIYOSHI, *September 21.*

. . . A CLOUDY DAY. I WAS SO happy to receive four letters yesterday. They may skip delivery for a few days, but I can stay calm because now I know that letters come in bunches sometimes. . . .

I wanted to eat yellow-fin sushi. But it cost 800 yen—I was flabbergasted! The regular tuna sushi costs 400 yen which is twice as much as the chicken-rice special—yellow-fin is four times as much! Since I'm not that crazy about yellow-fin, I've ordered sushi with regular tuna; it will be delivered about 7:30 p.m.—it is 6:20 p.m. now.

It's been a busy day. I finished the insurance form and took it to Dr. Shirabe's office for his signature—I'll get it back tomorrow; I got the receipts and converted yen to dollars, then went to the accounting office to deposit the check for $500, which came today. On top of it, Watanabe-sensei came to visit me and stayed till dinner time. Now I'm exhausted—it was a day of heavy labor! So you have to excuse me for this terrible penmanship. . . .

According to Watanabe-sensei, Kyushu University is planning an exchange program of young professors and assistant professors for the purpose of training them to become English/Japanese bilingual teachers at the university level. The American party would attend the lectures given in Japanese at Kyushu University, and in turn, he can teach English conversation. Under a two-year contract, his travel expenses and a $300 monthly stipend will be paid to him. The Japanese party will be from Kyushu University; under a one-year contract, he will study the English language and American literature. His travel expense and cost of living will be covered, and in return he will teach Japanese. I thought of San Jose State University as a possibility. Kyushu University will take exchange professors specializing not only in the English language but also in the history of the East or in any specialized study related to Japan. How about asking Mr. Delacroix if he can recommend someone? Or ask if he wants to take up this opportunity with his specialty in Oriental Art History.

So much for today. I'll write again tomorrow. . . .

From KIYOKO, *September 22.*

. . . I RECEIVED [YOUR SEPTEMBER 19] letter today. After dinner I went to Hayward, and also to Palo Alto, crossing the San Mateo Bridge. . . . Ōshima-san offered to take a box as large as a tangerine box with him so I made a package of about 17 pounds. The contents are a wool bathrobe, cashew nuts, almonds, two Gillette razors with extra blades, Almond Roca candies, orange powder, peanut candies, newspapers, chewing gum, and two salami rolls. The price sticker is still on each item, so please don't forget to take it off.

I'm glad to hear that the money has arrived. There will be another $100 which I sent a week later. Don't splurge on Hiroyuki just because you have extra money. I might say that I worry about your generosity.

I couldn't think of anything to give to Ōshima-san. However, he liked the Hawaiian punch that I served with the roast beef and was planning to take some home to Japan. Since I had some, I packed five bottles in a box and presented it to him. Mother and Mitsuko-san came with Yukiko and me. In the JAL group there is a man by the name of Tanaka Toshimichi who is from Ōmuta City in Fukuoka. He wanted to pay a visit to you when he goes to Kyushu University. I thanked him but told him not to make a special trip. I didn't do anything for him, but Hori-san took him around in San Francisco; only we, the poor, are so generous to others, I thought. Maybe we'll be rewarded someday. And even if there is no reward, the good feeling that comes from helping others is a reward by itself, I think.

I bought a box of California dried fruit as a send-off gift to Cecilia and her husband who are going to New York. It's rather pricey, but it's the right gift because she likes dried fruit. I took it to their house, but they were not home. I asked their neighbor, Nancy, to deliver it to them when they come home. They are leaving early in the morning so I won't see them off. . . .

Next week I'll start preparing another package to send to you. It may be better to buy winter clothes locally. Don't go out when it gets too cold.

I wrote about only day-to-day things today, but I'll have more time next week.

From Kiyoko, suffering from a deficiency of Kiyoshi, to Kiyoshi-san with a Kiyoko-deficiency syndrome.

From KIYOSHI, *September 22.*

STILL FRIDAY, SEPTEMBER 22. IT IS 10 minutes before eight o'clock at night. I thought I could mail the papers for the insurance, but I have to wait till tomorrow. The chief of the accounting office only wrote down his name on the paper so I asked that his title, "Head Treasurer," be added to it. Tomorrow is Saturday and the post office is open only in the morning. The other day I asked one of the patients to mail a letter by air from the post office in front of the hospital. Today I asked the same person to mail another letter. She said she would if she gets her treatment early enough. I didn't know that the post office across from the hospital is for domestic only, and last time she had to go all the way to the main office. I didn't know that, and I was overwhelmed with gratitude. She handed me change of about 100 yen for the medicine which I asked her to get also. I told her to keep it as a token of my appreciation. What a jerk I was! I apologized many times for my stupidity. I must repay her for her kindness. She has been staying in the hospital more than a year and a half and will go home soon. In spite of all that time, the treatment did not work; she still has a problem hearing in one of her ears. It is sad—she is only 22 years old. She is very clever in abacus calculation and has won prizes many times in regional competitions. Multiplication, division—she can handle them so easily; I've never met anyone like her. She helped me with the conversion of yen to dollars on the receipts.

There is another girl, also 22 years old, who has spent some time in this hospital undergoing plastic surgery on her nose. She is always in jolly spirits, laughing all the time; she makes people happy. I've been here for two months and have become one of the old-timers. These girls call me "Uncle" and come to see me often. They trust me because I receive them with a smile and say nothing improper. I've become a counselor to them.

Not like in America, male and female patients here can visit each other. I was surprised to see men go into the women's room freely and sometimes play chess on a woman's bed. They are well disciplined. When they come visit me, they sit on my bed and talk. Another surprise—they walk around the hall in pajamas! This is something I have never done; even in the summer time, I put a robe on over my pajamas when I went out of my room. However, I don't blame them because the summer here is unbearably hot. In the beginning it felt so unreal, but now I'm used to seeing it. Nowadays it is cooler so they put on *yukata*. I thought you would enjoy reading my observation on these local customs. They are using a bed for a chair; not only playing games on the bed, but also they take group photos on the bed— a scene Americans could never imagine! Nurses stop in and watch the game sometimes. I thought this is all proper. I'll send you a group photo that the high school girl across the hall took before she went home. It was taken in my room because I don't walk around much. The ringing in my ears has decreased a lot since I stay in my room most of the time. . . .

From KIYOSHI, *September 23.*

. . . I HAD MY FRIEND MAIL THE insurance form from the central post office. Since it is an important paper, I asked her to send it by registered air mail— it's costly but safer. I gave her 1,000 yen (about $3.00) for her two trips to the post office—besides, she helped me with her abacus. Last night she went out with two other girls and two men to a Chinese restaurant and to a dance hall after that. She said she had a good time. Things have changed so much from our days—they are enjoying life now! They go Dutch treat too. I was invited to come along but declined because of my hearing. Instead, I wrote letter

No. 65 *[dated September 22]* to you. (Before I forget, No. 64* was sent together with the insurance paper in one envelope. It may arrive after this letter because I didn't put the Mountain View Zip Code.) . . .

The episode about Yukiko and her sashimi made me smile. But I'm worried about your health, Kiyoko-san. We seem to get the same symptoms, like feeling chilled or getting headaches. It's so hard to get rid of these. Thank you for having Yukiko read my letters. In regard to the assimilated sound, it looks much better when I write it small—I'll remember that from now on. I'm so happy to hear that you liked the story about Robert Schumann. I think Clara was a great lady just as you are. . . .

Mother may want to consolidate her family, but I think it is impossible to buy a house large enough to keep two households in. Also you talked to my sister about a future wife for Henry—thank you very much. If my sister wants, it is possible to find a good one here. Japanese girls are much better than haughty American girls. Tell her that I'm sure she can find an honest and faithful young lady here for Henry. . . .

*No. 64 is missing. We surmise that it was a love letter that Kiyoko saved in a separate place for privacy.

From KIYOSHI, *September 24.*

. . . TOMORROW IS THE AUTUMN EQUINOX here in Japan. It is commonly said that the heat or the cold stays only up to the equinox; from now on it will be autumn. The lack of rain is causing the rice paddies to dry up, and water service is curtailed in some cities. Fortunately it has not happened in Fukuoka City. The Self Defense Force has been dispatched to Oga District of Kitakyushu City in order to distribute water. The joke column of a local paper carried the line, 水いらずで楽しんでいます。新婚の夫婦 ("We're enjoying it privately! From just-married"). . . . I get a kick out of Japanese joke columns. . . .

There is a nurse by the name of Yoshioka. She is 23 years old. . . . She said she wants to go to America someday. I told her I knew just the right person for her if she were older—I was thinking of Yotsuo-san. He is 40 and she is 23—well, he is too old for her. But he would take good care of his wife—what do you think? She is short and cute; she shows her teeth a little too much when she smiles; she has dimples like Mitsuyo-san. I think she is a good person. But she only finished middle school and has been working as a nurse

KIYOSHI *(far left)* WITH OTHER PATIENTS *at Kyushu University Hospital, fall 1967. The woman holding the child is Sachiko Shizuma. Photo courtesy of Yukiko Tokutomi Northon.*

to this day. She liked English in school. She has taken care of me very well from the first day on, maybe because Watanabe-sensei told her to do so. Anyway, I gave her Almond Roca candy and soap to take home. The other day I saw a woman of around 30 that looked like she was about your age—I think Japanese women tend to show aging early. Yotsuo-san would not take her. Sooner or later there will be another candidate for his wife; it's best to wait a little longer. Maybe ask Akira-san what is Yotsuo-san's preference for a wife. I will ask someone to take a photo of me with the nurse as my souvenir picture and send it to you. She looks nice. . . .

From Kiyoko, *September 25.*

There were no letters from you on Friday and Saturday; I bet a big bundle of letters will come on Monday. Today is Sunday. I got up late. I've rested well, but all day I could not suppress my anger at the post office. I spent the day cleaning here and there. I hope you are OK. I took laundry downstairs only to find that somebody had just started the machine. The same thing happened last Sunday. This is like living in an apartment complex with only one washing machine! Why don't people use the machine some other day; why don't they use it on Saturday? But nobody uses it on Saturday. I don't know whom to complain to—so I'm telling you, Kiyoshi-san. . . . I have never told them to do this and that; maybe keeping my anger inside is why I get sick to my stomach. The sun isn't hot anymore these days so I'm drying some things on the heater. Well, I've done enough venting of my grudge. . . .

Today Takemoto-san stopped by. He didn't know that you went to Japan for treatment. As usual he talked loudly and openly and enjoyed the tea that Yukiko served. You may hear from him since I gave him your address. He came to attend the Fall Festival of the Buddhist Association, where Yamamoto-san demonstrated how to make Japanese dolls. I saw a picture of Yamamoto-san in the newspaper; she looked pretty, not like the usual Madame Yamamoto. Please take a look at the photo when you get the newspaper.

Okumura-san is also teaching now in the Japanese Language School—there must be a serious lack of teachers. A few minutes ago your sister called and said that a Japanese teacher is wanted in the school in the Sanni building. I told her I would take the job if I had two bodies, and we laughed.

For the two-hour class, they pay $50 to $70 a month. They couldn't find anybody in the San Jose area. I'm glad that I teach Yukiko's class. Yukiko approves of my teaching style.

This is such an incoherent letter. I'll write again tomorrow after reading letters from you. I paid $36 for my traffic violation. I received a check from City College; I feel rich! . . .

I'm so lonely without you. If you were here, I wouldn't get so irritated —perhaps the lack of hormones causes it. You want a long letter, but last week I was too busy to write because of the JAL entertainment. I'm waiting for your tender letter to come, and I'll respond to it, don't worry!

From KIYOSHI, *September 25.*

. . . YESTERDAY WAS THE AUTUMN equinox and today is a holiday; no newspaper delivery today. Such a compensatory day off is something new making me think that Japan has changed a lot. However, there is no day off in the hospital, and the doctors came early to check the patients. . . .

Yesterday, Hiroyuki-san and Noriko-san came at 4:30 p.m. and gave me their wedding invitation. They stayed for about one hour. I had a chance to talk to them both about how you and I thought about marriage. Hiroyuki-san was very touched and asked me to talk about it at the wedding—I don't know. But I was very happy to read, "It was a good story; thank you. We will follow in your steps and do our best." . . . I wish the best of everything for them. I'm sure they will make a happy home. Noriko-san respects Hiroyuki-san and Hiroyuki-san loves her with tender care.

I'm glad that Yukiko is doing well in her school work. But she challenges you at times—she seems to be a bit stubborn. . . .

From KIYOKO, *September 26.*

. . . YESTERDAY I WROTE ABOUT MY laundry situation at home. I'm going to tell everybody to use the machine on Saturdays, not on Sundays. I don't want to spoil my Sunday anymore with this kind of meaningless strife.

Yukiko doesn't spend much time with TV anymore. She has been appointed to play the violin in the school orchestra. She wanted to quit but somehow is still playing. She has good auditory sensitivity. The other day on our way to Hayward, she wanted to listen to the radio. While I was searching for a musical station, she caught a note and already started to sing to it. I was surprised at her ability to catch notes so instantaneously. I'm encouraging her to continue playing the violin in the orchestra so that she will learn to finish something once she started.

Your documents for the insurance just arrived. Your airmail letter also arrived; it was remarkably quick since you put it in the mail only on September 24. I read through the document, entered the number eight, and delivered it to their office. It's handy to receive mail at work because the insurance office is here too. I read your letter up to the line, "If you can't read because people are around . . ." and put it in my bag to finish it at home. And there were three more letters dated the 22nd to the 24th waiting for me at home!

I enjoyed reading your letters referring to the Japanese customs. The other day when the temperature went up to 100°, American men had black suits on at work, whereas Japanese men would take off their jackets and be as natural as possible. Such a difference! Lately American women are going natural: their skirts get shorter, showing more of their legs; their neckline comes down lower—they are going back to nature. Of course, the men are enjoying looking at these "natural sights" so that both sides are benefiting. However, the unbearable sight is the middle-aged woman pretending to be young and showing legs three inches above her kneecaps that are miserably wrinkled. I am observing the people around me just like you do in the hospital.

There is a meeting this evening at the Buddhist Association concerning the Japanese Language School. I have to leave soon so I'm going to read your letter in my bag before going to bed. I'll write to you tomorrow.

From KIYOSHI, *September 26.*

. . . A BEAUTIFUL AUTUMN DAY! I told you about a girl who is having plastic surgery on her nose, didn't I? This morning she said: "*Oji-san*, won't you come up to the rooftop? The view is spectacular and it feels so good up there." So I went to the rooftop with her. You can see the whole city of Hakata from there. But unlike American cities, it is jumbled up without orderly streets—I wasn't particularly impressed. But the shoreline is beautiful. It is a typical Japanese seascape with tiny islands scattered here and there—just looking at it makes you feel good. I've been here for 70 days, but this is the first time I've gotten to see the view from the rooftop. This girl is so funny. She tells me that if you get a suntan in the fall, it is very hard to get rid of—girl talk, isn't it? She is so cheerful romping around all over the hospital. She knows that I write to you every day and says she wants to write to you too. She has no bias or anything—even toward her face with the broken nose—I admire her innocent nature. I pray that her plastic surgery will go successfully. She says "*Oji-san*, let's not give up, you and I!" And she adds, "When your hearing comes back, you'll be surprised to hear my devilish voice"; then she cracks up into laughter.

The girl who is an expert with the abacus goes home day after tomorrow. Her hearing is completely gone on one side and the ringing remains in the other side. It's a shame—she is still young and has a very nice personality. I hope someday a new improved treatment will help to restore her hearing. These two girls shared a room together for some time. The girl with the broken nose says she will be very lonely without a roommate—but I wonder if she ever feels lonely! They were so helpful to me so we three are going to have a sayonara party with sushi tonight or tomorrow night. Together with a man by the name of Yamato, they gave Yukiko a Hakata doll, did I tell you? I haven't opened it because it's so beautifully wrapped.

The high school student across the hall writes to me from time to time. She says she cannot concentrate on her studies because she has been away from studying the whole summer. . . .

What is Hisayo-san's situation now? No news from the Immigration Office? I think her application will be approved. How is Yukiko doing in school? It's about time she starts to have an interest in studying at home too. It must be hard on you when you have so much to do, but please guide her to study more. It was reported in a Japanese newspaper that a 19-year-old became an Assistant Professor of Mathematics at Stanford University. Was it reported in the American papers too? His salary is $15,000 a year. He has a doctor's degree from the Engineering School of Massachusetts University. Ask Hisayo-san—maybe she knows. . . .

From KIYOSHI, *September 27.*

... YESTERDAY THE CHECKS FOR $500 and $100 were returned to me because there were no personal seals on them. A rule is a rule—so I asked that cheerful girl with the broken nose to go get a seal for Tokutomi. Banks may be extra cautious because of a recent case of a forged check at Sanwa Bank. The accounting office at the hospital is not worried because the Sumitomo Bank is not denying payment of the balance. I told them that one's signature is more reliable and safer than a seal, and they agreed laughingly but asked me to get a seal because it's a rule.

Your letter came! It's about the delivery of lunch to Ōshima-san and JAL people. It was short, but enough to keep me going. . . .

I'm so pleased that they sought out your help in the Japanese Language School, and you told them that you would help them until they find a teacher; that was a good answer. It would be wonderful if everything goes smoothly like that. But be sure to take care of yourself, and don't overstrain yourself.

From KIYOSHI, *September 28.*

... IT'S PAST SIX P.M. I'M WRITING this because Ōshima-san and his daughter, Yumiko-san, came with the package you sent. Your letter that came yesterday mentioned the delivery of lunch to the JAL office and Ōshima-san's offer to deliver a package to me, but it seems like the package arrived here almost before your letter. I was surprised; I don't know how to thank everybody. Yumiko-san is a beautiful girl and carries herself gracefully although she has a large build. Ōshima-san looked so proud of her.

After Ōshima-san took his leave with his daughter, the talented girl with the abacus and her mother and sister came to say good-bye. While I was opening the package, there was the afternoon treatment with shots, then dinner. I finished reading the series "The Modern Day *Botchan*"* in the Japanese language newspaper that you sent, and now I'm writing this letter.

Regarding our present to Hiroyuki-san for his marriage: I was going to give him 20,000 yen. But as you suggest, I'll change it to 10,000 yen. We should follow the local custom; giving more than others is not necessarily good, is it? Somebody told me that sometimes relatives get together to make 10,000 yen. I've been paying an ample sum to Hiroyuki-san every time he helps me so I'll follow your suggestion. . . .

*Written by Natsume Sōseki about a young schoolteacher.

From KIYOSHI, *September 29.*

. . . ABOUT THE WASHING MACHINE: HOW about making a time table and display it above the machine? You can mention that the purpose of it is to avoid inconveniencing each other. Also, you can add that if one needs to use the machine on somebody else's day, coordinate the timing with that person. I would explain the situation beforehand to Mother so that it will go smoothly. It's your house, and if somebody uses the washing machine without asking your permission, naturally you would be angry. But getting angry doesn't solve anything; it only causes your stomach to cramp. Find a way to solve the unpleasant situation somehow.

You say even Okumura-san has been asked to teach at the Japanese Language School. It must be really hard to find teachers. Please be careful not to overdo it. I'm going to write down a method of drilling: 1. Questions and Answers to the entire class. 2. Q and A to each row—if they are sitting in rows. 3. Q and A to the individual student from Row 1 down to 2 and 3. 4. Have one of the better students stand up and exchange with him Q and A in depth repeating this exercise with a couple more of the better students. 5. Have one of the better students take the teacher's place, and you sit in his chair and have him conduct a Q and A drill—this animates the class and time goes fast. 6. Sing Japanese songs together and close the class.

I will write the basic form of Q and A drills and send it to you. You just follow it. If there aren't enough things to do, the class becomes unmanageable and the students may become lazy [and] inattentive, and play around. It is necessary to treat the students with a barrage of questions and answers; they will enjoy it. To get that effect, it is important to follow exactly the order and basic form of Q and A drills. . . .

From KIYOSHI, *September 30.*

. . . I WISH I CRAVED FOR FOOD AS much as I crave for you. Sometimes I miss you so much that I can't sleep. . . . If this was only a problem of hormone deficiency, anybody would do—but not me—I need Kiyoko-san! . . .

The patient who is having plastic surgery on her broken nose insists on writing to you. I gave her some paper to write on. She keeps saying that you must be a very good wife; she says she respects me because I don't look for frivolous affairs like a Japanese man would do. Sometimes I tell her your philosophy of life, and she is deeply moved. I told her there is nothing more beautiful than love between two people—but that love, I added, can easily become soiled if it is not nurtured tenderly by that couple. For a man and woman to fall in love, get married, strive together to make that love stronger and become a happy couple—that is the purpose of our life—that is the most beautiful life. While I was telling her this, I couldn't help but realize how lucky I am to have you as my wife and how beautiful our love is. . . .

From KIYOSHI, *September 30.*

. . . I HAD UNEXPECTED GUESTS TODAY: Matsuda-san, who took photos of me, and Tachibana-san, the high school student across the hall. Matsuda-san brought sweet buns from Saeki district in Ōita Prefecture, and Tachibana-san brought chestnuts and sweet persimmons from her garden along with cookies she baked. She is still in the career class which prepares students for a profession, but actually she wants to go to college and become a teacher for the blind and deaf-mute. She bought books and has been preparing for the entrance exams. I encouraged her. Matsuda-san works for a cement company. He apologized for not writing to me because his work took up all his time. It should be me who makes such an apology. He works overtime quite often, so much so that he has no time to play with his children—such a nice man.

I seem to lose these nice friends one after another. Ōtomo-san, who is an expert in abacus computation, has gone home too. Today Shizuma-san, who wrote you a letter, is going home overnight and says, "*Oji-san*, I'm sorry that you'll be left alone." She says laughingly that she wants a boyfriend, but I think it will be difficult to find one unless her nose is repaired—poor girl! Ōtomo-san had a couple of boyfriends, and they came to visit her. In the old days, most girls did not have a boyfriend so it was easy to accept life without one; but nowadays it is different. I feel sorry for the girls who do not have boyfriends. Shizuma-san doesn't like to sit still and is always tidying up her room. She comes to my room and puts things in their proper place too; she would be a good housewife. She would like working in some kind of trade and says she wants to do business together with her husband. She seems to be healthy; if she can find a man, she will do very well. In spite of her young age, she is rather conventional so she doesn't mind having a mother-in-law, she says. Also, she says she would be willing to build up a life from scratch together with her husband. When it comes to her looks, she is far below the average. She appreciates being treated as equal to any normal girl. I can't help but curse Heaven for its lack of equality and fairness. She respects me because I love my wife and write to her every day; she says we are more than ordinary lovers—and I don't show any interest in other women. She wants to find a husband like me and wants to become a good wife like you. The problem is that she is vulnerable to disappointment because she is so easily trapped by kind words from a man—poor girl. She would ask me what I think of him—what can I say to her? She is seeking a flower that is beyond reach. Men go instinctively for good-looking girls, not for girls with a golden heart; that instinct will never change throughout their marriage.

I don't know why I'm writing this way. I'll write again after dinner.

From KIYOSHI *[continuation of previous letter].*

SORRY I WROTE ABOUT UNIMPORTANT things while, in fact, all I could think of was about you and how I wanted to be at your side. Frustration drives me to say strange things. . . .

Are you completely cured of the cold? I'm still suffering from it. I know I can't rush it, but I can't help wishing it would go away. Tachibana-san's cousin also had tuberculosis and lost his hearing after taking some medicine. However, he has recovered from it and now works as a truck driver. It took him over six months to get well. I was glad to hear that story. I have a stubborn cold on top of it, but there is hope. My appetite will return, and I'll be full of energy so that Kiyoko-san . . .

[About half the page is cut off. Perhaps Kiyoko truncated the letter for the sake of privacy.]

Tell Yukiko that Daddy would be happier if she would write to him in Japanese. . . .

I love you so much. I can't say it enough.

From KIYOKO, *September 30.*

SATURDAY, THE 30TH, THE LAST DAY OF September. Today I received from you a rather despondent letter—I wonder if you will still be lonely when you read this. Letter No. 69 *[written September 26]* came yesterday. It told me that you went up to the rooftop, somebody gave you a Hakata doll for Yukiko (you've never told me this), a patient who is going into plastic surgery keeps herself in cheerful mood, etc.—everybody is trying his best in spite of the adverse situation. I think you are well disciplined by

American standards, but those patients reflect the Japanese culture itself in which the spiritual world and material world co-exist harmoniously so that they can face reality calmly.

To put trust in a commercially purchased seal rather than one's own signature seems to be ridiculous, but it is a Japanese custom and one has to accept it.

Cecilia and her husband are now traveling on the East Coast. They didn't have time to edit your Chinese letter before the trip. Her husband read it first and handed it to Cecilia without saying who it was from—he enjoyed watching her surprise and delight. They said your distinction between 爽快 and 快適 was correct. When they come back, I'll ask them further.

Regarding Hisayo's application to the Immigration Office: her extension is approved and her passport was returned to her. She is greatly relieved and waiting now for the bill from the lawyer.

I got a letter from Hiroyuki last Thursday. A photo of Noriko-san was in it—she looks like Hiroko-san, doesn't she? I'm going to get a card of congratulations on their wedding. Your sister wants to send the white candies to distribute at the wedding party. I'm going to get those for her. The candies will be wrapped two by two, and I'll send them to Hiroyuki by air mail. . . .

Yukiko brought home a paper from school; she is doing a little bit better than last year, but she still has some problems with multiplication. She talks about boys with other girls—they sometimes fight over the boys— she told me that last night, and I was flabbergasted. It's good that she talks about these things openly now—but I'd better watch out—she says she found a better boy than Salvador—what comes next, I wonder! The Japanese saying goes: "At seven years old, boys and girls must be separated." I don't know which is better, the Japanese way or the American way. . . .

に、きまし
たで、おなかが

紙面を理いという訳で提供し
ちらんの通り・目下発音の
鬢さんの手紙がつくでしょう。書

October

..

[*Autumn Loneliness*]

From KIYOSHI.

SUNDAY, OCTOBER FIRST. LAST NIGHT I PERSPIRED so much in my sleep, but I feel better this morning although my head is not clear. I don't know what this is. I'm disappointed to have this condition while I'm facing a more serious problem.

I just finished breakfast. I didn't have an appetite, and it didn't taste good at all. I bought two fresh eggs at the shop downstairs and slurped in only the yolks—don't I sound like an athlete?

How are you, Kiyoko-san? I've written a thank-you note to Mr. and Mrs. Ōshima and invited them to stay with us when they vacation in California next time.

I didn't get your letter yesterday so I'm hoping to have it today. Letters are delivered to the mailroom, but on Sundays sometimes nobody distributes them to the patients. But still I can hope. . . . Your letter is the only medicine that keeps me going. I wrote to you three times yesterday although they may not arrive at the same time—I posted one in the morning and the other two at night. I've written about three intimate letters thus far. Please keep them with utmost care so that no one sees them. I crave for a long one from you.

We have had a stretch of gloomy days here. There is no sign of rain, and the scarcity in the water supply is increasing day by day.

Reading Japanese newspapers, I notice a big change in people's thinking. Now they talk about self-defense and peace with military preparedness. On the other hand, enlightenment in sex is an eye-opening feature in the weekly magazines. Advertisements in the newspaper are focused fully on sex. There are too many magazines for female readers. Girls who ignore sex will be left behind. Articles emphasize graphically the joy of sexual encounters not only by both sexes, but also the same sex. The world has become inverted—a discreet love affair has become a thing of the past. Girls' behavior at the universities is astonishing. American universities are more conservative, more academic, I think. And their make-up—especially on the eyes! How grotesque! We must not raise Yukiko that way. Once you decorated the school principal's office with a seaweed container and straw—that simplicity is so much more beautiful and elegant. I want Yukiko to have that kind of esthetic appreciation. . . .

From KIYOSHI.

IT IS STILL OCTOBER FIRST. I'M TESTING TO SEE IF writing sideways might help to avoid the smear of the ink. The ink in this Japanese pen tends to run and make my hands dirty when I touch the letter. I bet you were thinking that I had become sloppy. I still have several more Japanese pens. . . .

Tanaka Toshimichi-san of JAL stopped by on his way to see his sister in Ōmuda. I am so grateful for the JAL people. He brought a big package of canned fruit to me which might cost over 1,000 yen. He gave me the airline sandwiches too. It was so thoughtful of him. He came to see me straight from Itatsuki Airport. He said he was so grateful to Mrs. Tokutomi. He leaves for Sendai in the morning. I'll mail a thank-you note this evening or in the morning. I am so touched by his visit, and this is because of the good will you expressed by that lunch service. Thank you, Kiyoko-san.

This is Sunday, and Hiroyuki-san might come. As you advised, I'm going to give him 10,000 yen in a ceremonial envelope for the wedding.

Yesterday the dentist who wants to go to America was released from the hospital. Now Shizuma-san, the girl with a broken nose, and I are the only long-time patients here. She comes back about 7:30 this evening.

I feel heavy in the head and tired. I wish I could run about with vigor like you do. I miss you, Kiyoko-san. Maybe a tender, loving letter from you might clear this depression away.

The ink still runs, but it doesn't get smeared if I write sideways. . . .

From KIYOSHI.

THIS IS STILL SUNDAY, OCTOBER FIRST. I HAD GIVEN up on a letter from you today, but about 4:30 p.m. when I was talking with Hiroyuki-san, it came! It made me so happy; I felt like I was resuscitated by it. You wrote: no letters Friday, Saturday, Sunday; you received two on Monday; on Tuesday an envelope containing the insurance documents and my passionate letter came to your mailbox at work; and to top it all, three letters were waiting at home. I'm so happy to hear that! You had not read my love letter at that point because you had to go to the Japanese Language School for a meeting, but you are going to read it before going to bed. The thought of you reading my special letter in our bed makes me feel warm all over with happiness. I'm anxiously waiting for your response to that letter. . . .

Yukiko must have an affinity for music if she can pick up a melody so quickly that it surprises you; it makes me happy too.

Hiroyuki-san and I talked about the wedding. Masayuki-san and your mother are attending the ceremony. I also talked to Hiroyuki-san about his work; I told him to suggest to the president of Fukuoka Storage that they expand their service to America where presently only Nihon Kōtsū is operating. Starting next year, 20,000 people are expected to use transportation services (I gave him a clip of the newspaper report). Fukuoka Storage might as well establish its own office in the States instead of working as a subcontractor to the American companies like Bekins Van Lines, Mayflower, and Allied Van. Hiroyuki-san thinks that after the American Military Forces go home, there will be not much business left for Fukuoka Storage. This is why I gave him the newspaper clipping. Besides, I thought you might have a close contact in the Northern California travel agencies. It is an opportune time for a Japanese company to expand its business to America. It depends on what the president says after reading the newspaper clip; but I told Hiroyuki-san that the president could assign him to California for a couple of years, and there is a good chance for the company to break into the monopoly of Nihon Kōtsū. . . .

From KIYOSHI, *October 2.*

. . . THE LAST DAY OF 43 YEARS of my life. I'll be 44 years old tomorrow! How do I feel? Nothing. If my hearing was back even slightly, I would feel better and look forward to my 44th year. The pronunciation of 44 in Japanese is *shijū-yon,* meaning "always well." I don't feel well at all. . . .

This morning, Professor Kawada made his rounds, and thanked me for the Gillette razor and candies. All I could think of was now it's October, but I'm not getting any better. . . .

I was going to continue this letter after reading yours—but it didn't come today. It's around 5:30 p.m., and I ate only the fish from the dinner served; I'll order out for something around eight o'clock.

I don't know what to write anymore. I think of you, only you, Kiyoko-san. I am so lonely—I don't know what to do—forgive me!

Maybe I should write a method of teaching the Japanese language. It might take my mind away from this loneliness.

· · ·

The secret of successful learning of a language is "extensive repetition," which means repeating <u>effectively</u>. That's why we have linguistic rules. Let's take, for example, "*Kore wa hon desu*: This is a book."

Q1. (Holding a book in your hand) *Kore **wa** hon desu ka, pen desu ka*: Is this a book, or a pen?

A. *Sore **wa** hon desu*: It is a book.

Q2. (Picking up something else) *Kore **mo** hon desu ka*: Is this a book too?

A. *Iie*: No.

Q3. (Picking up a different article) *Kore **ga** hon desu ka*: Is this a book?

A. *Iie*: No.

[Continued in next letter.]

Q4. (Repeat Question 3 and Answer "No" three times, picking up a different article each time.)

Q5. *Dewa, dore **ga** hon desu ka*: Then, which is a book?

A. *Sore **ga** hon desu*: That is a book.

(Up to this point, the practice has been on *wa, mo, ga*; but *wa* may need to be practiced more. Using the same articles that you used, go to the following exercise.)

Q6. (Showing something other than a book) *Kore mo hon desu ka*: Is this a book too?

A. *Iie*: No.

Q7. (Holding a book in hand) *Dewa, kore wa pen desu ka*: Then, is this a pen?

A. *Iie*: No.

Q8. (Holding a book in hand) *Dewa, kore wa naifu desu ka*: Then, is this a knife?

A. *Iie*: No.

Q9. (Holding a book in hand) *Dewa, kore wa enpitsu desu ka*: Then, is this a pencil?

A. *Iie*: No.

Q10. (Pointing at a desk) *Dewa, kore wa nan desu ka*: Then, what is this?

A. *Sore wa tsukue desu*: It is a desk.

This is the method of "no, no, no—then what?" I formulated this method using **wa, ga, mo**. This method can be applied to transitive verbs also.

I am lonely, Kiyoko-san.

From KIYOKO, *October 2.*

IT'S GOING TO BE A RAINY MONDAY. . . .

How are you, Kiyoshi-san? You might receive this letter very close to Hiroyuki's wedding. He wanted you to be at the ceremony, but I wrote a note saying, "Only Kiyoshi-san will know what his hearing condition is, so let him decide," and inserted it in the greeting card. Yukiko and I went to your sister's house and, together with Lily, we wrapped the candies two by two. In the morning Hisayo will take the box of candies to the post office. I'm going to get a few more things to fill up the package to you and mail it this week.

I read your special letter late at night in bed. . . . Even when I'm doing laundry or shopping, I feel you. . . . I feel your entire weight on me . . . what a thrill it is to lie under your chest . . . you should hear me call—"I want Kiyoshi-san!"

My head is whirling . . . I must change the subject. Pretty soon everybody will come back from lunch. Since Cecilia is away, I had lunch early and wrote this.

· · ·

When I got home, I found *[your September 28]* letter . . . and one from Shizuma Sachiko-san, the cheerful girl who is going to have plastic surgery on her nose. I was surprised to hear Ōshima-san visited you so soon. I thought maybe seeing Mitsuko-san here made him think of sending his daughter to school in the States. When will he come back to the States, I wonder? The remaining personnel in JAL go home after next week.

The wind has risen this afternoon, and it's going to be the first rainy day of this fall. Could you ask Hiroyuki or Noriko-san to get a pair of rain boots for Yukiko? I like Japanese rain gear for Yukiko.

I'm supposed to get paid $50 from the Japanese Language School. But Tsukiji-san's and mine were switched by mistake; Tsukiji-san just called to tell me that. I said that I had not yet opened the envelope; he teased me for not wanting the money. The truth was I just didn't have time to get to it. Everybody was late coming home today, including me. I was going to cook beef stew in the pressure cooker. Anyway we had dinner at around seven o'clock. From now on, I'll cook something on Sunday to warm up and serve on Monday. By the way, the above paragraph of my craving for love was prompted by your own comment in one of your letters which means we wrote it together. Reading it back, I feel relieved and satisfied—we will do it again. . . .

From KIYOSHI, *October 3.*

TUESDAY, OCTOBER THIRD, MY BIRTHDAY. Today, for the first time since I came here, your letter was delivered to me at around 10:30 in the morning. I was stunned, and deeply moved, and I cried. This was the best birthday present! It was written on Wednesday, September 26, the day after you went to the Japanese Language School to organize classes. I couldn't stop crying because you respect and love a man like me who is not good in anything; we are a happy couple only because you are so great. Who could pour love and respect and devotion on a man like me except Kiyoko-san—tears welled up, and I couldn't go on reading. It is you who are great, not me! . . . Thank you so much, Kiyoko-san, for your loving letter, especially on my birthday!

What a wonderful birthday it is! The letters were never delivered so early before, but today, on my birthday, it happened. This could be the beginning of a lucky streak; I will guard this opportunity tenderly. I even feel that your love will cure my hearing problem.

I would like to talk about the Japanese Language School. Please discuss the following with the teachers, Tokunaga and Hōjō. The Japanese Language School is not showing even half of the expected result. How about arranging a short training course on a Method of Teaching the Japanese Language for the teachers at the Buddhist Assemblies in the State of California?

Tell Tokunaga-sensei and Hōjō-sensei that your husband's closest friend is a professor of linguistics at Kyushu University. His teaching method is highly respected in Japan; he could be invited during his summer break to give regional training courses to Japanese teachers state-wide. Tell them I think it will bring a tremendous result, and show them what the syllabus would look like. For one week they can attend the lecture and practice the Japanese method of language education. I think a $2,000 honorarium is reasonable for travel and lectures for two months. This will lead to more

Cousins Yukiko Tokutomi and Lily Hoshino dressed for Obon, on the steps of the Tokutomi house in San Jose's Japantown, 1963. Photo courtesy of Yukiko Tokutomi Northon.

active classroom exchanges and increased academic results. Watanabe-sensei also will attend some classroom training sessions. The prestige of the Japanese Language School of the Buddhist Assemblies will increase tremendously. Make a memo of these points and explain it to them—they might show interest. As you said, the present status of the Japanese Language Schools is far below standard. Something has to be done. . . .

From KIYOKO, *October 4.*

. . . YESTERDAY WAS YOUR BIRTHDAY—I was thinking of you all day—so much so that a couple of times in the office I put your birth date on the papers I was working on. Today I didn't make any mistakes. Last night after dinner I went out to get medicine for my nose because it bothered me due to a lingering cold and went to bed without taking a bath. After the rain it is getting chilly here too, and it will be winter very soon.

I've just been to the post office to mail some medicine to you, but the package was smaller than regulation size so I couldn't send it. . . .

There were a few things from you that needed my reply so I'll start on it now. Mr. Delacroix is in Europe so that I can't discuss with him the exchange proposal with the Kyushu University. In Hisayo's opinion, the exchange of professors at the state university level will be difficult due to the stringent fiscal policy enforced by Governor Reagan; it would be better to negotiate with private universities. Kiyoshi-san can do it, but I'm not sure if I can carry on this type of high-level negotiation. I wonder if it could be done successfully between the universities. . . .

Please feel relaxed because I keep your letters of importance with me all the time.

Since I started to teach Japanese conversation, I feel a little uncomfortable speaking in English; it's strange! Please send your syllabus as soon as possible. There are students who have attended the Japanese Language School for five or seven years, but they still cannot speak Japanese. It will be nice if I can improve this situation a little bit. . . .

From KIYOSHI, *October 4.*

. . . I HAVE INTERESTING NEWS TODAY. Two nights ago, a patient in this ward came to see me together with the girl with the broken nose. This patient is a singer of folk songs and regularly appears on NHK and other TV stations. She is highly rated as a new type of folk singer in newspapers such as the *Mainichi*, the *Yomiuri* and the *Nishi-Nihon*. She sings the traditional folk songs with a new style and arrangement so that they appeal to modern listeners. Her record will come out this November from the Grand Record Co. She wants to spread her art to America. So I wrote to Hirose-san about this and advised the singer to send a tape to him before the record comes out to the public. She was very grateful for this. She is only 22 years old and her stage name is Koi Machiko—her real name is Shigehisa Machiko. She is the new singer on the program of NHK called "Songs of Kyushu." Since her debut in June, she has been on the program every month; she took October off due to an operation on her throat but will return to the program in November.

I have never had a conversation with a talent in the entertainment world. But she became very interested in my reference to Hirose-san and wanted to be introduced to him. She may want to have an overseas agent now that her record is coming out in the States too. Please phone Hirose-san several days after receiving this letter. Let's find out if she is really a promising singer although she couldn't be too bad since she appears on NHK TV. It may be a good business opportunity for Hirose-san too. I told him to have On-odera-san listen to the tape. Also this Japanese singer will be on the radio this Saturday and Sunday; listen to the broadcast and let me know what you think. . . .

From KIYOKO, *October 5.*

. . . I RECEIVED NOS. 77 AND 78, both written on October first. No. 77 was written sideways. You seem to be unable to pull yourself together yet. Perhaps it's psychological? I could be wrong, but maybe you are worried because you can't attend Hiroyuki's wedding? If so, I think you have to change your thinking—make it more self-centered and concentrate on your own health. . . .

About the refund of the airfare—I think it is better that you write to them directly instead of me trying to explain in my poor English. You can tell them that the insurance will cover it as long as the doctor certifies it. You could describe the treatment you are getting there. . . .

Our Yukiko is not a good student. She must have been told, or she volunteered, to bring a sample of volcanic stones that she found. So she called Cousin Hoshino for help—but she didn't know the name of the stone, nor did she try to find the description of the stone she wanted to show. I had to help her with a dictionary and make her write it down—it was a riot! I almost lost my temper. Now she is playing with a ball she made with torn hose. She doesn't care. I told her that I was writing to Daddy what she was doing, or not doing. She says, "Can I say I'm sorry to Daddy?" I don't know what to think—I only get tight in the stomach. I must relax and teach her to use a dictionary as a way of studying.

I had a slight argument with an American woman in the office today. She apologized at the end, but ill feelings are still left between us. She was late this morning and missed the instruction session. I told her about the instructions related to her work. "Don't tell me what I should do," she said. I had told her about the instruction which she missed, and said, "What's wrong with letting each other know what was missed?" I could have said, "You should get up earlier in the morning!" But I didn't because once in a while I myself oversleep too. She comes late though sometimes three mornings in a row. It's not fun to argue with a woman because afterward she tries to humor me. Not fun with a man either, but I can at least say, "You are a man, aren't you?"

I'm sorry to end the letter this way.

From KIYOSHI, *October 5.*

. . . I'M WORRIED ABOUT YUKIKO. She is so young, and yet already she talks about boys; she fights with other girls about boys—what's going on?! Instead of setting rules of good and bad, tell her some heartwarming anecdotes or beautiful love stories—it might work better. It has to be corrected before she becomes older. Memories of childhood should be more naive and pure and pretty. I want her to spend time collecting insects and plants or studying some subject with the passion of youth. It's all right if she is attracted to a boy for his achievement but not because of his handsome or cute looks. The way she is now, I'm afraid she might join a go-go or hippy group; she might end up chasing one man after another, leading a wild life without love. It will be too late to turn back once she steps foot into such a rough life. Please do something now! I'm not saying that she must avoid boys; as I wrote earlier, she should find a boy whom she can respect and adore for his sincerity and achievement. . . .

I'm depressed today because of Yukiko's situation. She is my only daughter. It makes me feel left out just to think that she might start a life completely foreign to mine. I don't want to be an unsympathetic, headstrong daddy to her. I understand a child's interest in the other sex. But I can't approve of reckless, superficial love. I want her to find clean love. I feel so bad that I lost my hearing at this important juncture in our life.

From KIYOSHI, *October 6.*

I HAVE SAD NEWS. MATSUMURA-SAN, MIYAZAKI-SAN, and Nakayama-san of Japan Airlines died in a plane crash during their training session. Miyazaki-san who lived in Imari once came to see me. Nakayama-san used to live near Dr. Kurimura. I found out about this accident last night from the newspaper. I was just skimming through the report of a plane crash: first the name Matsumura caught my attention; then, Nakayama and Miyazaki—all familiar names. I was struck dumb with shock. That Matsumura-san, who was so concerned about me and came to see me here twice and sent me a card telling me of his completion of the written tests and of his first leave out of the training school—I haven't had a chance to write him back! He took such good care of me on the plane when I flew into Japan; and in Tokyo, he was the one who stayed with me until I boarded another plane to Fukuoka. A few days later he came to see me in the hospital with a basket of fruit; on another occasion he brought special cookies from Kumamoto—and always with a broad smile—I just can't believe that he is gone. I wrote a letter to his wife last night. You must have read about this plane crash in the Japanese newspaper; maybe you could send a letter of condolence to Mrs. Matsumura. Miyazaki-san came to see me too with a book. Nakayama-san looked into the news of Dr. Kurimura's family for me. All of them, such kind and good men!

Kiyoko-san, this is all I can write today. I am still in such shock.

From KIYOKO, *October 7.*

. . . ONE LONELY LETTER ARRIVED TODAY. It was written on the second and has No. 79 on it. Even before opening it, I felt your loneliness seeping out of it. I just finished my lunch after coming home from the Japanese Language School. Yesterday morning I sent 15 bags and medicine for your ears by air mail; this morning I had Hisayo send a package by sea mail. The package contains winter underwear, three white shirts, peanuts, coffee candies, art work by Yukiko, newspapers, an old blue sweater, a package of almond candy prepared for Hiroyuki's wedding, two sticks of salami —all these together with 60 stoma bags. I hope it arrives without any problems. I wrote down the price for each item so as to avoid any questions.

Hisayo was charged $110 by the lawyer for her case with the Immigration Office. But she can pay in installments. . . . Shall we give her $20 for her graduation? It has been difficult to make ends meet every month, but it has eased up a little this month leaving us with about $80 extra.

The delivery of mail is getting slack, and it will get worse as it approaches year's end. I am writing at least every other day. Don't become like dried-up violets; they might revive with some water, but old leaves and tiny leaves give up and die. Many of our violets are budding now.

I tried your syllabus on my students at the Japanese Language School. Yukiko is very good at it. I had a 30-minute session using the days of the week as the subject and a 20-minute session using pencils and other classroom items. I have two grades of students in my class, one of which is ages 14 and 15. Some can study by themselves, but I would rather teach them also. I've never experienced having different grades in my class, and I need to consult with American teachers about how they are handling this situation. Do you have any ideas?

I wanted to tell you this before, but the pen you invented is working nicely. I wouldn't use any other pen to write the children's names. It's old now and not suitable for fine letters, but it is very good for writing on name cards. I wish you could make another one before the ink runs out on this one.

Mr. Shichisaburō Hideshima died yesterday. He was 83. Today's paper reported on the death of three employees of JAL in a plane crash during their training flight. The accident happened in Yamagata Prefecture. I hope they are not the ones we know.

Betting on the World Series is popular in my work place too. Cecilia and her husband are in Boston right now. Everybody is talking about his enthusiasm for baseball and jokingly is betting on whether he keeps the portable radio on while sightseeing or wondering if he persuaded Cecilia to watch the game at the stadium. The Giants are not doing well this season.

Mr. Dave Smith called last evening. He had a checkup at the hospital and was given an OK to resume his full schedule of activities so he keeps himself busy going to school. He sends his best wishes and says of you, "He can pull himself up very well and he probably is doing OK in Japan too." Such a nice man! He was amazed to see the long address of the hospital.

Kiyoshi-san, let's hold on together at this difficult time. . . .

From KIYOSHI, *October 7.*

. . . AFTER 11 O'CLOCK LAST NIGHT there was a scattered rain shower accompanied by thunder, and the dry season is finally over in North Kyushu. Also this morning we had a little rain. I'm sure everybody is giving a sigh of relief. Operations had been cut short in the factories and water service to homes shut off; it has been a hard, long summer.

I'm mailing some photos today. Shizuma-san with a bandage on her nose is the only one left here now. She is 22 years old. She has written to you already so I won't describe her any further. Ōtomo Eiko-san, 23 years old, is the one who is the expert on the abacus; she went to the post office for me. Both girls looked after me like their own uncle. Ōtomo-san was suffering from being totally deaf in one ear, ringing of the ears, and frequent headaches —poor girl, a girl with such a gentle nature—she is staying home without further medical attention. Watanabe Sayoko-san, 21 years old, a girl studying English at a community college, stayed in the hospital for only two weeks after surgery on her tonsils. She wants to go to America, but her English is so poor. She showed me how the students in English class talk among themselves, signing behind the teacher's back; I enjoyed this demonstration very much. Next is Tachibana-san, 17 years old; you know about her. The last one is Matsumoto Hiroko-san, 20 years old. Of the group she is in the worst condition. She is scheduled to have a complicated heart operation in a few months. When she had surgery on her tonsils, she had some serious after-surgery complications that made everybody worried. Right now she is home preparing for the next big operation. I pray for its success!

Next about the men: first Matsuda-san—he must be slightly younger than me. Yamato-san, 26 years old, had an inflammation in one ear; now he's back to work in a construction business. He is the one Shizuma-san fell in love with at first sight. I'm not sure if Yamato-san felt the same way about her. He comes back as an out-patient and stops by to see me—a very nice person. Yamamoto-san, 26 years old, is a dentist; well informed in world affairs and hopes to go to America to study. He has one ear inflamed perma-nently and had difficulty in standing straight with his eyes closed, but he has no problem walking with his eyes open. He said he was getting better and went home last week. There is one more man—but he's not in this picture—Hinashi Yoshiharu-san who studies economics at Kyushu University. He was hospitalized for inflammation of the ear and recently went home. He is bright. He used to stop by my room to read my English newspaper, and we would talk; he still comes to see me quite often. I told him to get a job at the Sumitomo Bank and come to America. He says he is not smart enough to go abroad and work, but he is a nice young man and definitely one of those whom I would like to have come to America. . . .

From KIYOSHI, *October 8.*

SUNDAY, OCTOBER 8, THE DAY OF Hiroyuki-san's wedding. I had the nurse Yoshioka-san send a congratulation message to Hiroyuki-san by phone. . . .

When Hiroyuki-san comes next time, I'll ask him to get a pair of rain boots for Yukiko. You don't have to send me the vitamin supplements. You take them and gain your energy back—I have enough supplements here. My cold is almost gone. The problem may be from a "deficiency of Kiyoko-san."

I received a post card of EXPO '67 from Cecilia and her husband the day before yesterday. It is in beautiful English—perhaps her husband wrote it. It says they understood my Chinese very well. . . .

I've written so far two syllabi using intransitive verbs. Next I plan to outline the case of transitive verbs. An important point is that a syllabus must contain a surprise quality so that it attracts the student's attention. In other words, the questions and answers must proceed like this: "no," "no," "no," "then what?"—"no," "no," "no," "then where?"—"no," "no," "no," "then why?" I will continue on this tomorrow. . . .

From KIYOKO, *October 9.*

. . . I CAN'T BELIEVE THE JAL accident happened to people whom we knew. The names were not mentioned in the paper here. I opened that air letter wrongly by mistake so that your message was cut up everywhere. I read each section of the cut-up letter and felt something grave had happened; but I didn't know what it was until I connected each line to make sense. It was unreal. I am so sad—why, I hadn't even thanked them yet! I feel the despair of their families as though they were mine. I called the JAL office in Hayward but no answer.

I'm sorry I made you so worried over Yukiko. But she knows how we think. She will be OK if we hold on to our belief and let her know it—there will be a chance for her to learn self-control. Lately she wants to go out in the evening. I try to persuade her not to go, but I think she is lonely at home. The other night I allowed her to go out to see Mrs. Eckford, and she stayed there for about two hours. We go to the Japanese Language School together, and she gets invited to attend Sunday school. She is happy there because she meets many students from the Language School. She has attended Sunday school twice so far. I try to fill her after-school hours as much as possible. Strangely she has stopped being glued to the television these days. I bought workbooks of math and spelling the other day for her to study at home. I wish I could have more time with her. . . .

I came straight home today because I was so sleepy, and I forgot to bring home a letter that I started in the office. Tomorrow I'll continue that letter and mail it to you. I should get the photos from you tomorrow. I've been looking for a nice card for Shizuma-san; failing that, I'll write a letter to her. I wonder what was the cause of her nose surgery. She must be wondering why I haven't answered her letter in spite of writing to you often. To tell you the truth, I have barely enough time to write to you; please explain it to her. About the singer of the folk songs—Hirose-san might get in touch with me; I'll phone him toward the end of this week. . . .

It is getting chilly here in the morning and evening. The front of our house is covered with fallen leaves. I miss you, Kiyoshi-san. You seem to be more energetic and back to your old self now—it makes me very happy!

From KIYOSHI, *October 9.*

. . . IT IS A BEAUTIFUL AUTUMN DAY but the mountains are covered with smog. Today is the first day of married life for Hiroyuki-san and Noriko-san. I wish them the best! . . .

Today's newspaper reported that in Haneda one of the demonstrators died in a collision with the police. They were students trying to stop Prime Minister Satō's visit to Southeast Asia, particularly to South Vietnam. You might have read about it. The editorials are very critical of the student demonstrations. There was a big one at Saga University too. Things are so different these days: the police intervention on campus, boycotts against exams, clashes with professors, and disrespect for professors, calling them "Hey, you!" Watanabe-sensei told me that nowadays the students don't greet the professors because they regard the professors as hired hands who are paid to teach them. In the old days there were some professors who showed off their authority, but the present situation is extremely impersonal; I think I am a liberal, but I can't understand this trend. The arrogance and meanness of the old academic atmosphere should be cleared away, but losing warm human relationships on the campus is something to be avoided. I think the older generation should be respected and cared for—or am I getting old myself? The reporters write about the low standards of the university students; for example, some cannot even recite the alphabet in its entirety. They also write about the phenomenal increase in the number of universities and the unsatisfactory policy in which one can matriculate as long as one pays the tuition. What is the purpose of starting a university—to educate people or to make money—I don't understand. . . .

I am thinking of coming home if no improvement is made by next month. If there is some improvement, I will stay longer. This is the time to make a decision one way or other. I will try hard to get better; if I come home with no improvement, please don't feel disappointed. If I decide to stay longer, please support my decision. I need your love. . . .

From KIYOSHI, *October 9.*

TODAY I'M GOING TO SHOW YOU HOW TO CONDUCT a class on transitive verbs (verbs accompanied by an object). Let's use the most typical verb "to have."

 1. Write the following two groups of sentences on the blackboard:

  Ichirō **wa** *hon o motte imasu*: Ichirō has a book.

  Jirō **mo** *hon o motte imasu*: Jirō too has a book.

  Saburō **wa** *hon o motte imasen*: Saburō does not have a book.

  Shirō **ga** *hon o motte imasu*: Shirō has a book.

  Hanako **wa** *pen o motte imasu*: Hanako has a pen.

  Masako **mo** *pen o motte imasu*: Masako too has a pen.

  Nobuko **wa** *pen o motte imasen*: Nobuko does not have a pen.

  Keiko **ga** *pen o motte imasu*: Keiko has a pen.

 2. Drill the class following the forms below:

  Q. *Ichirō* **wa** *hon o motte imasu ka, pen o motte imasu ka*:
   Does Ichirō have a book, or does he have a pen?

  A. *Ichirō* **wa** *hon o motte imasu*: Ichirō has a book.

  Q. *Hanako* **mo** *hon o motte imasu ka*: Does Hanako too have a book?

  A. *Iie, Hanako* **wa** *hon o motte imasen*: No, Hanako does not have a book.

  Q. *Dewa, Masako* **ga** *hon o motte imasu ka*: Then, does Masako have a book?

  A. *Iie, Masako* **wa** *hon o motte imasen*: No, Masako does not have a book.

  Q. *Nobuko* **ga** *hon o motte imasu ka*: Does Nobuko have a book?

  A. *Iie, Nobuko* **wa** *hon o motte imasen*: No, Nobuko does not have a book.

  Q. *Dewa, dare* **ga** *hon o motte imasu ka*: Then, who has a book?

  A. *Jirō* **ga** *hon o motte imasu*: Jirō has a book.

Q. *Shirō **mo** hon o motte imasu ka*: Does Shirō too have a book?

A. *Hai, sō desu*: Yes, he does. OR—*Hai, Shirō **mo** hon o motte imasu*: Yes, Shirō too has a book.

Up to this point, you have had enough drilling on the particle *ga*, but not enough on *wa*; so continue as follows:

Q. *Soredewa, Hanako **wa** tokei o motte imasu ka*: Then, does Hanako have a watch?

A. *Iie, Hanako **wa** tokei o motte imasen*: No, Hanako does not have a watch.

Q. *Hanako **wa** naifu o motte imasu ka*: Does Hanako have a knife?

A. *Iie, Hanako **wa** naifu **wa** motte imasen*: No, Hanako does not have a knife.

Q. *Hanako **wa** rajio o motte imasu ka*: Does Hanako have a radio?

A. *Iie, Hanako **wa** rajio **wa** motte imasen*: Hanako does not have a radio.

You may pronounce ra-ji-oh in the English way, ray-dee-oh.*

Q. *Dewa, Hanako **wa** nani o motte imasu ka*: Then, what does Hanako have?

A. *Hanako **wa** pen o motte imasu*: Hanako has a pen.

Q. *Masako **mo** pen o motte imasu ka*: Does Masako too have a pen?

A. *Hai, sō desu*: Yes, she does. OR—*Hai, Masako **mo** pen o motte imasu*: Yes, Masako too has a pen.

END

Drill the entire class, asking one student one question, passing from row to row from left to right, from front to back; have a few students go over all the questions and answers. Lastly select one student to become the teacher and repeat the drills—he (or she) will conduct the class excellently, even better than Nagasaki-san or Tsukiji-san. The students will take part in the class actively and the one or two hours will fly by quickly, I assure you. At the end have them sing a Japanese song. I would like Tokunaga-sensei to observe this class and this method of teaching. Tell him that you are teaching your class the relationship of the subject and the transitive verb—you will get an A+. Start the question and answer part with Ichirō and Hanako; quickly move on to the next question and answer by Jirō and Masako; thus the pair changes with each question and answer. You can expand this drill as much as you want. Time will go fast, and most importantly, this method will keep the students busy and involved in the class. Students will be glad to be involved and have fun too. Praise them at the end of the class period. Tell them they speak as well as Japanese kids do; they will be happy to hear that. Most importantly you must know the drill thoroughly so that the questions and answers will flow smoothly.

Lastly, you place your finger on *wa* on the blackboard, point to your eye with another finger, and ask "*Kore wa me desu ka*: Is this an eye?" Repeat the question pointing to the mouth, to the hand, etc. Similarly place your finger on *ga* on the board, and ask "*Kore ga me desu ka*: Is this an eye?"

*In Japan, it is pronounced "ra-ji-o", and Kiyoshi himself spelled it so in katakana, the Japanese alphabet. In Japanese-American society in California, Japanese speakers commonly use "ray-dee-oh," mixing the English pronunciation in a Japanese sentence.

From KIYOKO, *October 9/10.*

YESTERDAY I WAS THINKING OF HIROYUKI'S WEDDING while doing laundry and cleaning. I finished those in good time and was about to write to you when Mitsuyo and her family came unannounced. So, I couldn't do anything until after five o'clock when they went home. Akira-san wanted to take a ride to somewhere so everybody joined him. They were going to eat something on the way but didn't. Fortunately my roast beef was just about to be done—so we laughed that they followed the smell of the roast. . . .

It would be nice if Watanabe-sensei could give a summer course on methods of teaching the Japanese language. But I doubt if he considers teaching methods to be an important educational skill. If a specialist in that field happened to be in this area, I might think of taking his course. But our school is not a real school; it's not run by rules nor managed like a regular school. Yet they want the students to be able to speak Japanese—it's absurd! We who have experience in teaching are in disbelief. I don't see other teachers at school. I go straight to the classroom; at 12 o'clock, I end the class and hurry home—if I stayed there any longer, I'd be left in an empty building. Nobody cares what other teachers are teaching or how they are teaching. You won't find anyone in this Buddhist School in San Jose who wants to take training courses to improve his or her teaching method.

For example, Okumura-san: he is taking lessons in golf from a pro golfer so that he can play with the head of the bank. He is paying $6.00 for ½ hour. That's why he leaves school as quickly as possible. Nagasaki-san: as you remember, he thinks nobody is a better teacher than he because he has the longest experience in teaching. Tsukiji-san might want to continue his studies if he has time. I'll talk to Tokunaga-sensei about it on the day of the Parents' Association [meeting].

The school district in Campbell could not find a teacher and put an ad in the paper. Apparently there are many parents who want to have children learn Japanese, but if they are having difficulty in finding a teacher, it is hopeless. It's better that the parents speak Japanese to their children at home. Something is wrong. Like in Japan, people speak Japanese all the time but are eager to learn English. I wish I had mastered a way to teach Japanese. Tokunaga-sensei and a couple of others do not understand my feeling because they don't teach. If I were to succeed in teaching, they would realize how important the teaching method is. . . .

Yukiko says that you should start getting her reward of a camera and a watch ready because she is doing very well in school—I do hope so. She is doing better than last year. I should get her report card soon.

Today's paper reported that there was a huge demonstration in Haneda Airport. In spite of the drought, a record crop of rice is reported also, and at the top of the list is Saga Prefecture. I wonder if it is true. . . .

From KIYOSHI, *October 10.*

. . . LAST NIGHT I WROTE A SYLLABUS on the use of particles. After going to bed, I kept thinking of the final drill on the use of [は]**wa**. The following is the improved format:

Q. *Ichirō **wa** hon o motte imasu ka, pen o motte imasu ka*: Does Ichirō have a book, or does he have a pen?

A. *Ichirō **wa** hon o motte imasu*: Ichirō has a book.

Q. *Jirō **mo** hon o motte imasu ka*: Does Jirō too have a book?

A. *Iie, Jirō **wa** hon o motte imasen*: No, Jirō does not have a book.

Repeat the above question and answer twice using the girls' names, always ending with a negative answer. And conclude this section as follows:

Q. *Dewa, dare ga hon o motte imasu ka*: Then, who has a book?
A. *Ichirō ga hon o motte imasu*: Ichirō has a book.

Additional usage of *wa*:

Q. *Dewa, jirō wa pen o motte imasu ka, naifu o motte imasu ka*: Then, does Jirō have a pen, or does he have a knife?
A. *Jirō wa pen o motte imasu:* Jirō has a pen.
Q. *Saburō mo pen o motte imasu ka*: Does Saburō too have a pen?
A. *Iie, Saburō wa pen o motte imasen*: No, Saburō does not have a pen.
Q. *Dewa, Saburō wa naifu o motte imasu ka*: Then, does Saburō have a knife?
A. *Iie, Saburō wa naifu o motte imasen*: No, Saburō does not have a knife.
Q. *Saburō wa rajio o motte imasu ka*: Does Saburō have a radio?
A. *Iie, Saburō wa rajio o motte imasen*: No, Saburō does not have a radio.
Q. *Dewa, Saburō wa nani o motte imasu ka*: Then, what does Saburō have?
A. *Saburō wa enpitsu o motte imasu*: Saburō has a pencil.
Q. *Shirō mo enpitsu o motte imasu ka*: Does Shirō too have a pencil?
A. *Hai, sō desu:* Yes, he does. OR— *Hai, Shirō mo enpitsu o motte imasu*: Yes, Shirō too has a pencil.

Conduct the questions and answers like this. Please make a clean note for yourself.
The next drill is related to ". . . *desu*: it is . . ."

Kore wa hon desu ka, pen desu ka. Sore wa hon desu.
Is this a book or a pen? It is a book.
Kore mo hon desu ka. Iie, sore wa hon de wa arimasen.
Is this a book too? No, it is not a book.
Dewa, kore ga hon desu ka. Iie, sore wa hon de wa arimasen.
Then, is this a book? No, it is not a book.

*Soredewa, dore **ga** hon desu ka. Sore **ga** hon desu.*
Then, which one is a book? That is a book.
*Kore **mo** hon desu ka. Hai, sō desu.*
Is this a book too? Yes, it is.
*Soredewa, kore **wa** pen desu ka, soretomo naifu desu ka. Sore **wa** pen desu.*
Then, is this a pen, or a knife? It is a pen.
*Kore **mo** pen desu ka. Iie, sore **wa** pen de **wa** arimasen.*
Is this a pen too? No, it is not a pen.
*Dewa, kore **wa** naifu desu ka. Iie, sore **wa** naifu de **wa** arimasen.*
Then, is this a knife? No, it is not a knife.
*Dewa, kore **wa** rajio desu ka. Iie, sore **wa** rajio de **wa** arimasen.*
Then, is this a radio? No, it is not a radio.
*Soredewa, kore **wa** nan desu ka. Sore **wa** ningyō desu.*
Then, what is this? It is a doll.
*Kore **mo** ningyō desu ka. Hai, sō desu.*
Is this a doll too? Yes, it is.

I think this drill is much better with the particles *wa, mo* and *ga* being presented systematically. Use this format also for the verb "to have."

From KIYOSHI, *October 10.*

THIS IS A CONTINUATION OF NO. 86, A PART OF a syllabus for a Japanese conversation class. It takes a lot of thinking because it has to be tightly organized to be effective. After going to bed, I realized that the same format could be used for everything. It's a simple logic, and it would result in a well-organized classroom performance. I think it would be fun to prepare a textbook following this format. In order to make classroom exercises easy, teachers need a textbook with sample sentences to write on the blackboard. Based on this theory, we could write a textbook for teachers on how to practice drills in their classroom. This classroom drill format could be applied to all other particles too. I think I can write a unique Tokutomi method. I may not be an expert in linguistics but you, Kiyoko-san, recognize my capability, don't you? I have found a method of drills on the particles *wa, ga,* and *mo,* with the subjective case. There are a lot of teachers who can teach *wa* and *ga* separately as they are used in the subjective case, but nobody has come up with a syllabus to work on *wa, ga,* and *mo* together

with the subject. *Wa* and *ga* have been sticking out like ulcers scaring foreigners away from learning Japanese. They can understand the grammatical
use of *wa* and *ga* with respect to the subject, but they are not able to get a
good command of these particles in conversation. That's why an exhaustive
drilling is necessary so that they can use the particles without thinking. The
same thing goes for *ni* and *o*. It also applies to their use in an explanatory
sentence. *ni* I'd like to work on this carefully.

I feel so much better these days. I must restore my strength so that my
hearing too becomes improved. Maybe it's too soon to mention this, but it's
been five days now since my hearing came back to some degree. I thought
the loss of hearing was a side effect of the histamine treatment, but it was
because of my bad cold. The doctor didn't think that histamine or *karikurein*
had an ill effect on my hearing because an ear-and-nose specialist does not
use any drugs that might have that kind of side effect. Come to think of it, I
felt generally well when my hearing was way down. In my diary I wrote I
felt ill due to histamine and *karikurein*; but at the same time I wrote I heard
the rustle of my pillow and the sound of a fan. And when I stopped taking
karikurein and histamine, my hearing stopped too. I had a consultation with
the doctor a week ago, and now I am back on the *karikurein* and histamine
treatment again. A week ago I started taking one histamine pill a day, and
not only have I had no ill effect from it or from *karikurein*, but also I feel
much better now. Tomorrow I'll increase the intake of histamine to two
pills, and probably I'll have no side effect. Not only that, I have been hearing
a faint sound in my left ear for five days now. Yesterday I could hear the
ventilation making a noise like "peeee . . . peeee. . . ." Actually it should
sound "suuuu . . . suuuu . . . ," but I don't care how it should sound—I *heard*
something! It makes me happy! It will take time to get my hearing back, but
these signs give me hope. I will be very careful so as not to upset this
improvement. . . .

From KIYOSHI, *October 11.*

... DID I MENTION IN YESTERDAY'S letter that Dr. Yoshida came to see me from the sanatorium in Mei-no-hama? This may be repetitious, but I'm going to tell you anyway. He came unexpectedly and thanked me for the razor and Almond Roca that I asked Hiroyuki-san to deliver to him. Dr. Yoshida brought me some cookies famous in Kyoto where his wife is from.

We discussed my case extensively. If the tuberculosis virus is extracted from the side of my chest for five days periodically over three to five months, and the test proves to be negative, the chest will be closed. On the other hand, if it is positive, the lung would be completely extracted six months after opening the chest. The recovery time would be three to six months from that point, and the recovery rate is 80 to 90%. I told Dr. Yoshida the recovery from the chest problem would be nice, but right now I can't say anything about it because I don't know how the treatment of my hearing will turn out. Maybe by the middle of next month I will know if my hearing is coming back or not. I told him that then I'll write to him. I'm suffering from my hearing problem right now, and I don't want to have any other problems on top of it. Besides I don't want to be separated from you anymore, Kiyoko-san. It would be different if I could be sure that there is hope that my hearing will recover. Right now I think only of my hearing. . . .

The weather here has been so nice. It would be wonderful if I got my hearing back, and you and I and Yukiko could go on a tour and enjoy these autumn days in Japan. . . .

From KIYOSHI, *October 11.*

... I'VE TOLD YOU THAT I FEEL much better lately. The only trouble was my throat. There was nothing unusual except the presence of a lump which felt hard when I touched it. I was afraid that it might develop into cancer. At the very beginning after arriving here at this hospital, I told many doctors about this, but nobody checked it thoroughly. I was afraid of a frightening diagnosis. Besides I didn't think I had the strength to go through another treatment on top of my ear treatment. But I was troubled with the possibility of having cancer.

Then I began to feel much better lately, so much so that I decided to take a chance and ask the doctor to have a look at my throat. I thought it would be better to treat it now rather than waiting until I am back in America. I made up my mind last night after mulling this over. It was a tough decision on my part!

The doctor examined it very carefully. Drawing a picture of the inside of my mouth on the blackboard, he told me that it was normal to have a lump there. I told the doctor that I was frightened of the possibility of cancer, and he laughed. Also I told him that my general health had improved, and my intake of histamine has increased to two tablets a day as before. I don't expect any problem from this, and *karikurein* has had no ill effect either. I told him also that the ringing in my ears has decreased, and I can hear a ticking noise in the left ear. I said there is a good chance that I'll get some of my hearing back if the count goes up by 10 points within one month. Then the doctor said it would take only three weeks to get it to that point if the repair work on the carbon dioxide inhaler is completed. He was sure that it would increase 10 or 15 points then. It was so assuring. After all, I was thinking of the recovery speed without CO_2 inhalation. Now it looks like the inhaler is going to be repaired too! I am more hopeful now.

In any case, this month is the key to successful treatment. . . .

From KIYOSHI, *October 11.*

. . . YOUR LETTER OF OCTOBER FIFTH arrived. I decided to write one more time because I thought it necessary. It is about the letter to Dr. Childrey. If my condition were improving, I could write him about the treatment and prognosis, etc., but in my present condition, I don't feel like writing to him. If I write to him, I'd have to explain what's going on, and I have no desire to do that. . . . My present condition is so bad that just the thought of it causes my head to ache. So, Kiyoko-san, I drafted the letter below; please copy it and show it to Dr. Childrey as your own request:

"Would you please write a certification for my husband to send to my insurance company. As I told you, since treatment is not available in the United States, my husband went to Japan to have carbon dioxide inhalation for deafness caused by medication, such as streptomycin and kanamycin. The insurance will also pay the transportation. At present, carbon dioxide inhalation treatment for such a case is only available in Japan and Germany.

"I would appreciate it very much if you could write a certification for my husband. Of course I will be very happy to pay the fee for your certification."

If the doctor asks how I am doing, tell him that it takes a little time, but I am getting better little by little. I'm sorry to ask you to do this, but I really hope we can get a certification from him somehow.

From KIYOKO, *October 12.*

. . . TODAY WAS OPEN HOUSE AT Yukiko's school. I went there from Mountain View and observed her class. The teacher is young but strict. She leads the class with the awareness befitting the fifth grade. The class is made of all fifth-graders, which helps a lot. Yukiko does not do homework; but this morning she did all right on the blackboard with the spelling and multiplication. I was relieved. The teacher complimented Yukiko saying that she is bright, but she lacks concentration and makes careless mistakes. She also says Yukiko does not speak up loudly or clearly enough. I asked Yukiko about this; she says she feels shy and not comfortable with this new teacher. Judging from her make-up and her determination, the teacher gives an impression of being cold, and Yukiko is intimidated by this. Since she is withdrawn, she was not elected to be a hostess—yet that's what she wants to be. I wish she had one-tenth of my confidence. Someday she will.

I stopped by the house at lunchtime and found your letters and a photo being delivered. The syllabus on teaching Japanese conversation using transitive verbs will help me a great deal. Last Saturday I had the older students listen to music and had them look up words that they knew in the dictionary—but it wasn't successful. I was just thinking that it's better to put the two groups together and practice conversation. Will you please write one teaching plan every week? I'll pay you $25 a month! Anyway, I like the idea of us working together to improve the methods used to teach Japanese. You make the plans, and I carry them out in the class—perfect teamwork.

I was expecting the photo to be of a group of sick people. But everybody looks so healthy and cheerful that I couldn't believe it. I am so happy to note that you have not changed much. By the way, what is it that's hung on the door of a cabinet by what looks like a bathroom? A profile of a beautiful woman on top, and below it, a mirror? I could see a few folded cranes that you might have made when you had nothing to do.

Ōtomo-san seems to be a nice person; she could have a busy life if she could only use her hearing fully. Your description of Ōtomo-san is perfect; a nice personality, but she asks for too much. Tachibana-san carries an air of grace and kindness like a princess. The other two girls do not seem to have the thoughtfulness of Ōtomo-san or Tachibana-san—maybe I am prejudiced. Matsuda-san is exactly as I imagined. The other two men are typical Japanese young men—so likable. And, lastly my Kiyoshi-san— valiantly faces the situation with a bright smile—my precious Kiyoshi-san—I love you and respect you! I may lose hope in everything else, but not in Kiyoshi-san: this feeling will stay forever. I feel that my everlasting love for Kiyoshi-san and his for me are written on the sky—or emitted clearly into the universe. What a strange way to describe my feeling, but I will write again.

From KIYOSHI, *October 13.*

THE GIRL WITH HER BROKEN NOSE CAME TO SEE me and asked if I knew what day today was. I said I didn't know. She said it was Friday, the 13th, and the day Jesus Christ was crucified. I was surprised; maybe nowadays Japanese people know more about the western culture than we suspect.

How are you, Kiyoko-san? I feel very good. In today's treatment, I could hear the ticking sound in my left ear better than yesterday. If I start to hear a steady hissing sound, it would be better—I'm sure I'll get there! . . .

The death of Hideshima Shichisaburō-san was reported here too. He became famous and several years ago he was awarded a medal for his achievement. The plane crash of JAL during the training session was shocking news. Of all the people, Matsumura-san, Miyazaki-san and Nakayama-san were the closest to us—I couldn't believe it.

Every day I read about the American World Series in the English newspaper. The score was 3-even as of yesterday. It's going to be an exciting game between Saint Louis and Boston. . . .

I'm glad to hear that you are doing all right at the Japanese Language School. I'm writing a textbook of my own method of teaching. I don't have yet an outline of the finished text, but I'll keep writing as far as I can. Divide an intransitive verb into perfect and imperfect, do the same with a transitive verb, and prepare systematic exercises—I think it will work. The first volume will have only the present tense. The particles are the most unique element in the Japanese language; therefore if those are mastered well, the rest follows easily. If the particles are not mastered, you will end up with funny Japanese (even if other parts are correct). In any case, I'm going to work on this project very slowly. . . .

From KIYOSHI, *October 13.*

. . . HOW LONG AGO WAS IT, I wonder—a patient gave me a plant before she left the hospital. It has beautiful leaves and is only 15 or 20 cm tall. I cut a leaf from it and put it in a jar with some water. If this were a flower, I would have been sure that roots would come out, but I wasn't sure in this case because this was a tree. People came to see this leaf in a jar wondering what in the world I was doing. Nobody believed that I would succeed; even the patient who gave this plant to me thought it was useless. The plant didn't have enough dirt to begin with so that its leaves had begun to fall. However, the leaf that I put in water has been doing all right except for its tip. Still everybody thought it would wilt eventually. I prayed it wouldn't. For me, it was a symbol of my own ear—if it takes root, my hearing will come back; if not, I remain deaf. I told the person who gave this plant to me that a root should come out if only to hold up my prayer; she said it wouldn't. Then yesterday I took the leaf out of the jar without much thought. What do you think I saw, Kiyoko-san—a tiny root of about two millimeters sprouting out from one spot! It took two and a half months to come out. I almost cried. I'm telling myself that I will be cured; even if everyone gives up on me, I won't give up—I will be cured! A tiny shoot is coming out from the leaf—the green, beautiful leaf with white lines like veins!

I'm going to bring this sprout home, soaked in water, in a flat, plastic container carefully carrying it in my pocket. I am so encouraged by this tiny leaf—now I know I will be cured. I asked the head nurse today for the carbon dioxide gas inhaler to be repaired quickly; I will repeat this request over and over until it is done. I must concentrate on this—help me, Kiyoko-san.

I'm going to write another letter because I have something else to tell you.

From KIYOSHI, *October 13.*

... IT'S 5:30 P.M. HERE. I SENT for fried pork for dinner. It was 190 yen. The meat was thin—it's made to look large with a thick coating—but it tasted delicious. It cost 53 cents with delivery so it wasn't bad. It was served with potato salad and shredded cabbage, plus three slices of cucumber. I'm a bit worried because I spend about 200 yen every day for food. Milk is not included in food so it is not covered by insurance. Milk costs 90 yen a day and ice 50 yen. On top of these—this daily mail. It costs a lot, but I'm going to close my eyes to it because it is so important to me. During the summer, cleaning cost a lot because I changed clothes every day; now I change every three days, and spend 70 yen for one set of tops and bottoms. If the pajamas are very dirty, they charge 100 yen. I changed three or four times last summer when I had a fever; once they were very dirty, and they charged it separately.

The average spending is between 150 and 200 yen a day—the 200 yen includes some incidentals. I heard from the doctor about an enzyme that is good for metastasis so I bought the enzyme called *Lēben.* How much do you think it was? 4,000 yen for one bottle! I'm supposed to take three bottles so it'll be 1,200 yen!

Let's stop talking about money. I'm so sorry, Kiyoko-san.

Next, about Yotsuo-san's bride-to-be. I'm so surprised to learn that the nurses are all single women. The head nurse is 37 or 38; of her assistants, one is about 35 and the other about 25. Under them there are a number of nurses about 22 years old—and none of them are married! Probably they just missed the chance. Being with doctors and medical technicians all the time, they must have lost interest in ordinary men. Perhaps they expected too much from marriage, and chances slipped away from them. They are all nice women. The head nurse—her family name is Shibata—is a pretty lady. I can't understand why she is still single. Her assistant is a very earnest person and modest and natural. It is rumored that she will become the head nurse of a new ward soon to be built. The other assistant is modest and gentle, and a fine lady—but also single. Unfortunately there isn't anybody between 27 and 31; if I wait a little longer, maybe somebody might show up.

Tomorrow Shizuma-san will go get my favorite fish, *akamutsu,* and cook it for me. I just mentioned that I was craving *akamutsu,* and she offered to do it. I'm going to eat five or six *akamutsu.* Don't worry—of course I pay for the fish and the cooking. Now that Hiroyuki-san has a wife, I can ask him to bring some cooked fish. . . .

From KIYOSHI, *October 14.*

. . . YESTERDAY I WROTE ABOUT MY daily expenses. I'm afraid it might be much more. For example, I forgot to include the cost of fruit and a newspaper. It's scary not to know the exact amount. I don't think I'm spending $100 a month, but it is at least over $60. I am so sorry, Kiyoko-san. I'll prepare a balance sheet again some other time.

. . . The painter Sakurai, that notorious man in San Francisco, is back in Fukuoka—I suppose he was born in Fukuoka. He will stay here for about one year; then he plans to go back to America. He still has an untrimmed beard and brags about the hippies in San Francisco.

St. Louis won the World Series, didn't they? I hoped they would win, and they did! The batter, Cepeda, who was mistreated by the Giants, now plays with St. Louis. Once he left the Giants, he jumped to the top level among batters. The Giants' head coach has lost face completely. I enjoyed the game.

This is Saturday. Hiroyuki-san and Noriko-san may come today. I hope they become a happy couple like we are. I read in yesterday's paper something I keep saying: "Happiness in marriage must be built by the two; it does not just grow between them." This was in the column called "*Shunjū Yoroku,*" equivalent to "*Tensei Jingo*" in *Nishi-Nihon* newspaper—I was so pleased. . . . I'm glad that somebody famous has the same idea—I say "love" and he says "happiness," but we both mean the same thing. You and I share this thing called "love" or "happiness." We don't have anything to show off to others, but the happiness of our love is priceless. I thank you, and respect you, Kiyoko-san. You are my everlasting love. I am a lucky man!

From KIYOSHI, *October 14.*

. . . SHIZUMA-SAN WENT TO THE market for fish today, and her roommate cooked it with shoyu. But they didn't have *akamutsu* at the market. Instead, she bought five *itsutsusaki* and paid 480 yen. I ate two of them, she ate one, and two are left for tomorrow. I read your letter to her, adding and modifying the lines here and there. She was very happy.

You say Yukiko wants to go out at night. I think she is lonely. Encourage her to read the encyclopedia; ask her to look up "oxygen," for example; tell her, "It should be fun—and please let me know what it says." I think it will stir up her interest. Multiple and single hibernation of insects, the age of the earth, the history of the mankind, etc.—there are so many interesting facts in the encyclopedia that it would stimulate even grown-ups. *LIFE* published a *Dictionary of Physical Science* some years ago. I wish we had bought it then, but we didn't have the money. I would like her to be interested in something good; I would like her to become a thinking child, a creative child. Even the story of electricity has many interesting facets. This is a critical time in her life. You have more than enough things to do, but please think of a better way to guide Yukiko; I will do the same. We cannot just tell her, "Don't do this and that." The best way is to show her things she might become interested in so that she will stay away from undesirable activities. You cannot encourage her too much either. If you force her, she will rebel and lose interest. Let her do what she shows interest in; praise her when she reports back on her research, and show your honest interest so that she will do more research. Anyhow, we must come up with countermeasures against the present situation regarding Yukiko. I hate to leave so much for you to bear on your shoulders, but until I come home, please try.

I have not written to my mother because I didn't feel well for so long. But finally I wrote her the other day and told her that I was feeling better and that my hearing is slightly improving too. She is getting old. Please, Kiyoko-san, look after her. I'll write you again tomorrow. Take care of yourself.

From Kiyoko, *October 15.*

Thank you for the detailed teaching plan for a Japanese conversation class. It helps me a great deal. . . . Three letters written on the 11th and the one written on the 12th arrived all at once last Friday. I'm going to put them in my notebook in the order of my teaching schedule. Last Friday I entered the particles は (wa), を (o), も (mo), with transitive verbs. Each time I get a syllabus from you, I'll enter it in this book.

Friday evening I went to see the movie *Yukiyama Silk of Rokujō* [六条ゆきやま紬], played by Takamine Hideko. It was not as good as *To Be Poor, Pure, and Beautiful* [貧しく、清く、美しく]. After that, I saw *The Tale of Genji* on TV, and the next morning at nine a.m., I was teaching Japanese at school. I was so sleepy on Saturday afternoon, I took a nap together with Yukiko, but we slept through the afternoon and into the night. I usually write to you on Saturday, but I could not—I am so sorry!

I'm happy to hear that you feel much better these days. If you feel good even without having the help of the inhalation machine, you can certainly recover your hearing. Catching cold can damage one's health so much—it's amazing. But I'm glad that you have had no bad aftereffects from that cold. You must be relieved too. Eat well and store up energy before the cold winter arrives.

Looking back, your medicine was causing a bad effect on your blood vessels. Maybe that's why blood didn't reach your ears where the vessels are so fine. Come to think of it, around the end of February the color of your face became darkish, and your hearing loss started around that time, I think. Now you look so much better in the photo—I can see you laughing out loud surrounded by girls calling you *oji-san*. You are so anxious to get my letters—in spite of that you look very happy in the photo. I'm looking at the photo while writing this letter.

You've told me about the initial examination done by Dr. Yoshida, but what you tell me here is something new. Do you have more concrete results from the examination now? Does what they extracted from your side now show a positive result? It's important to have your hearing cured, but if your lung still has problems, your hearing will be affected. I can see that both may not be treated at the same time, but how about preparing for the lung too? For example, we may be able to ask them to start the cultivation process which usually takes five months. Can you ask that of Dr. Yoshida?

If the test is negative, you might get well without surgery. If your hearing gets better first, you will have the advantage of choosing the next step for your lung. But for now at least, the testing part of the lung treatment could be started.

Regarding your throat, I'm glad that your suspicion was cleared in laughter. I bet you felt relieved. . . .

From KIYOSHI, October 15.

. . . THE STATES MAY RAISE TAXES, according to the English newspaper. President Johnson says that if taxes are not raised, inflation will affect the cost of living and that will be worse than raising taxes. The cost of the Vietnam War is rising sky high, and President Johnson is facing reelection next year. He is increasing the bombing of North Vietnam to force them to come to the negotiating table, but they don't budge; instead the American casualties are rising, etc. What a headache!

I notice that Japan is becoming conservative. A professor who glorified life so much that he led an anti-war group is now the target of contempt by the students of the U. of Kyushu. This was reported in the newspaper.

The letters from Ōshima-san and Tanaka Toshimichi-san just arrived. According to them, babies were born just recently to both Nakayama-san and Miyazaki-san. Nakayama-san's family took my condolence letter addressed to the three families in Japan. Ōshima-san is going to investigate the accident by taking the same route flying the same type of airplane that caused the said accident. Tanaka-san says he cannot forget Kiyoko-san's lunch party in Oakland, and he is sure that all three seniors, now deceased, would fully agree with him. It is a courteous thank-you note reflecting the sincere nature of the JAL employees. We are the lucky ones who got to know them. Ōshima-san also wrote that the lunch party must have been a happy memory to all three of the deceased. . . .

From KIYOKO, October 15.

MITSUYO CALLED ME ABOUT 11 O'CLOCK IN THE morning. She wanted to stop by on her way to San Jose. I did the laundry and housecleaning quickly and waited for her and her family. She brought six boxes of ripe strawberries so that I had to give some away right away. Even so, about half are still in the icebox. She came to San Jose to see a flower arrangement exhibit of the Ikenobō School. I was amazed that even Akira-san came along, and I went to the exhibit with them. . . . I was going to cook ham for dinner, but they wanted to take me out. So after Hisayo came home, we all went to Spivey's Restaurant. It was so hot in San Jose—a little over 90°. It was nice to eat out rather than cooking at home. . . .

Yukiko was helping Ginny Nakajima, who is Hisayo's friend and is studying children's development in the arts at San Jose State University, by doing sketches for Ginny's school project. Mitsuyo's family stopped by after Yukiko came home, and she and the boys were so happy to see each other. At the dinner table in the restaurant, Yukiko was asking Glen what kind of textbooks he was using. I was pleased to note that her interest has become more adultlike. . . .

I read your letter again and discovered that I have not answered the following as yet. It's about the claim for the airline tickets. Since you wrote a draft for me, I'll make a clean copy and send it. Every time I see that doctor, my English evaporates into air! I must be psychologically intimidated. A letter can explain the situation much better. The doctor told us frankly that he wished he knew more about the insurance so that he could help us. But I feel very inferior to those doctors at the Stanford University Hospital. . . .

Enjoy the autumn in Japan. I wish we were there too—all three of us. Last Friday I deposited another $100 dreaming of such a trip for us. You, too, hang onto your dream, Kiyoshi-san!

From KIYOSHI, *October 16.*

DR. KAWADA MADE HIS ROUNDS THIS MORNING ABOUT nine o'clock. We are going to continue the present treatment since I've become much better lately. I feel so good this morning! My temperature is 36.1—normal. I have a slight problem with my hearing because I read so much yesterday—it was foolish of me. Reading books is not good for me. But I put my hands on them because I am lonely; it's like eating peanuts—once I start, I can't stop. . . .

Yesterday was Shizuma-san's birthday. I treated her to *tonkatsu,* a special at 280 yen each—she was so pleased. . . .

Hiroyuki-san and Noriko-san didn't come. They work every day including a half-day on Saturday so I guess Sunday is the day they do housework. I wish them a happy marriage! When they come, I will ask them to get rain boots for Yukiko. . . .

From KIYOSHI, *October 16.*

. . . I HAVE GOOD NEWS TODAY. It is about a possible candidate for Yotsuo-san's future wife. I wrote last time that there was no lady in the age range of 27 to 32 here, but I was wrong. There is a nurse in the Treatment Room. She is better-than-average looking with double-folded eyes; she is cheerful and kind and professional—she takes care of changing my dirty bag. She is a hard worker. I thought she was about 23 years old because she has some pimples on her face. She appeared to be just right for Yotsuo-san except for her age. But I thought she might know somebody among her friends that would be the right age. When she came to my room to change my bandage today, I told her that I was looking for a lady of about 27 to 32 years old who might marry one of my relatives. I told her that if she were that old she would be the best candidate, but she would be too young for my relative. She laughed and said that she was an old lady of age 27. I was so surprised. She listened to me thoughtfully as I described Yotsuo-san and said that she didn't know what to say because it was unexpected. Then she added that she couldn't even imagine what life in America would be like. She said she wanted to think about it. I was impressed very much by her rational attitude. I don't think she has a boyfriend. Her name is Ōsaki-san, and she was born in Miyazaki-ken. After high school, she took a regular nursing course. She doesn't mind dirtying her hands (in Japan the nurses do not put on gloves) and changes my soiled bags without showing any disgust—for which I am so grateful! It seems that she doesn't mind farming. I don't think Yotsuo-san's family would find anybody better than this candidate. If they don't like her, they might as well give up searching for a wife for him. Will you tell them on the phone about this possible candidate and find out what the parents and, more importantly, Yotsuo-san himself thinks about this possibility. Check also with Akira-san and his family about what they think. By the way, Ōsaki-san has a complexion similar to Kiyoko-san's. I'm waiting for your reply. I'll write you tomorrow.

From KIYOKO, *October 17.*

. . . I WAS IMPRESSED BY YOUR STORY on the shoot of a tiny root from a leaf. If you had given up and thrown it away, you could not have had such a result. Even our obsession, if it is constructive, can bring a good result. We have to avoid hardening our mental flexibility; rejoice when a root peeks out and be happy again when a leaf comes out. Of course at the base of all the excitement, one has to have a sense of attachment, as you had, for that leaf.

I was pleased to hear your report on eating fish. It sounds delicious! It is autumn now when food is abundant and delicious. Please enjoy! Maybe it's better to order out because hospital cooking tends to kill all the flavor.

I almost forgot this—we received the second check from the insurance company. They covered $336.60 against $353.82 medical cost. The deductible was only $17.22, and I am so glad! Let me know when the next payment day is; until then, I shall deposit this somewhere. I called the insurance company to let them know we received this check, and they wished you a speedy recovery. You spoke about some medicine that costs 4,000 yen—is it not covered by the insurance? If it is good for you, get it; there is no point in turning our back on an excellent medicine. Getting well is our first objective. The insurance will cover it. In spite of your being in the hospital, we did make a deposit of $100 in the bank—it's wonderful! Next time, I'll deposit some in the Tokyo Bank.

Today Yukiko is studying, for a change. She is practicing common nouns and proper nouns. The class is gradually moving on to more intricate grammar. Yukiko seems to understand the differences, but she cannot cite the definitions yet. I told her to consult with her teacher tomorrow. I think her teaching plan is well constructed.

I am a little bit restless—maybe I'm approaching that time. It's the dry season in California, and wildfires are threatening the south. My nose is dried up. Hisayo said that anti-war sentiment is mounting at [San Jose] State University; she was watching the 11 o'clock news. I'm glad that we don't have to worry over being left behind because news is broadcast instantly and in detail. Please remember me to Watanabe-sensei. I should write to him but have not found the time yet. I'm not a slow writer, but somehow I have not done it yet. I've sent a comic card to Shizuma-san; has it arrived? She may need a translator. Since I don't have much to say to her, I decided to send a card. My long letters are saved only for Kiyoshi-san. I miss you!

From KIYOSHI, *October 17.*

HOW ARE YOU, KIYOKO-SAN? I WISH I COULD say "I'm OK," but I can't. Last night I had some fever, and I feel weak today. This won't last long— maybe I'll feel better tomorrow.

Yesterday I wrote about a possible candidate for Yotsuo-san's bride. I'm not sure if the girl will say "yes," but I think she would be a good candidate. Her looks are better than ordinary; she is kind to others and cheerful at work. . . . She doesn't look flippant or nervous, and, of course, not saucy. With her looks, I can imagine that she has had one or two boyfriends; after all, she is 27 and single. I think nowadays, it is normal. If a man expects a virgin from a woman of that age, he will be either deceived or accept her as she is. . . .

Hinashi-san, a student who studies economics at the University of Kyushu, came to see me today. I don't know why but he comes to see me frequently. He brought a couple of books for me to read, and I'm grateful for that. Shizuma-san wants to write to you so I gave her one air letter. I said to her that my wife is very busy so that she may not be able to write back. Don't be bothered with a reply; it would be sufficient to add a line or two addressed to her when you write to me.

Calligraphy has become a fashionable cultural activity here in Japan. It might be interesting if you organized a group in conjunction with the Buddhists' Association. If you do it together with Saitō-san, it would be a first-class gathering. You are too busy right now, but it may be worth considering. . . .

From KIYOSHI*, October 18.*

THREE MONTHS HAVE PASSED SINCE I CHECKED INTO this hospital. Yesterday I asked Dr. Shirabe if the inhaler for carbonic acid gas was ready. He said he was discussing with the technical team the possibility of using only one pump, instead of two, through which patients can inhale the regulated amount of carbon dioxide and oxygen, and he is now looking for a mechanic who can change the design of the pump. I don't have any luck, do I! I may get well without this machine, but I came here specifically to try using one of the only two inhalers in the world.

I wrote yesterday that I didn't feel well. But today I'm all right. How about you, Kiyoko-san? And how are Yukiko and Hisayo-san? You be careful with driving—I bet you are still vexed over that traffic ticket. Think about it from time to time and take it as a warning. . . .

Some time ago a young man threw himself into the Kegon Falls . . . leaving behind a note saying that he failed to understand Life. Last night I felt I could understand Life. 人生 (life) means Man lives. Respect for life is its foundation. Where did that life come from? It came from sex. And sex based on love is the source of life. True love between a man and a woman creates another beautiful happy life. Love is the supreme source of life—it is that simple. . . . After the lights were turned out last night, I was thinking of us—how well we worked together to build this happiness. Then I thought of that young man who killed himself because he could not comprehend what life was to him. I started to question it myself—is life really incomprehensible? I could answer it very easily, and I was so happy. . . .

It's such a simple question, like Newton's question about an apple, for example. For ordinary people, an apple falls, and that's the end. But to Newton, who questioned for a long time why it falls, it was the starting point to his discovery of the theory of universal gravitation. . . . I'm not saying that I am as great as Newton. [But] as for the love between us, I thought about our mutual effort; and since I think about it all the time, it was easy to arrive at this understanding of life. We are so lucky. This is a victory that we share.

From KIYOSHI, *October 18.*

. . . YOUR LETTER OF SATURDAY SAID that one you started to write at work would be mailed on Sunday; therefore the mail might not be in order. I thought that it would arrive on this Sunday, or Monday at the latest. But none came, and this is already Wednesday. As I always say, you don't have to write a long letter; a quick note of two or three lines will do. Just tell me that you are busy or you are sick; that way at least I know how you are, and I will not be upset. . . .

I wonder how Yukiko is doing. I wanted to be a good father to her, and now I have lost my hearing; I can't describe enough how sad I am.

I will write to you tomorrow. I'm waiting for your letter.

From KIYOKO, *October 19.*

. . . DOES READING BOOKS MAKE your hearing worse? But writing letters does not? I can't believe that reading has such a bad effect on you; maybe it is the content of the books that makes you ill. Did the story of Robert and Clara Schumann have an ill effect on your hearing? The other day I read their story in the *Mainichi North America.* It was an abbreviated version of what you wrote to me.

Your teaching plan on Japanese conversation is very helpful, particularly now that I am teaching. If it doesn't bother your hearing too much, please continue. Last night I talked with Tsukiji-san on the phone about his class with mixed grade levels. He has one group read Japanese while the other practices writing. I thought it would not help in teaching conversation. . . . My way is to let them listen to sentences and give answers— an exercise through the ears all the way through. I give them handouts only for them to review the conversation at home. The other day we had fun. A student mimicked my way of talking as he answered loudly. I said it was like teaching children in Japan. He thought I might get mad and didn't know how to take my response.

I wanted to finish this letter and mail it tonight, but I worked together with Hisayo instead to help with Yukiko's school project. We worked on it till 11:30. Yukiko had made her old dress into a costume for Pilgrims in the Thanksgiving display, and she was very proud of it. But some classmate said it was junk. Yukiko came home crying. Hisayo took her to the NB store, bought new material, and then we all started to work. I made a pattern for the dummy and helped to sew the dress. Hisayo made a little Bible with red leather. Yukiko was so happy. Tomorrow is the show. My goodness, we barely made it!

I felt light-headed all day today—maybe because of the approach of that monthly thing—knocking over a glass of milk, confusing people's names, etc. I told somebody that he was looking for himself. I said he himself was looking for him. He said "Oh yeah?" while looking around! I made Linda laugh because I said "I am dishing wash." Nowadays she is well settled in, and we are getting along fine. You may sense that your wife is doing OK. . . .

From KIYOSHI, *October 19.*

. . . A BEAUTIFUL AUTUMN DAY IN Japan. I was so depressed yesterday because I didn't get your letter. I tried to think it over and get back to my senses. I'm not in the best condition, but I feel all right. I'll be back to my normal self if your letter comes today.

Are you all right, Kiyoko-san? How is Yukiko? How is her school work? I wonder how she is handling her homework. I think that she has good comprehension. I think that if she has a good teacher, she will achieve quite a high standard of scholarship. If she took after you, she would be a good student. I guess she took after me! A girl child tends to take after the father and a boy child after the mother, so they say. Maybe it is true.

Today's newspaper reports the latest news of the Russian space program—the landing of Venus No. 4 on the planet Venus. . . .

The second page is filled with the news on the Vietnam War. The singer Joan Baez was arrested in Oakland. On the 21st there will be an anti-war demonstration in front of the Pentagon, and over 70,000 people are expected to join this anti-war movement. It is said that the government is going to take a tough position against the demonstrators. . . . On the domestic side, there is the problem of segregation. With these problems, what will become of America? Maybe they made a very small mistake at the very beginning; maybe that mistake became larger because it was wrong from the beginning; maybe things got worse as the government tried to patch up that wrong start.

A similar analysis can be applied to our life. It's so important to have a correct start. Take my case, for example: my life is developing in a bad sequence of events because I had tuberculosis. I hope it stops at some point, and in reverse, develops toward a healthy life. The bad circumstances have become so convoluted that it takes more and more of our energy. But we cannot give up. It looks just like the Vietnam War—all the nations connected to the U.S. are drawn into it—like you are drawn into my undesirable sequence of events.

This is not a pleasant thought. When I don't have a letter from you, I don't know what to think. I feel despondent; even my body feels heavy. Can't you write just a few lines? Have I become such a burden to you? I am so sad.

What a deplorable letter! I am so depressed.

From KIYOSHI, *October 19.*

. . . YOUR LETTERS CAME FINALLY! . . . I was so exhausted from expectation and anxiety. I felt better after I read them. I'm glad you are all right.

Thank you for going to the open house event at Yukiko's school. I think it is important to keep close contact with the school. About her neglecting her homework—every day check with her at the dinner table to see if she has finished it. Tell her to finish her homework before dinner time, and after dinner, take a look at it. How is she doing with multiplication and division? I think this is the most important period for learning these basics. . . .

I am so glad that you like my way of teaching Japanese conversation. Your approval is what I value most, and the respect I get from you is the best encouragement I can have. . . .

Writing a syllabus is important, but practicing in the classroom is also important. Drill the whole class by row from front to back and left to right; call on each student, and finish by having a student teach the class. I developed this method when I was teaching English in Japan; it was very effective, particularly the way it utilized time in the classroom. Book, pen, knife, pencil, notebook, desk, chair, window, blackboard, etc.—present these objects by threes—it will help you tremendously. When you ask これは＿＿＿ですか (*kore wa ＿＿＿ desu ka*) [Is this ＿＿＿?], you have to be prepared to follow with どれが＿＿＿ですか (*dore ga ＿＿＿ desu ka*) [Which is ＿＿＿?], それが＿＿＿です (*sore ga ＿＿＿ desu*) [That is ＿＿＿.] and これも＿＿＿ですか (*kore mo ＿＿＿ desu ka*) [Is this ＿＿＿ too?]. Therefore you need three objects to carry on the conversation. One round takes seven or eight minutes; 80 minutes fly by easily. I'll continue with this teaching plan. I'm so happy to know we are working together. It is just like us.

To answer your question about my room—the profile of a beautiful woman is on a calendar that the pharmacy gave me—also hanging is a ball that Ōtomo-san gave me (it's a pretty ball that her friend made by hand)—I wrote about it some days ago. Ōtomo-san is the best among the patients of college age. She writes to me from time to time, but her health is unstable with frequent headaches.

Please talk to the school about Watanabe-sensei and of a possible invitation to him to give seminars in America; just to listen to him would make attending the session worthwhile. He would be very pleased if you helped to arrange an invitation. If the Buddhist Association arranged a lecture tour, the Golden Gate Gakuen and the Gyōsei Gakuen would want to invite him also. . . .

From KIYOSHI, *October 20.*

. . . THE ALL-JAPAN BASEBALL SEASON starts tomorrow with Kyojin against Hankyū. The newspaper says Kyojin will win. The hot news is about Twiggy from London who wears a mini-skirt as short as 20 inches high above her knees. The mayor of Oakland and his wife are visiting Fukuoka, the sister city of Oakland. They are overwhelmed by the famous Japanese entertainment for foreign visitors. They were thrilled to find the similarity of their park in Oakland to Ōhori Park here. Among the topics discussed is the exchange of students and of teachers teaching the first grade to high school level. . . .

The anti-war demonstration in Washington, D.C., planned for the 21st, appears to be a colossal event; over 10,000 military and police are being mobilized. The Japanese paper shows a keen interest in the movement. Also reported is that the New York Democrats will lead a nationwide anti-Johnson-for-the-next-president movement. Is it true? . . .

The other day I wrote that I take oxygen that costs 4,000 yen, didn't I? The pharmacist who sells that medicine told me yesterday that he made mention of me to a Professor Horita. According to Dr. Horita, there are many cases of displaced vertebrae among the patients who have lost their hearing after taking a certain medicine; the vertebrae are the center of the nervous system. When the vertebrae are displaced, the nerves connected to the ears lose their proper function. Dr. Horita told the pharmacist that I need to have a chiropractic adjustment on my vertebrae. I'm going to talk to Dr. Shirabe about this. I know my vertebrae are not straight after the operation I had years ago. Dr. Horita's theory makes sense. . . .

From KIYOKO, *October 21.*

. . . YESTERDAY I RECEIVED FOUR letters, one written on the 14th, two on the 15th, and one on the 16th. In the letter that came last Thursday, you were saying that your temperature was 36.1 and you felt good. Now you say you are not feeling well—I don't understand. Today I received the one you wrote on the 17th, two on the 18th, and one on the 19th.

Yukiko angrily reports that Debora is jealous of the new dress in the tableau and says that Yukiko must have bought it. I told Yukiko that maybe she should invite Debora to the house. I think the life of children at this age is rough as they are not able to conceal their raw emotion. . . . It appears that Yukiko withdrew her work from the display after these arguments.

I think your idea on the encyclopedia is excellent—we should buy it this year. By the way, Yukiko's handwriting and her use of paper are improving greatly, as the teacher promised at the Parent-Teacher Association meeting to emphasize this. The papers that she brought home yesterday prove it, and she didn't make many mistakes either.

About the bride-candidate for Yotsuo-san: I think I should go see him and his family and describe her to them. It's after two p.m. now, but as soon as I finish this letter, I'll go. I think she sounds good for Yotsuo-san, but I don't know whether he wants a bride from Japan. Maybe you should send me a photo of the lady. I forgot which is first; the lady should see the man's photo first, or the other way around. But in this case, since you talked to the lady about Yotsuo-san already, it may be better to send his photo to you. We'll decide after I have talked to them this afternoon.

You are lonely for my letters—I am so sorry that I'm slow in writing while you've written more than 100 letters already.

Early yesterday morning I went to have an x-ray taken. The technicians there as well as the nurses were surprised to hear about you, and everybody wished for your quick recovery. The technician said that it was not easy to imagine what you've been through unless one has had the same experience. I fully agree with her. I said that sometimes I could not fathom your pain and anxiety even though I am your wife. . . .

From KIYOSHI, *October 21.*

SATURDAY, OCTOBER 21, 9:15 A.M. — A BEAUTIFUL AUTUMN day with just a speck of clouds. I feel great! How are you, Kiyoko-san? . . .

Prime Minister Yoshida of Japan died yesterday, and the paper is filled with articles on him. He was the first Prime Minister to govern the country five times in succession, surpassing Prime Minister Itō Hakubun who headed three successive cabinets. Yoshida was a dictator; he would call out to others, "You idiot!" and throw his glass of water at the press corps. But he was a great leader leaving great work behind. He reminds me of Churchill in Britain who understood humor too. I think Yoshida was Japan's best Prime Minister.

In the comics section in yesterday's evening paper, there was one about a jump in the price of vegetables because of the long dry season. There was a funny line: "The price of vegetables jumps—now it's my turn!" signed by 大根役者 (daikon *yakusha)* meaning a poor actor on the stage. I laughed and laughed.

I now have the receipts of another month's spending—I'm going to mail them to you next week. . . . Next month I'll know better whether I should continue this treatment or not, and then we can talk about sending more money. First I'll see if the oxygen works or not. . . .

From KIYOSHI, *October 21.*

. . . IT IS 5:35 IN THE AFTERNOON. I rested after dinner and wrote a letter to Yukiko. How are you, Kiyoko-san? This is the time of the day when I miss you so much.

Today being Saturday, several former patients came to visit my ward as outpatients. It was like a month or two ago here. Everybody looked well. Ōtomo-san remembered that this was about the time I have to convert my hospital expenses from the receipts into dollars and brought her abacus with her. She finished the conversion within five minutes—it is quite an art and stupendous just to watch her! After that, Shizuma-san and Ōtomo-san and I had lunch together. After three p.m. the group went to town. I was invited but declined. I needed some rest, but also I wasn't enthusiastic about romping around with such young people. . . .

Dr. Shirabe told me today that the carbon dioxide inhaler may be ready next week. He will be going to Tokyo to attend a medical society meeting for 10 days starting tomorrow. Some other doctor will take over in his absence. . . .

A man called Yamato-san (in the photo) also came today and gave me a 1968 notebook of the Railway Mutual Benefit Association. There is a list of statistics in it. A 44-year-old male will continue to live for 28.56 years more, and a 39-year-old female for 37 years more. An age-100 male, 0.59 years more; a female, 0.67 years; a 90-year-old male, 2.14 years; a female, 2.46 years. Every year you are told how many more years you would live. I have 28 more years to go—I will make it healthy, happy, and purposeful. How about that?

From KIYOSHI, *October 22.*

. . . I HOPE THE USE OF THE carbon dioxide inhaler starts this week.

Here in Japan people are carried away now by baseball—the Nihon Series. Yesterday Kyojin won. Premier Satō took over after Premier Yoshida's death. He went to Vietnam but stayed there for only three hours and went to Ōiso after returning. Other news is about the anti-Vietnam-War march in America and a prediction of the demonstration on the last day of the event: the government's estimate is 10 to 20 thousand people as opposed to the organizers' estimate of 70 to 80 thousand. Some troubles in Oakland are reported too. How about your area?

Anyway, how are you, Kiyoko-san? It is 9:45 a.m. here; and 4:45 p.m. in America. You must be getting ready to go home. I try to imagine every move you are making. . . .

How are you coming with the Japanese Language School? Is my input working? I don't think it is necessary to separate the upper class and the lower class. It could be that the lower class may do better than the upper class. If conversation is the objective, as Tokunaga-sensei says, there is no need to separate them. You stick only to questions and answers. It is like a child learning to speak through a drill with his mother. It does not come from learning to read and understanding sentences. Reading and understanding may help to enrich knowledge, but it is quite different from speaking. You have to change your method depending on your objective. For conversation, question and answer is the only way.

I'm thinking of the progressive form now. Teaching it together with the imperative form will make an interesting exercise. For example, you tell one of the students, Hanako-san, to stand up:

花子さん、立ってください。
hanako-san, tatte kudasai.
Hanako-san, please stand up.

Then ask the class a chain of questions:

花子さんは立っていますか
hanako-san wa tatte imasu ka
Is Hanako-san standing?

花子さんは座っていますか
hanako-san wa suwatte imasu ka
Is Hanako-san sitting down?

Next have Hanako-san go to the door slowly:

花子さん、ドアの所に行ってください。
hanako-san, doa no tokoro ni itte kudasai.
Hanako-san, please go to the door.

While she is walking to the door, ask the class:

花子さんはドアの所に行っていますか、窓の所に行っていますか
hanako-san wa doa no tokoro ni itte imasu ka, mado no tokoro ni itte imasu ka
Is Hanako-san walking toward the door, or toward the window?

Now tell Hanako-san to open the door slowly:

花子さん、ドアをゆっくり開けてください。
hanako-san, doa o yukkuri ake te kudasai.
Hanako-san, please open the door slowly.

While she is opening the door slowly, ask the class:

花子さんはドアをあけていますか、窓をあけていますか

hanako-san wa doa o ake te imasu ka, mado o ake te imasu ka

Is Hanako-san opening the door, or opening the window?

Do the above exercise for "return to your seat" and "sit down on the seat" actions. In other words, make the students move around using the imperative form and carry on the questions and answers in progressive form. This should be very effective as well as a lot of fun. If we delve into it further, I'm sure we can find many effective methods of teaching conversation. . . .

From KIYOKO, *October 23.*

. . . ON SATURDAY I WENT TO Watsonville to talk to Yotsuo-san. He was alone loading boxes on the truck. He said that he had no preference or worry over marrying a Japanese, but he worries about his earnings. I told him he didn't have to worry about the cost of the air ticket because he could pay in installments. He will talk to his family and will let me know. His situation is different from three years ago so it may work this time, I hope. . . .

Yukiko didn't go to school today because of overeating again. She should feel better tomorrow. I think she is at the age now to be troubled with stomachaches—I remember Hiroyuki at Yukiko's age ate more than seven *botamochi* and vomited from overeating. I myself have a record of eating seven cups of *gumeshi*, but I didn't have a stomachache. Last Friday evening we had sukiyaki, and Yukiko, disregarding my warning, ate twice as much as the others. By the way, the death of both Hideshima Shichisaburō-san and Premier Yoshida was caused by overeating at parties. I told Mother not to eat too much at her parties. I think food should be served sparely to elderly people. Somebody wrote about it in the newspaper after Hideshima-san's death. . . .

Yesterday I was cutting articles from the newspaper to help Yukiko with her homework—and I read a report that our space program or the Apollo Project, as it's called, that has been in progress may have to be disbanded because of the success of the Russian Program. The report says that the progress on our project has been sacrificed due to the Vietnam War. Doesn't it look like America got stung by a bee on her already painful wound although she sent gentlemanly applause to Russia? . . .

From KIYOSHI, *October 23.*

. . . HIROYUKI-SAN AND HIS WIFE came yesterday. They came around 4:15 p.m. and stayed till five p.m. Ōtomo-san's group took leave at four. I saw them to the door, and there Hiroyuki-san and Noriko-san were just coming in. They brought a large box of カステラ (*kasutera*) and a lot of photos of their honeymoon to Miyazaki and Kagoshima. Their wedding photo will be mailed to us later. I sent the *kasutera* to the nurses' station because I can't eat that much by myself.

I am invited to Hiroyuki-san's place this Saturday for a dinner of 鯛 (*tai*). 鯛 is expensive, about 500 yen for one fish. I gave them 2,000 yen ($5.50) for four fish; three to cook and one for sashimi because they have just spent so much for the wedding. I feel better this way.

I asked them to get a pair of boots for Yukiko. Noriko-san asked about the size. Do you want the kind that goes over the shoes? Noriko-san is thinking of the kind that you wear without shoes. Please describe what you want in detail. . . .

Ōtomo-san stayed with her relatives for two nights. She came to see me again and gave me a pamphlet on the clinical study done on the ultrashort-wave treatment (超短波治療) at Tokyo Imperial University. According to this, applying the ultrashort wave to the affected body part, the capillary vessels there expand more than 10 times their size. And even the injection of a strong agent like adrenalin cannot hold back this enlargement by the short wave. I'm going to ask the doctor about this today. I am very much interested in the data from the clinical study at the best university in the country. This electronic treatment costs a little over $200. There is a list of symptoms among which mine is included. If the doctor recommends it, I would like to buy it, of course, with your permission.

I will write again after talking to the doctor.

From KIYOSHI, *October 23.*

. . . SOON AFTER I FINISHED THE earlier letter, Watanabe-sensei came to see me. I asked him to read the pamphlet on the ultrashort-wave machine. When Dr. Sakamoto came to give me a shot, I asked him also to read it, and the two doctors discussed it. Dr. Sakamoto said that one has to make sure that there won't be any harmful side effects; particularly in the case of the ears, one has to watch out for excess circulation of the blood. For ordinary injuries, this treatment should work well. He said that I might purchase the machine and have a hospital technician operate it for me. The final approval of this treatment, however, should come with the unanimous approval of professors, assistant professors, the physician-in-charge, the head of the physicians, and Sakamoto-sensei. The price is 79,000 yen. The insurance may cover it, at least partially, as a medical and surgical supply.

I have 174,000 yen left at the hospital accounting office. Subtracting my monthly expense of 24,000 yen and the hospital cost of between 100,000 to 110,000 yen, I will have 40,000 yen left after November 15. I will need another 40,000 yen if I buy the machine at the beginning of November. Can you send me $500? It will cover the hospital cost of $320 for the following month, $150 toward the cost of the machine, and $65 for my personal expenses. You don't have to wire the money; regular air mail will do. This should cover my hospital stay till December 15. I'm sorry for this extra expense, but I want to try everything I can to be cured.

Next, about Watanabe-sensei. I told him that you feel very bad not to have thanked him in writing, and that you barely have time to write to me even. Today's letter from you (the one you wrote on the 17th) expresses your regret, and I showed it to him. He said don't worry about it. He was very happy to hear that we are working together on the project of teaching Japanese conversation based on his method. I told him that you are thinking of asking Tokunaga-sensei of the Buddhist Association to observe your class hoping that the association will sponsor Watanabe-sensei's visit to California. I hope that will happen. Sensei and I also talked about the program of exchanging teachers. But I'll write about it tomorrow since I'm running out of space. I'm so grateful to Watanabe-sensei, particularly talking about the ultrashort-wave treatment with Sakamoto-sensei. . . .

From KIYOSHI, *October 23.*

. . . I HOPE YOU ARE NOT TIRED of reading my letters! The following *waka* has stuck in my mind for all these years and makes me long for you more.

来しかたも	*koshi kata mo*
行方も知らぬ	*yukue mo shiranu*
沖に出て	*oki ni dete*
あわれいずくに	*aware izuku ni*
君を恋うらん	*kimi wo kouran*

I don't know
where I was
or where I'll be—
in the open sea, floating . . .
I miss you so!

わびぬれば   *wabi nureba*
いまはたおなじ   *ima hata onaji*
なにはなる   *naniwa naru*
みをつくしても   *mi wo tsukushitemo*
あわんとぞ思う   *awan tozo omou*

lonely . . .
passing now
by the familiar Osaka waterway,
I want to meet you
even if I die from rowing

みし夢を   *mishi yume wo*
あう夜ありやと   *au yo ariya to*
なげくまに   *nageku ma ni*
目さえあわでぞ   *me sae awadezo*
ころもへにける   *koromo he ni keru*

I dream of you . . .
but never met you
at night,
not even a glance at each other . . .
just passing by

海恋し   *umi koishi*
水色の空   *mizuiro no sora*
たそがれて   *tasogare te*
われに語らう   *ware ni katarau*
星ひとつあり   *hoshi hitotsu ari*

I miss the sea.
the blue sky is
getting dark . . .
a star
is talking to me

I'm amazed at myself because I still remember these poems. I recited these poems to you, remember? And I said, "Promise not to forget me—you have not changed—I am not changed—please do not change ever!" How about this daddy?! One time you said to me, "Kiyoshi-san, you remember so well what you learned in school. I've forgotten everything." Then I said, "I am slow-witted, but I don't forget quickly." Do you remember now?

I am impressed myself—this 44-year-old man! I still remember things that I learned in my teens; maybe I can still sing my high school song! The first and second *waka* are very good expressions of my yearning for you. I miss you so much.

Now, let's talk about Watanabe-sensei. I told him about the tightening of spending in the state universities, as Hisayo-san once mentioned. Among the private colleges, Sensei picked Santa Clara University and Mills College, and he wants to find out the following:

> 1. Is Japanese taught presently, or are there plans to offer a course in the future?
>
> 2. Is there a teacher-exchange program presently, or will there be one?

Ask Hisayo-san to phone the two colleges and say:

> 1. "Does your school have a Japanese-language course?" If the answer is no, then:
> 2. "Are you planning to have one someday?"
> 3. "Does your school have an interest in an exchange program with one of the leading universities in Japan?" If the answer is maybe, then:
> 4. "A friend of mine who is a professor at Kyushu University is looking for a college that has an interest in an exchange program with his university. He will be very happy to write to your college (or university) and explain the program."

Please ask Hisayo-san to phone the college. She can repeat what I wrote word for word. She should know which office of these colleges to call.

From KIYOSHI, *October 24.*

... SHIZUMA-SAN CAME THIS afternoon and told me about last week's party. Getting together nowadays is so different from when we were young. First of all, cafes and dance halls have become their gathering places. In our day, a dance hall was a place for special people; it was sort of a forbidden place for ordinary folks. Now everybody goes there just like going to a restaurant. Shizuma-san asked if I danced. When I said "No," she looked puzzled. She said I should practice so she and I can go dancing. I was shocked! She is good at dancing American dances such as the Monkey and the Go-Go, she says. And, of course, she can dance to blues, waltz, or tango music. The group had a really good time. She asked, "*Oji-san*, do you know how to cheek dance?" I said "No." She said, "Last time we saw a really hot pair!" and laughed loudly. "They were dancing in front of us," she continued, "and we thought the man was chewing gum while he danced—but no, he was chewing the woman's ear!" ...

Her openness and cheerfulness are something! I talked about the search for candidates for Yotsuo-san's wife—Ōtomo-san and Tachibana-san were still with us. Shizuma-san jumped up and said, "I want to be one of the candidates!" I told her, "But he is 40! Be serious, and think of yourself." She is so open. . . .

She respects us very much and told a lady doctor about us. She wants to have a married life like ours. I told her that such a marriage can be realized only when two people together put their effort into building a happy marriage. She listened to me very attentively. I told her that one cannot find the happiness of love just by dreaming—one has to work for it. . . .

From KIYOKO, *October 25.*

... TWO LETTERS, DATED October 21 and 22, and one to Yukiko arrived yesterday. I'm so relieved to hear that you feel much better. I'm deeply impressed by Ōtomo-san. Yukiko read your letter without my help—she had only two questions. I asked her to summarize the content, and she gave me the gist of what you wrote.

This is going to be a hasty letter. I have been summoned by the school. It says that Mitsuko-san tends to be late to school because she oversleeps; she skips classes when she cannot make it or she does not like the subject. Her counselor is furious—but Mitsuko-san herself is not disturbed at all.

I told her about the summons and asked what was going on. She said, "It's the teacher's fault. Probably she marked me as absent when I was late to mathematics class. You don't have to skip work to see the counselor. I'll see her myself because it is my problem." My blood pressure soared, and I almost got sick. Evidently this is the second incident and the administration office is considering invalidating her student visa. Mitsuko-san is not perturbed at all and says "I didn't do anything wrong." At this I lost my temper and told her, "You were wrong—you failed to fulfill your responsibility as a student!" I'll be in school at eight o'clock in the morning. I just shampooed my hair and dried it. I am not going to tell this to Yoshimitsu-san.

I read an article about high school and college students in modern Japan in *Bungei-shunjū* [文芸春秋] that Mitsuyo passed on to me. According to this article, there is an increasing number of students who are repeating the same grade with *ryūnen* [留年] marks (repeat the grade), or they don't go to school at all and receive *rakudai* [落第] marks (flunk the course). These students insist that they won't go to school unless they like the courses. They think that schools in America are even more relaxed—isn't it absurd! I'd better calm down, and see the counselor tomorrow. Yukiko has been bothering me also with this and that while I'm writing this letter. I told her, "Don't bother me!" She said, "OK, finish your letter," and now she is mumbling something in her bed. This is such an unpleasant evening.

So, Hiroyuki and Noriko-san finally came to see you. Did they say anything about the candies that we specially wrapped and sent by air mail for the wedding? Since your sister paid for the candy, I must write to Hiroyuki about it. When you go for *tai-ryōri* [鯛料理] with him, please mention it. Try *tai-no-sashimi* on hot rice with seaweed, put shoyu over it, and pour hot green tea—it is delicious!

Today we received a book from Nōtomi Zenroku-san called *Around the World Surveying Education*. It is a travel log written by several people. . . . I'll make a copy tomorrow and send it to you.* I have a chance to write a thank-you note to Nōtomi-san, but I'd like you to draft it.

The length of Yukiko's foot is slightly less than 9 inches. . . .

*See attachment to Kiyoko's letter of October 26.

From KIYOSHI, *October 25.*

. . . THE INSURANCE PAPERS ARE ready now. I'll have Shizuma-san mail them from the post office in Tenjin-machi. I'm going to give her 200 yen for the taxi and other expenses. . . .

It appears that the Israelis and the Arabs are fighting again at the Suez Canal. There are troubles everywhere. President Johnson seems to have stepped forward to suppress America's anti-war movement. In New York about 50,000 demonstrators gathered to support the war in Vietnam giving the impression of hawks and doves starting to engage in a melee. Why can't we live peacefully?! It seems that man is born only to be killed by another man—it is sad. Why can't the world become one united entity? I guess each nation's rights and interests are preventing that from happening. I just don't like the killing—I wish young people in their twenties would stand up against the war, not just in America but in Russia and in all other parts of the world. . . .

These days I ponder often on my future and our future. I feel hopeful sometimes—other times I feel desperately lonely. I know there is no reason to feel abandoned, but sometimes I can't help it. It is because I've been separated from you for such a long time. But I'm trying to see the bright side. One has to hold on tight to his life till his last day. . . .

I had a conversation the other day with Ōtomo-san about this abandoned feeling. She too is suffering headaches and ringing in her ears. I told her that for her to rest is to work. For her, resting doesn't mean doing nothing—it means she is resting to get better. We all have to do our best in whatever situation we are placed in. We shouldn't give up our hope to get better. She is 23 years old. The medical world improves constantly; someday her young body will answer to some new medicine, and she will be cured. We must try hard till the last moment of life—we must not give it up. Try to live until we draw our last breath in. (I tell this to myself.) . . .

From KIYOSHI, *October 26.*

I'M SO GLAD THAT YUKIKO HAS BECOME A BETTER student at school. The teacher's "push" is more effective than the parents'. Students are lucky if their teacher has that push. . . .

About her sewing a garment for a display dummy—she made a dress of an imaginative style, but its merit was not appreciated by the class, or her teacher. It was unfortunate, but you can't do much about it because the judgment was hinged upon the level of the teacher's esthetic taste. We should praise Yukiko's originality, which the teacher missed, and encourage her creativity. The teacher has an influence on Yukiko in other areas such as handwriting and the use of paper. I am very pleased by this report. I think your talk with the teacher at the school's Open House made for a good result here. Please consult her and get the opinions of others to find the best encyclopedia for Yukiko. Also, when *LIFE* magazine publishes the complete collection of the *Science Encyclopedia* again, we must buy it this time.

I'm grateful that you made a special trip to Watsonville on account of Yotsuo-san's future wife. I look forward to hearing more about the results of your talk.

You said that you went to take another x-ray; how often do you have x-rays? Is this for some new problems? I'm concerned—please tell me more about it.

When I see Hiroyuki-san next time, I'll ask him to get the medicine for piles. I'm thinking of buying the following books: a dictionary of archaic words, a Chinese and Japanese dictionary of ancient events and proverbs, a dictionary of synonyms, and 20 files to give to our friends who sent me off with money. We might need about 10 of these at home to organize our papers. Also I'm thinking of things for Yukiko. I will ask Hiroyuki-san to send these to America. The other day I wrote that my projected expenses till the middle of December would be about $500. Could you please send me another $100 for these purchases when you can?

I feel good today. Hankyū won one game, and it is getting more exciting to watch. If they win today, it will be even more interesting.

Shizuma-san came to see me. She wants me to advise her about a man she is in love with. . . . I'll write more about this later. . . .

From KIYOSHI, *October 26.*

. . . I'M GLAD TO HEAR THAT your Japanese class is going well. (I stopped here and had dinner.) Tonight or tomorrow I am going to write on the progressive form. Nothing makes me more content than helping you and making you happy.

In this morning's letter, I mentioned Shizuma-san. I feel so sorry for her. She and Ōtomo-san shared a room for more than a year. It must have been hard for Shizuma-san, at times, because Ōtomo-san was popular among the men. Shizuma-san went out of her way to help some of the men patients, but all departed without showing any interest in her. Now she is engrossed in taking care of a liver patient who is under complete rest, but he does not show any sign of interest in her, or even gratitude for her, even though she does errands for him. He tells her that he had a relationship with more than 10 women and lived together with one of them for about 10 months; he said he would like to get married and maintain a home with a woman, but he will not stop having relationships outside of marriage. Shizuma-san was shocked to hear him say such a thing, but she cannot stop herself from adoring him. She has never had sex with a man. Last night she came to see me and asked me to talk to him. I told her that forcing a relationship does not work any more than forcing a bud by prying it open. She was in tears and said, "I want to have a boyfriend." I felt so sorry for her. She says, "I don't mind living with his mother, or that he has 10 other women—I just want to have a boyfriend like everybody else." Poor girl . . . it must be so hard to be left alone that way—maybe the loneliness she suffers is way beyond our comprehension. I used to tell her that she was still young, etc., etc.—but it doesn't work anymore. What do you think I should tell her? She respects what I have to say, and that makes just offering her soothing words all the more difficult. On the one hand there is a girl who is transported with the joy of love; on the other, there is a girl who longs for a companion even though no one pays the slightest attention to her; it is not fair! Ōtomo-san has a serious health problem, but everybody loves her; no one wants Shizuma-san even though she is in good health—which girl is unfortunate, I wonder. Ōtomo-san even thinks of death; Shizuma-san cries for want of a boyfriend—I think I understand both of them.

   This turned out to be a sad letter. I can't help but think how lucky I am to have you! . . .

From KIYOKO, *October 26.*

. . . THE TEACHERS ARE EXTREMELY perturbed by Mitsuko-san because her attendance in her classes is so poor. She was asked why she didn't come to class for three consecutive days; her answer was "because of nervous prostration." That made the teacher amused, but it was not an acceptable answer, of course. Mitsuko-san started to challenge the teacher in rough language so I had to tell her in Japanese, "Don't talk that way as you might make the teacher angry." She cut her morning class for 10 consecutive days so far, and this is the last warning from the school.

We came home. Mitsuko-san looked undisturbed as if nothing had happened. I couldn't believe it! In school she was so mad that her face turned pale. I don't know what to make of her. At least it's better than crying, or fretting, or becoming unruly.

I am sending a copy from the book that I mentioned in my last letter. I enclosed a photo of Yukiko that was taken at Hisayo's graduation ceremony. . . .

I'm sorry for these hasty letters. I think the super electronic machine that you wrote about sounds good, but what did the doctor say? Did you ask him about your misaligned vertebrae too? I'm anxiously waiting for your next letter on this. . . .

I miss your cheerful smiling face!

[Enclosed: *Education in the World—a Diary of my Tour in Europe and America*, by Nōtomi Zenroku.]

"VISIT TO KIYOSHI TOKUTOMI'S RESIDENCE"

Tuesday, August 24th. It was near evening when we arrived at San Francisco Airport from Chicago flying over the Rocky Mountains and crossing the continent of America. Mr. Tokutomi was waiting at my hotel. Ten years had passed since I saw him last at the train station when he left Saga City. He is a fine gentleman. I taught him at the Saga Shihan School (a teacher's school at the junior college level). After the end of the war, he was teaching at Nabeshima Middle School. Some years later, he and his mother returned to San Francisco where he was born.

I accepted his invitation, and we drove to San Jose where his house is. It took about one hour. The road was nicely paved so that we drove probably at about 80 kilometer per hour.

It turned out that Mrs. Tokutomi was one of my students at the Women's School of Saga Shihan. She read my postcard and knew that I was coming. But she was not home because she had already made plans to visit Japan with a Japanese-American tour group. I decided to see her in Saga when I return home. It was after eight o'clock at night when we reached Mr. Tokutomi's house. His mother and Mr. and Mrs. Tsukiji Eiichi were waiting for us. Mr. Tsukiji is a close friend of Mr. Tokukomi, and his parents are from Nakahara in Saga Prefecture.

We had good conversation in the drawing room enjoying the buffet dinner that Mr. Tokutomi's mother had prepared. We talked about the Japanese residents in California successfully engaged in various jobs, and their children—how they are making high grades competing with Americans in the American education system. We talked about the teachers in Saga Shihan whom we both knew; about the alumni; about Saga City and Saga Prefecture.

Mr. Tokutomi is presently employed by a trading company because the State of California requires the strictest teaching credentials in the United States. Mrs. Tokutomi works at a precision machinery company after passing a test as one of the top two out of 60 applicants for the position; the other successful applicant was a German lady.

Mr. Tsukiji graduated from a university in America and Tokyo University in Japan. He speaks English and Japanese equally well.

It was a wonderful evening reminiscing about the old days. When Mr. and Mrs. Tsukiji took their leave, it was after 11 o'clock. I took a bath and went to bed about half past twelve. The Tokutomis' bed and bath are about the same as the ones in the hotels where we had stayed. The next morning I got up at seven. After breakfast, Mr. Tokutomi drove me back to San Francisco.

From KIYOSHI, *October 27.*

. . . I HAD A PHONE CALL yesterday from an unexpected person. Can you guess who it was? I couldn't go to the phone, but the nurse brought a note. It was Haruta-san; he's in Japan with a tour group. The nurse forgot to ask him where he was staying, but I think he was calling from Fukuoka. It was a pleasant surprise.

About the nurse who could be a good candidate for Yotsuo-san's wife—she wrote me a letter asking for time to think. She is an exceptionally nice girl. It must be very difficult to decide. She says it would take courage to accept this proposal right away, and so she could use a little more time to think it over. Her letter shows her sincerity, so much so that I wish she could accept this offer. Should I talk to her again, I wonder. I guess I should wait for your letter which should come today or tomorrow.

The baseball season has moved into an interesting stage. The Hankyū team is in the lead now, 3 to 2; it will be 3-3 if they lose tomorrow. We might see an exciting game in the final match. Kyojin is still the favorite, though. The venue moves to Osaka today, and tomorrow the sixth game will be there. Everybody, including me, is excited.

The big news around here is about a student from Kyushu University School of Medicine being detained in the United States. It was reported in detail in the *Asahi-shinbun* and other local papers. A professor in the United States published as his own a joint thesis prepared together with Dr. Hazama. Utterly dejected, Dr. Hazama wanted to return to Japan, but he was held up for various reasons until another joint researcher was found. However, the new researcher turned down the offer of the position when he heard about the conduct of the U.S. professor. Dr. Hazama's application for returning home was held up again, and this dispute is now in the courts. It is customary to take one's thesis back to his home country, and this type of obstruction is unheard of. This is an unfortunate incident after the promising start of the Japan-America Exchange of Scholars Program. The U.S. professor had been awarded a huge sum of money from the Bureau of U.S. Aeronautics because of Dr. Hazama's research, but that payment has been stopped now. Therefore the professor is taking all sorts of merciless steps to win his case. Here in Japan, a fund-raising campaign has been started in order to help Dr. Hazama. To have a man like this U.S. professor is a great embarrassment to America.

From KIYOSHI, *October 28.*

. . . HIROYUKI-SAN LEFT A MESSAGE at the office saying that he would pick me up at around six o'clock tonight. I look forward to having a dinner of sea bream with them.

How are you, Kiyoko-san? I am getting better. Yesterday Shizuma-san brought a lady's magazine called *Mademoiselle* [which] has many articles worth reading. The one I read was about Shimazaki Tōson. I didn't know much about Tōson except for his poem called "Chikuma-gawa" (千曲川) with that famous line, "White cloud in the sky over the Komoro Castle . . . I wander around with a heavy heart . . ." (小諸なる小城のほとり、雲白くゆうし悲しむ) and a novel entitled *Transgression* (破戒). I was shocked to read in this magazine an article about his countless affairs including with his niece who bore a child by him. Nonetheless the public adored him as a poet and writer in spite of the criticism of Akutagawa Ryūnosuke and a few others. Maybe the public accepted him because of his sincerity. His novel *New Life* (新生) is about his account of this illicit love affair.

I am happy to note that Hayashi Takeshi (a painter) is one of the recipients of the Order of Cultural Merit. It was reported in the newspaper today. He had refused to belong to any artists' group and worked alone all these years. That is why he was not recommended to the Academy of Japan and lived penniless for so long in spite of producing works superior in style and skill. When I read it I shouted, "He made it!" Now the Academy will have to embrace him because of this award. A man who works hard and produces the best products stays poor in our society. I think the decoration for Hayashi Takeshi helps to open people's eyes. He said, "My wife is very happy. The life of a painter's wife is so miserable, so much so that I think this award should go to her." How about that! I couldn't help but cry when I read this. I wish those artists and writers who lead loose lives chasing after women in the name of art would learn from Hayashi what a true artist's life is. It is a hard life. The Hayashis didn't have enough to eat; they were delivering bottles of milk to homes until 15 years ago. Takeshi says, "My wife gave up everything just to be with me . . . she is like a little girl, innocent and trusting." He has such a friendly, wrinkled, even charming face. Mrs. Hayashi said, "We toasted the Decoration—he was crying and hugged me tight." How about that, Kiyoko-san! Here is a painter who doesn't care how he looks—he just keeps working with paint all over him. His wife says, "He is crazy about painting; he will keep painting until he is 135 years old." She understands him so well . . . they shared hardship together for 50 years. I was so touched that I couldn't hold back the tears and couldn't read the print anymore. . . . I was so disappointed every time the Academy refused to include Hayashi Takeshi as a member. To Master Hayashi, however, it didn't matter one way or other. He must be so grateful for his wife's understanding of his need to be a painter. You can see one of his paintings in the magazine *Bungei-shunjū*, which we have. . . .

From KIYOKO, *October 29.*

. . . HALLOWEEN IS JUST AROUND the corner. I received two letters on Friday and learned that Watanabe-sensei came to see you. I wish we could have given him a better report from the Japanese Language School. It will take a year or so before the students get used to the freestyle conversation in the class. I conduct the class informally around the question-and-answer exchange, but some students tell me that they miss the textbooks.

Yesterday after school I went to the cemetery; and today your mother observed the 37th anniversary of your father's death at the gravesite inviting relatives to the house for a box lunch from Ginza. We just finished cleaning up. I wanted to write to you yesterday after a quick stop at the grocery, but I couldn't because I was so sleepy—I went to sleep without eating dinner. . . . I've been extremely tense for the last few days and could feel the exhaustion spread from the center of my head. But sleeping without having dinner might have helped—today I felt much better. I was able to do the laundry, clean the house better than usual, get ready for the grave visit 15 minutes early—so efficient—not like the usual Kiyoko. Maybe I've grown up at last. But it is somewhat uncomfortable if everything is done so perfectly. Thank God I'm still late reaching the office. . . .

Yesterday I had a chance to learn about the trends of young Japanese through your description of Shizuma-san. It is so different from our days, isn't it? However, when we were young, older people envied us. The situation is not much different.

A week ago Sunday in Hirose-san's TV program, "The Great Couple," there was a story about a man who sent love poems in the form of *waka* in *Man'yo* style to propose marriage. I thought it was such an elegant story— but now even my Kiyoshi-san sends me a bunch of *waka*! And here I am—a graduate of the Japanese Literature Department—forgetting all that I studied. I'm amazed at Kiyoshi-san's power of retention. . . .

Tokunaga-sensei of the Buddhist School makes me self-conscious—he thinks I am different from other teachers in the school. He now reads the Scriptures in Chinese; but at Grandfather's memorial service, he didn't do that. This is just between you and me. . . .

From KIYOSHI, *October 29.*

. . . I'M ABOUT TO LOSE CONFIDENCE. I came here three months ago to receive the carbonic acid treatment, but the machine is still not working—it is a serious blow to me. . . . But I am thinking of the alternative treatment with a machine using high-frequency waves. According to the pamphlet and literature on the machine, it doesn't appear to cause any bad side effects. It is used for treating inflammation of the tympanum so I can't think there would be any harm in using it for my ears. The doctor said that one has to be very careful not to over-stimulate the blood flow to the ear, which is very delicate. But there isn't any such warning stated in the literature. It is said that the blood circulation of capillary vessels will get better by 140% by the inhalation of the carbonic gas, whereas the application of the high-frequency waves produces almost 10 times the effect of carbonic gas inhalation. . . . I'm going to consult with Dr. Shirabe who will be back in the middle of this week. If they are afraid of over-stimulation, they wouldn't use it to treat an inflammation of the tympanum. But I've seen them using it on both ears. The result is very satisfactory—and it is due to stimulation of blood circulation. I must find something to make my condition improve.

As I wrote last time, I have enough money to last till November 15 if I don't buy the machine. If I buy the machine, I would like to have $500 extra together with the hospital expenses for December. Although I said not to rush earlier, please send it by air mail. I know I'm getting impatient. But I'm trying to calm myself down.

I visited Hiroyuki-san and Noriko-san yesterday. They treated me so well. They served sea bream sprinkled with salt and roasted. On top of it, sashimi and soup—they were so good! The seasoning was done by Noriko-san, and she is a good cook. Too bad they didn't have lemon—even so it was very tasty. I was happy to see them helping each other. We talked about the old days. Mutō-san is still teaching Japanese. Setsuko-san is also a teacher of Japanese—the standard of teaching is lower these days! Imaizumi-san was not bad then. But it appears that you were the last one who could teach Japanese well.

Yesterday Tachibana-san came to see me. She gave me a scroll as a birthday present. I told her that my birthday was the third of October—she thought it was November third. She is such a nice girl. Hinashi-san of Kyushu University also came to see me with several books by Kawabata Yasunari and Inoue Yasushi. He comes to see me so often—once every week or 10 days. I can't believe that I have visitors of such talent as he. I have not given him anything—not even a candy.

From KIYOSHI, *October 30.*

... KIYOKO-SAN, WHO DO YOU think came to see me today? I don't know where to start or how to report this event—Mrs. Matsumura and her father and Mayumi-*chan* came to see me! What a graceful family! I heard that the Japanese people had changed, and nowadays they have an attitude that's very impersonal. Maybe a certain group of the population has changed, but there are still some people who hold on to the traditional values and virtues. The Matsumuras brought a huge basket full of fruit. It is I who should have done something to express my condolence. We talked about how he [Mr. Matsumura] and I met, his visit to my house in San Jose, his help on my flight to Japan, and his visit to see me in the hospital. I showed the photo of Mayumi-*chan* which I keep in my wallet, and the letters that he sent me here. They were in tears—so was I. I read them your letter about the training accident and told them that you were so upset.

I can't find words to describe their noble intent to visit me in spite of their own grief. Please write them and give them your condolence and your gratitude for their visit to the hospital.

Dr. Shirabe returned today from the conference. I talked with him about the treatment using the ultrashort-wave machine. He didn't show any interest in it, maybe because the university has its own policy; besides they don't have funds to purchase the machine. However, I'd like to try it myself. I've been taking Arlidrin to stimulate the blood circulation. It works because a few hours after taking it, the ringing in my ears goes away. But it doesn't last long. The warning on its effectiveness is printed even in the literature. I highly respect the results of the clinical experiment at Tokyo University. Also other universities recognize the results of the experiment. But Dr. Shirabe told me not to use the machine as long as I am a patient here. Since the carbon inhalation machine is still out of order, I have no other route but using this ultrashort-wave treatment. But I have to purchase the machine, according to Dr. Sakamoto. On top of these problems, there will be a change of my physician-in-charge. There is no one who looks after me with responsibility.

In any case, please send the money because I want to get the machine and try it. I will talk to Dr. Sakamoto, who is the head of the doctors in this ward. I should not give up until I have tried everything I can. No, I will not give up! . . .

From KIYOKO, *October 31.*

TONIGHT IS HALLOWEEN NIGHT; A NUMBER OF BUNNIES and hippies are strolling on the streets. Yesterday I received so many letters from you—six in all, including the teaching plan of the progressive form. Which letter shall I respond to first?

First, the insurance papers. I received them in the office mailbox and took them to the insurance company after adding a little more to what you declared.

I'm sorry for Ōtomo-san who seems to have lost her hope for recovery. She might be just appealing for your sympathy—I hope so.

My x-ray appointment is one of those scheduled ones. The next one will be in April next year. I'm OK; please don't worry.

You seem to have started on the shopping list. I'd better let you know what we want. First, an electric rice cooker that serves five people for your sister; Cecilia wants a small rice server, *ohitsu*, the kind you see in the Restaurant Ginza; I want a larger one—about 30 centimeters in diameter for our family. Take your time—maybe have Hiroyuki help you instead of you going to the department store yourself. I will send $500 for the ultrashort-wave machine first, and after that, some more money for this shopping.

You must have opened counseling services in the hospital—and the business appears to get busier and more complicated! It is a very involved profession even for a healthy person, and you have to fight against your own health problems on top of that. The treatment for a case like Shizuma-san (a mental case) is difficult, but I'll try. She is overly anxious to find a boyfriend so that she scares men away, don't you think? I can understand her desire to be like all the other girls. But everybody is endowed with a nice side—some day someone will notice it. Until then, she should concentrate on nurturing herself culturally and mentally. . . . Tell her that if she chases after men, they will run away from her—tell her to cool off. If she can believe that someday the right man will come to her, and she prepares herself for that moment, she will become more attractive to men. Looking for a man so obviously is not only selling herself cheap but also forcing herself onto him.

You said that Haruta-san called. Just about when you left for Japan, there was a message from him on our telephone, but I might have forgotten to tell you. When I finished making the costume for Yukiko's school display some days ago, I thought I should phone the Harutas and thank them for their message. It was about nine o'clock in the evening. For about two and half hours I had to listen to Mrs. Haruta's complaints about her husband and mother-in-law. Maybe her menopause did this, but she said we have a much better life than they do. I told her that we didn't have problems like hers. Mrs. Haruta was staying home while her husband and his mother were in Japan. She was opposed to their trip to Japan and became consumed with jealousy toward his mother. I am so blessed, Kiyoshi-san, because I don't have such problems. I feel sorry for Mrs. Haruta who at her age, 50 or more, has an unhappy marriage. . . .

From KIYOSHI, *October 31.*

. . . I RECEIVED YOUR LETTER today with photos, and the one about the summons from school. Also a package arrived. I didn't have to pay a tax; furthermore it was delivered to the room.

Today's letter was a huge surprise. You received a summons from Mitsuko's school—it was like a bolt from the blue! Mitsuko doesn't prepare for her lessons, skips classes, etc—what's happening? No wonder the teachers are upset. I can't believe that Mitsuko is blaming her teachers, and even goes at you! What is my mother saying? If Mitsuko's grades are poor in spite of her effort, we can help her, but this is different. If there is no way to straighten her out, we may have to give up on her. If she continues to stay with us, we may fall into a pit of hating each other—my mother's worry and concern would double and drive her to nothing but despair. Isn't she already disappointed in Mitsuko? Please talk with my mother. If the school has issued the last warning, what can we do? One who receives a warning must try to correct his way. But, as *Yokozuna* Futabayama said, "One who is told not to will do anyway." Do you think we still have a chance to change Mitsuko's behavior? I don't think so. Anyhow don't say anything and just observe the situation for now. If the school sends a dismissal notice, don't respond to it; the best way is just send Mitsuko back to Japan without saying anything.

I am so shocked. Bad habits of going to bed late and leaving her room untidy, etc., don't mean anything compared to this. She lost the privilege of being a student by skipping school, ignoring her homework, and fighting with her teachers. Suppose she studied diligently and got high marks, but became pregnant. We could rescue her from such a situation, but not one like this.

How is Yukiko? I was happy to hear how nicely she read aloud my letter written in Japanese.

My physician-in-charge is now a young doctor called Torii-sensei. I have not yet talked with him about the ultrashort-wave machine, but I will. Since Sakamoto-sensei says I can try the machine as long as there is no side effect, I want to try it. Sakamoto-sensei is the head of the doctors in my ward and has to OK it. I cannot stay here forever without doing anything to treat my hearing.

Today is the birthday of Hinashi-san of Kyushu University. Shizuma-san wanted to surprise him with a present. I chipped in some money for a flower vase, and she took it to him. He came to see me today and gave me an hourglass to thank me for the birthday present. He is a nice young man, modest and yet brilliant. I gave him a bag of candy. He wants me to use this hourglass when I take my temperature. A great idea!

Thank you for the copy from the travel diary written by Nōtomi Zenroku-san. I wrote to Mrs. Matsumura and her father today. . . .

- これ⊞本ですか ぺ く
  これ⊞本です。
- こん⊞本ですか？
  いいえ、それ⊞本で
- では、これ⑰本ですか
  いいえ、それ⊞本
- (いけ) これ⊞本ですか
  いいえ、それ⊞本
- それでは、ど⑰⊞本です
  それ⊞本です。
- これ⑤本ですか？
  はい、そうです。

November

..

[THE *Long Night*]

From KIYOSHI, *November 1.*

... A BEAUTIFUL DAY BUT THE mountain is covered with smog. We used to say, "The clear autumn sky; the air is filled with the fragrance of chrysanthemums," but nowadays it is rare to have such a day. . . .

I am still stunned by yesterday's letter about Mitsuko. She skipped classes for 10 days without permission?! What nerve she has! How daring she is! I was thinking about it all day yesterday and came to a conclusion that we, as the responsible third party, should not get involved in this case. Instead we should ask my mother to write a letter to Japan. In it, be sure to mention that Mother is writing to ask their guidance so that whatever she says will not cause friction between the families. . . . Or, maybe we should wait until we receive a dismissal notice, and then just send her back to Japan? Maybe that is better than writing letters now to the family and going through unpleasant exchanges. Shall we take a hands-off position and wait for the expulsion note?

Come to think of it, my mother is unlucky. I feel sorry for her, losing her husband when she was very young. She lived through the hardship, which she still carries like a cross on her back. We had good intentions of trying to help Mother. But it looks like this is just more pain and sorrow for her. So is the best way for us to remain indifferent to the case? . . . Or, respect Mother's good intentions and go along with her wish to offer the child our help? Now everybody is in trouble—I can't let it go easily by just saying, "Sorry, we can't help." I don't know—what do you think, Kiyoko-san? Are we wrong? It's a difficult situation, isn't it?

This is a strange and indecisive letter—please think about the case carefully. I'll write again tomorrow. I'm reading the *Dictionary of Folklore and Proverbs* now. It's very interesting.

From KIYOKO, *November 2.*

. . . SUMMERTIME IS OVER, AND it is dark when I come home from work. Winter is approaching, but the weather is unusually warm—maybe this is Indian summer. I received the letter you wrote last Sunday, October 29. . . . You don't seem to be so happy now, but you must be patient. Dr. Shirabe might bring back new information from the conference for your treatment. Your idea is correct most of the time so that the high-frequency electrical machine may be good for your treatment. But if you become so irritated, nothing will work for you. Try to calm down when you talk to the doctors so that they will want to help you enthusiastically. Our health insurance coverage is very good so there is no reason to lose confidence in your recovery. . . .

You had a splendid dinner at Hiroyuki's with *tai* (鯛) accompanied by *funa* (鮒) wrapped in seaweed! I bet the family has aged now. But I bet they talked about the old days fondly, which I'm sure you enjoyed. I still remember the rambling talks that Mutō-sensei gave in his class. He has been teaching for so long—he must be the head of the teachers by now. He had great confidence in himself and thought his way was the only way.

Last night I taught Yukiko fractions. We practiced on it a little this evening too. Now it will be easy to move into multiplications. She joined the Girl Scouts and attends the meetings once a week after school. She has not caught a cold yet this winter. She says that she made the 50-yard dash in nine minutes. She says she can do pushups 15 times—so I asked her to show me. She does her "pushups" with her knees on the floor!! She says only the boys do regular pushups. This is AMERICA!

I wish Yukiko would work hard on her mathematics, but she says she is studying French now. For what? For entertainment? I know I am cynical. On the 16th I'll see Yukiko's teacher about her report card.

Remember some time ago we worked together to part the roots of a violet? Now all of them are blooming. I stuck toothpicks in the pot to mark them. Maybe it is the kind that blooms easily, but they are pink and have blossoms as large as an inch and half—they are so gorgeous! Jane took the same violet with purple flowers. But she didn't say anything at the memorial service the other day though she was looking at ours very carefully. This pink violet is much larger and so majestic. . . .

From KIYOSHI, *November 2.*

. . . TIME WENT BY SO SLOWLY when I was counting day by day, but now looking back on the first, the second, and the third month, it seems the three months flew by very quickly.

Today is a gloomy, dull day here. Since Shizuma-san will go out today, I asked her to get the medicine for hemorrhoids for Mother, air letters, and five books. The other day I bought a dictionary of fables and proverbs, and I'm enjoying reading it. So I bought dictionaries of synonyms, expressions in the sentence, playing with words, myths and legends, and a book of poems by Takamura Kōtarō, which seems to be an excellent collection. The dictionaries of playing with words and the myths and legends are to be read together with Yukiko. You will like the dictionaries of synonyms as well as the dictionary of expressions in a sentence. I asked Shizuma-san to get the poetry collection of Kōtarō's wife, Chieko, since you recommended it, but maybe the bookstore didn't have it. Kōtarō's book also has many beautiful poems about his yearning for his wife. You talked about Kōtarō's wife many times, but I had forgotten her name. One day a patient in this hospital came to see me together with Shizuma-san. When she mentioned *Chieko-shō* (智恵子抄), I said that you had liked the collection. I wanted to read it too. It is beautiful to keep loving one's own wife so deeply—even though she has become insane. . . .

I enjoyed reading your story about your office. I bet you look like an honor student there! . . .

From KIYOSHI, *November 3.*

. . . TODAY IS CULTURE DAY IN Japan—the day of awarding decorations to the cultural achievers. The Nishi-Nihon Newspaper Company received one. I was interested in the one given to Prof. Kiyoshi Fujikawa who is an expert on seaweed. He developed the seaweed industry in the Ariake Sea; also the seas surrounding the Korean Peninsula. The seaweed we buy in America could be a product of his research. His work went against the widely held opinion that raising seaweed around the coast of Jinsen, Korea, would fail because of the severe action of the tide there. The tide ebbs and flows violently in the Sea of Ariake, but because of this professor's research, now Fukuoka Prefecture is top on the list of seaweed producers. The research involved so much work, starting with the prevention of diseases. He waded into the sea himself, and now at age 76, he still works in the water together with the young folks. He has a degree in chemistry, and he is dedicated to the cultivation of seaweed. He began by analyzing seaweed and finding a high presence of protein in it. Protein is made with a large quantity of nitrogen; but there is not much nitrogen in the sea. Then why does seaweed contain so much protein? This was the starting question of his research. His hope is to cultivate seaweed in the open sea as well as on land. The latter he has successfully done at his home, and now he is working on a way to mass-produce the land-grown seaweed. Isn't he great?

We tend to give up too easily. In the face of the hard work of these great people, our self-inflicted depression is laughable. I get sad because my hearing is gone, and I feel as though I'm at the end of the road. I must look at my situation more closely and do my best in whatever is left for me to do in my life. . . .

Yesterday I started to take a solution of sodium bicarbonate by injection. This is to enlarge the blood vessels of the brain by sending CO_2 there. This is part of the initial plan along with the inhalation of the carbonic gas. The doctor is young and aggressive. He explains the medical situation until I understand. Also he is urging the administration to speed up the repair of the inhalation machine. He told me that these two treatments must be given side by side in order to see improvement. For which I am anxiously waiting also. . . .

I'm reading the *Dictionary of Folklore and Proverbs.* Chinese and Japanese proverbs are particularly fun and educational. Wait till you read them yourself—I think I bought a good book. . . .

From KIYOSHI, *November 3.*

EVERYBODY IS ENJOYING THE THREE-DAY HOLIDAY. ABOUT six p.m. the girls came to invite me to go see the folk dance in front of the hospital. I thought it was just around the corner, but we walked about 10 min. The hospital is in the large campus of Kyushu University.

Firewood was piled up to make a huge cube, and people danced around it. It was about five meters high. The square was as spacious as the GEM parking lot, and faces in the crowd were illuminated nicely by the bonfire. The hospital employees, the nurses, men and women from the town danced around the fire. It was very impressive. I was just watching, and a young woman signaled me to join the line. I signaled back to say "No." Modern Japan is so different from our days. People are young and open and enjoying life. I thought it very nice. There was no atmosphere of decadence. I thought it is nice that men and women can meet this way and select a partner for life. I wanted to bless all of them. . . .

I packed Mother's medicine to mail. It's small so that I can send it by air mail. She will be happy. I addressed it to you so please give it to her, read the prescription, and explain it to her. I'm going to ask Shizuma-san to mail it.

I was enjoying reading the dictionary today. Do you remember the TV program called "Joke Classroom"? In it, there was a play on words, *mono-azuke* (物預け), "leave things in one's care." It should be said *mono-wa-tsuke*, "buy things on credit," according to this dictionary. There are many similar puns in this book. . . .

From KIYOKO, *November 4.*

. . . I AM STILL GLOWING AFTER talking with you on the phone. Yukiko found out that you called. She was mad at me because she didn't have a chance to talk to Daddy.

You wrote me that Mrs. Matsumura and her father came to see you. Last night I wrote her a letter of condolence and a thank-you note for her visit to the hospital. What a gracious family they are!

Dr. Shirabe's opposition to the ultrashort-wave treatment tells me his own concern is for himself and his position. Now I'm not sure if he can be trusted. Please be guarded and find the best way.

Mitsuko-san's case has been quiet recently. Mother will send her home if and when she is ordered home. Mother sponsored her to come to America because she was asked to do so. If Mitsuko-san fails to comply with the rules and is ordered to return home, that's her fault. I think Mother feels relaxed now. I feel sorry for Mitsuko-san, but I'm going to see how she carries on alone. I have warned her that she will be sent back home if she cannot get along with the people around her. I also told her that I won't tell anything to anybody so she should try hard. She said "Thank you." I've left it there. I talked with your sister, but not to Yoshimitsu-san. I'm not going to say anything to him. . . .

You said you had not received my letters for some days. I hope you've got some since we talked on the phone. I was so happy to hear your voice, and so sad that you couldn't hear mine—I was so emotional that I don't remember now what you were saying. It is one o'clock in the morning. Yukiko was angry because she could not talk to you on the phone. But now she is sleeping, breathing peacefully. . . .

From KIYOSHI, *November 4.*

. . . IT IS 9:35 AM—JUST finished reading the newspaper. It reported on the citizens' vote in San Francisco on the Vietnam War—whether you are for the war, or against it, or immediate withdrawal. Are you really discussing these policies there? Vice President Humphrey immediately stated publicly that American policy will not change because of the citizens' vote. But the paper pointed out the difficult position the White House is in.

Another issue was the scarcity of jobs for Japanese women. Only two graduates of the Kyushu University found jobs. . . . It is said that businesses that used to hire females are now avoiding them.

The students who have degrees from foreign countries are shunned. For, if the company needs special skills, it would send its own employees to foreign universities to study because they can trust them better than foreigners. Japan has changed! Her advancement in the academic, political, economical arenas is so remarkable that educating her sons and daughters in foreign countries does not help the country anymore. Upon college graduation, one takes a job in a company while another advances to a university abroad for several years' study and obtains a PhD degree. The latter returns home but cannot find a job while the former has already advanced to the position of a section chief—this is the reality.

The problem with high school graduates is that there are too many more men than women—the ratio is eight to one. It is easier for girls to find husbands. However college graduates have tough competition in finding jobs. This is why you should not come back to Japan. If all you want is to get married and stay home as a housewife, it's all right. But if you want to find a good job and still keep studying, this is not the place to live. . . .

Dr. Yasuda made his rounds today, and I had a chance to show him the pamphlet of the machine for the high-frequency treatment. He showed keen interest in it. I think there are many different reactions depending on the person. He wanted to study it and borrowed it from me. When he was my physician-in-charge, my hearing was getting better. . . .

From KIYOSHI, *November 5.*

A CLOUDY DAY ENCLOSED IN SMOG—STRANGE WEATHER. I am lonely because there was no letter from you yesterday. I hope I'll get one today. When I don't hear from you, I feel as though I've been chased to the end of the road, and I want to give up on everything—even my life. I must not think this way even if my hearing does not come back. I was talking bravely to Ōtomo-san when she wanted to die; and here I am—I feel I am at the bottom—I want to die! It is sad.

Let me stop talking about dying. Are you all right? How is Yukiko? I'm sure she is all right. How about her school work?

The morning paper here reported that the editors of *San Francisco Chronicle* who oppose the Vietnam War publicized their statement on an ad page. They collected funds among themselves to buy the space in order to express their position against the war and against their own newspaper which supports it. Did you read about it? It appears it is going to become a political issue in the coming election.

Here in Japan, it is the time of harvesting rice. Saga Prefecture was the top prefecture for the production of rice for five years in a row. But because of a long spell of dry weather, they lost that position. In order to maintain the leading position, they used an excessive amount of chemicals, and there are cases of liver inflammation among the farmers. The general opinion is that they went too far trying to keep up their record of production. It is necessary now to reevaluate their policy.

Another topic is gambling with fighting cocks in Kineshima District. It is well organized, led by the chiefs of the district. They have lookouts; the money bet for the fight is transferred immediately to somewhere else so that it does not look like gambling; there is constant communication by telephone—even women are taking part in this scheme. It is a business of several billion yen a year; over one million yen is handled per night. They are targeting the farmers' income. This has become a social issue involving the chiefs of the district.

According to the newspaper report, the cost of salmon roe will come down by 30%. Black beans also will be cheaper. Other delicacies for New Year's entertainment will be the same. Anything changed on your side? . . .

From KIYOSHI, *November 6.*

. . . I WAS FRETTING OVER MY situation and decided to call you yesterday. I'm glad you are OK. I can't figure out why the mail is not being delivered regularly. . . .

It was close to nine p.m. when the lines were finally connected so it must have been around midnight your time. I'm so sorry to have wakened you. I was relieved to be able to reach you. I so wished to hear your voice! I'm glad you could hear mine. I was overwhelmed while I spoke—by enormous sadness—I cannot describe it fully. . . .

If no significant improvement is made in my hearing by the middle of December, I'm coming home. In the meantime, Dr. Torii is checking with the mechanic on the CO_2 machine. Also I'd like to find out from Dr. Yasuda about the pamphlet on the treatment using ultrashort waves. I will let you know as soon as I hear from them.

I am thinking of sending home my summer clothes. . . .

From KIYOSHI, *November 6.*

. . . I JUST READ YOUR LETTERS written on October 29 and the night of Halloween. Thank you so very much—I've been brought back to life again! I was so depressed and beaten. When I called you yesterday, I could tell that you were all right, but reading letters like these makes me doubly happy and relieved.

I'm going to write this letter quickly so that Shizuma-san can post this when she goes to town about three o'clock. When Dr. Torii came around today to give me the injection, he said that the inhalator may be back in operation in a few days. Maybe because of the injection, the ringing in my ears now seems to have been reduced a little bit. I wish I could restore my hearing by taking CO_2 using the inhalator along with this injection. . . .

In regard to shopping—two rice containers for Cecilia and for us also two of the same in different sizes. I'll get the rice cooker for five servings made by National. If you want anything else, let me know as soon as possible. I want to spend one day doing shopping. . . .

So, Haruta-san took his mother on the trip instead of his wife? I can't blame her for becoming so angry. She and her husband don't seem to work together deciding when and how they make trips. In a sense, it is worse than going out with a girlfriend. You and I are so lucky. I feel sorry for Mrs. Haruta. Maybe all healthy men are like Mr. Haruta? Do I behave differently because of my poor health? I don't think so.

The time is up—I have to stop writing. I'll write again tomorrow. . . .

From KIYOKO, *November 7.*

. . . I WISH I HAD A BOOK ON science and electricity, a book easy enough for me to understand so that I can teach Yukiko. Right now she is experimenting with powdered soap, dissolving it in a soap box, and letting it dry to make a bar of soap. I wish I could teach her how to make soap.

Today we went to the gas station to fill the tank. While we had the bulb changed for one of the headlights, Yukiko asked if gasoline was water. Hanada-san said it was something made from oil. She asked him then what it was that was left after taking the gasoline out. I know there are many by-products from heavy oil, but I wish I had a book of science like the one I used to have. I don't remember those things anymore! One time Yukiko asked me to take her to an open house at Fairchild so she could learn about electricity. I told her that Daddy would love to hear this. I could teach her these things immediately if I had those books.

One other thing that I meant to tell you, but I missed the chance until now: she made a violin using a box. She cut out the center and tightly stretched nylon cord and rubber bands over it so that it produces sounds close to the scale. She is very proud of this.

Lately she is actively participating in the Girl Scouts. She wants to get the uniform. Since I deposited some money in the bank the other day, my cash is low right now. I'll wait till this weekend and get a uniform for her.

What is your plan for Christmas? If you still have to be in the hospital, I want to send you a package. Also I have to decide whether I should continue sending the newspaper to you. You say that Dr. Yasuda showed a keen interest in the high-frequency treatment. The hospital is still trying to repair the inhalator; maybe we could help them by getting the parts for the inhalator from America. It is such a travesty if they are hesitating to ask around out of pride because they are Kyushu University. My patience is about to run out! It has nothing to do with luck, Kiyoshi-san. Let us look for a way out of this situation.

Henry came home with a decoration for escaping from the communists in Vietnam. I'm glad he came home unhurt with or without the decoration. Today's paper is filled with interesting topics: a conversation with the recipients of the cultural achievement award and a photo, the case for Proposition P*, the case of Professor Hazama, etc. About Proposition P, there are different opinions—Japan and America are against it, [Canada] is for it . . . Japan and America oppose it on the ground that ending the war in Vietnam will not solve the problem.

My mother wrote thanking me for the candy that I sent to Hiroyuki and Noriko-san. Hiroyuki kept his word not to tell my mother about your situation. She writes, "Kiyoshi-san must be very busy. I'm sorry I have not written sooner." I am relieved. . . .

*Proposition P on the 1967 San Francisco ballot called for a unilateral withdrawal of U.S. forces from Vietnam.

From KIYOSHI, *November 7.*

. . . IT HAS BEEN 130 DAYS since I checked into this hospital. I've lost my sense of time. Thank you for the two letters delivered today. I'm glad you are OK. I'm just about the same.

Yesterday I had the medicine for Mother sent by air mail. Shizuma-san helped me.

I bought a Japanese-language dictionary. It is an excellent book—I'm so glad that I bought this. The Academy of Japanese Language compiled it, and many first-class scholars took part in writing it. Tokieda Seiki was the head of the 190 editors, among which were Kindaichi Kyōsuke and Kindaichi Haruhiko. The content is as follows: sounds, symbols, words, linguistics, pronunciation, characters, grammar, style, vocabulary, dialects, topological words, everyday language, general problems of languages, problems unique to the Japanese language, literature, education, folklore, games, social psychology, mass communication, experimental psychology, entertainments, documents, data, letters, machines, names of books, names of magazines. It is gigantic—1,250 pages. It cost 2,500 yen, which is about $8.50. We would be charged at least $50 in the States for a book of this quality. I want to show this to you as soon as possible. This book will explain everything as far as the Japanese language is concerned.

Today's local paper reported an increase in jobless teachers. Last year's record shows that 40% of graduates could not find teaching positions. This year that figure will go even higher. The teachers of elementary, middle, and high schools have problems also.

The farmers in Hyōgo Prefecture are complaining about the rise in their costs. They had purchased mowers for rice plants paying an exorbitant price, but found they cannot use them because the plants bend down. Hiring manpower costs 2 or 3,000 yen. On top of it, this year's harvest was reduced drastically due to the drought. I wonder how the Nabeshima area is taking this harsh reality.

Today is Election Day in San Francisco. But the voters are more concerned about the Vietnam War than electing the mayor. Is it true? I'll know in a few days, won't I?

How is the Japanese conversation class coming along? If the conversation gets sidetracked, you can follow it as much as you want because children remember such diversions better. Shall I get a bulletin board, maybe a secondhand one? It would be interesting to make textbooks using stencil paper. Tokunaga-sensei and the Buddhist School will be pleased to note our ingenuity. How about starting to prepare for next year's Literature Day? We can write an appropriate script. I can help you. I want to concentrate the rest of my life on something related to the Japanese language. It will be worth doing. I can make it meaningful; besides it gives me great joy to work with you.

Yesterday I bought the poetry books of Nakahara Chūya, Kitahara Hakushū, and Takamura Chieko published by Iwanami and Shinchō; the total was $2.70 or 80 yen. I'll get the book by Ishikawa Takuboku in a few days. I think reading poems and studying Japanese will become my future work. I wish my hearing would come back; if not, it will be good to study Japanese quietly. . . .

From KIYOSHI, *November 7.*

. . . YOUR LETTER CAME THIS morning—the one you wrote on November second. Also I received a letter from Mrs. Matsumura saying that she sent me three books along with her wish that I get well soon so that I can go home to you and Yukiko. I don't know if these books are her late husband's books or new ones.

Tachibana-san wrote me also. She says she is my niece and I am her uncle! Isn't that sweet? She was so pleased because I asked her to find a dictionary of old proverbs, a sequel to what you have. She says, "I'm so happy to do something for you. I haven't done anything for you so it makes me very happy to look for the dictionary. Please don't hesitate to ask me because you are like my uncle. Tell me to do this and that like you would tell your niece, and don't hesitate to point out to me if I'm doing something wrong." She is 17 years old. I feel I am ancient. I should try to be a good uncle to everybody! Shizuma-san calls me "*Oji-san*" too. The head nurse advised her to call me "Tokutomi-san." So she sometimes calls me Tokutomi-san with the accent on the second "o" and laughs.

Tachibana-san didn't get a good grade in English. She says, "*Oji-san*, please don't be disappointed. I wasn't sure if I should tell you this, but English is so difficult for me. *Gomennasai!*" . . . Tachibana-san closed her letter saying, "Please give my love to Mrs. Tokutomi and Yukiko-*chan*."

Yukiko seems to work hard without even catching cold—I'm so happy. I would be happier if she put her heart in her studies too. I look forward to hearing about the results of her school work on the 16th.

The dictionary and the poetry collections are all so good—they help me to deal with boredom. . . .

From KIYOKO, *November 8.*

. . . THE SUN GOES DOWN SO EARLY these days. The frenetic year's end is just around the corner. Streets are already decorated for Christmas, and our mailbox is full of holiday advertisements. . . .

Last Saturday I went to San Leandro . . . so that I was unable to take my letter to the post office until Sunday. That night you phoned me. I'm sure it made you feel even worse because you couldn't hear my voice. I think we'd better not use the phone because it will make us sadder. Your voice was clear—just like the usual Kiyoshi-san.

If the inhalator is repaired, you won't have to come home right away. But it is a good idea for your homecoming to coincide with Ōshima-san's visit to America. If the treatment stagnates, as it has been, you might as well come home. But don't lose hope. It must be hard on you, but you are my Kiyoshi-san, even should you lose your arms—even your nose— you are my Kiyoshi-san. Don't forget that. Come home to me with your cheerful smile. I can hardly wait to see the things you are buying for our home.

I finished a draft of the letter to Dr. Childrey but have not made a clean copy to mail out because I don't have time—I am carrying it in my bag. I'll make time somehow. The same with the inquiries on Watanabe-sensei's chance to come to America as an exchange professor. That note is still in my bag also. I'm sorry. I just cannot find time to do all these things. I used to find time in the office to write letters or talk with somebody on the phone. Not any more.

To compensate for it, however, I got a raise today. With the addition of $25, my earnings are $595 a month. The citation checks "Excellent" on all accounts. The supervisor said that it could have been a $50 raise and brought my earnings to $620 if there were no Austerity Program. I told her that my husband's praise would make up the balance. . . .

The name of the mayor of San Francisco is Alioto. He is a lawyer and a Democrat. Cleveland [Ohio] and Gary [Indiana] elected African-American mayors; both are Democrats. Proposition P was not successful, collecting only one third of the votes—they say the failure was due to the semantics of the proposition itself. . . .

From KIYOSHI, *November 8.*

. . . ACCORDING TO THE NEWSPAPER, this is the first day of the winter season. They say it's going to be a harsh winter. . . .

Yesterday I was reading my newly purchased dictionary of the Japanese language. I am glad to have found the following passage about the Japanese that foreigners speak:

> "The Japanese language used by foreigners tends to be somewhat awkward. It is natural that they use odd phrasing abundantly in the early stages of learning this language. However, in some cases it does not go away even if one lives in Japan a long time and keeps studying the language. The awkward phrasing appears in writing too, but it is more noticeable in conversation, especially in diction and pronunciation. It is caused mostly by the influence of their mother tongue, usually by trying to translate it directly into Japanese. For example, *shiken wo ukeru* (I am tested) vs. *shiken wo toru* (I take a test). The latter is not correct. This type of awkward phrasing occurs due to the wrong use of particles. Some examples are: I study in the library, 図書館で勉強する (*toshokan de benkyō suru*) vs. 図書館に勉強する (*toshokan ni benkyō suru*); I walk around town, 町を散歩する (*machi o sanpo suru*) vs. 町で散歩する (*machi de sanpo suru*)."

Remember, Kiyoko-san, the exercise on the particles *ni, o,* and *de* that I prepared? It is so important to practice the particles. I remember that I wrote to teach the application of the particles *ni* and *o, o* and *de,* and *de* and *ni*—this is the best way to teach the particles to prevent making mistakes. Do you remember? Reading the above passage in the dictionary, I learned that my theory was right. This will give me confidence when I write a textbook. I was so pleased.

The dictionary touches upon the specific feature of Japanese pronunciation, but I have not yet come across a passage saying that the particles are the characteristic components of the sentence structure in Japanese language. I have confidence in my theory on the pronunciation. Let's think about the sentence 私は本をもっています (*watashi wa hon o motte imasu*) [I have a book]. We cannot change the English word order, but in Japanese we can say 本を持っています、私は:

hon o motte imasu, watashi wa, or

motte imasu, watashi wa hon o, or

motte imasu, hon o, watashi wa.

This is because of the particle, I believe. Even though the changing word order does not change the meaning, it does stress different components of the sentence. I'm sure you would agree with me. I think I can compile an excellent textbook. I'm going to do that. . . .

From KIYOSHI, *November 8.*

. . . I SPENT ALL DAY READING books and thinking about my textbook on the Japanese language.

In the *Dictionary of Word Play*, there is a heading called 回文 (*kaibun*), in which sound is the same whether you read from top to bottom or bottom to top. I was surprised to see so many phrases, sentences, and poems written this way. People must have enjoyed this word game in the old days. It is impressive. The sentence that Tamaru-san likes to cite is in this book too: 草くさの　名は知らぬらし　花のさくさく (*kusa kusa no na wa shiranurashi hana no saku saku*). But he omitted the middle of the sentence which goes this way: 草くさの　名はしらぬらし　花守も　名はしらぬらし　花のさくさく (*kusa kusa no na wa shiranurashi hanamori mo na wa shiranurashi hana no saku saku*). [Nobody knows the name of the weed; even the gardener doesn't know it—the weeds in full bloom.]

長き夜の　遠のねふりの　みなめさめ　波乗り船の　音のよきかな (*nagaki yo no tō no nefuri no mina mesame naminori fune no oto no yoki kana*). [After the long night everyone is awake and refreshed . . . the sound of the boat riding on the waves.] I thought this *waka* was in 万葉集 *Man'yōshū*, but it was in the *Topography of Japan*. There are so many nice *kaibun* in this book.

Some more examples: 繁る葉を　かざして岩間　闇くだく　深山は出し 坂もはるけし (*shigeru ha o kazashite iwama yami kudaku miyama wa ideshi saka mo harukeshi*).* [Thick foliage above the boulders casting its shadow and broken into pieces . . . Coming out of the deep mountain, I can see the distant slope.] Isn't this amazing?

Another interesting word game is the Silly Questions and Answers. Here is an example:

煎餅 せんべい (*senbei*) [one-thousand rice cracker]

Question—(*kore wa nan to iimasu ka*) [What do you call this?], pointing at one **rice cracker.**

Answer—(*sore wa senbei to iimasu.*) [It is called **one-thousand rice cracker.**]

It is similar to calling a bun まんじゅう (*manjū*) **ten-thousand buns** even if it is only **one bun.** How about the next one? There is **a pear.** But the pear is called *nashi* which means there is **nothing.** Another one: you **bought** 瓜うり (*uri*)—but *uri* also means to **sell.**

As I was writing the above, Shizuma-san came to visit. Now it is Thursday, November ninth, 9:30 a.m. I finished reading the newspaper. The result of the citizens' anti-war poll in San Francisco is reported to be 70,000 "Yes" and 130,000 "No." . . . More interesting news is the mayoral election in Cleveland; an African American was chosen over the grandson of President Taft. I think it was a big surprise. A lot of the white folks voted for him too. The support for President Johnson seems to be waning. It is normal that the opposition party gets an advantage in the mid-term election in America, but the support to Johnson is crumbling. I was surprised to learn that more than 50% of the populace wants him to step down, according to the Gallup survey. At this point he cannot win against any candidate from the Republicans.

I am learning many Japanese words lately. Indian summer is 小春日和 (*koharu-biyori*) and *koharu* means October in the lunar calendar. I am enjoying reading the dictionary. I think about writing a Japanese textbook quite often. I think it would be nice to include a nursery song with a score at the end of each chapter. Since it will be published in America, this would be a good idea. Also I am envisioning some unique features for this textbook. Easy-to-learn Japanese is my focal point. My textbook will have many unusual features. . . .

*From the collection of Fujiwara Takanobu, servant of the Imperial Court [This is Kiyoshi's addition.]

From KIYOSHI, *November 9.*

. . . THANK YOU FOR WRITING to Mrs. Matsumura thanking her for all the things she and her husband did for us. My heart aches for her—she lost her husband so unexpectedly—it is not like losing an irresponsible, good-for-nothing husband. Mrs. Matsumura respected her husband very much, and he was a very considerate gentleman who took such good care of her and the family. I can believe it from the way he took care of me. He must have loved her very much. It is a cruel world, isn't it?

Today Dr. Yasuda brought several medical books to explain to me how the high-frequency treatment works. I am so grateful for his deep concern. He said that inhalation of carbon dioxide increases the flow of the blood 60 times, which is 10 times better than the high-frequency treatment. He said that I should try the inhalation of carbon dioxide for a month, and see the result. He has discussed this matter with Dr. Torii, who also came to see me today to tell me that we are set to resume the treatment tomorrow as soon as the attachment is found. I am so happy to see the positive attitude of the staff. Instead of dismissing the pamphlets on the high-frequency machine, Dr. Yasuda went through the medical books and told me to read certain paragraphs in them—here is a doctor who shows his professional excellence and a real concern for the patient! I told him about your support and encouragement. He was moved. He stayed in my room for about an hour and we kept talking. Dr. Torii is also working hard on my case. I am so grateful for these people.

Unexpectedly Tachibana-san came to see me today. She will be back in the hospital after December 14. She brought me the dictionary of archaic Japanese that I asked her to find. It is written by Kindaichi Kyōsuke, published by Sanseidō; the price is 650 yen. . . .

I look forward to having the carbon dioxide treatment tomorrow or the day after tomorrow. Kiyoko-san, thank you for your encouragement with such tender love. I will try my best.

From KIYOSHI, *November 10.*

... THIS IS THE FIRST DAY OF the long-distance relay race of Kyushu Island. It goes around the entire island and takes 10 days. Everybody is excited about it. It is predicted that the championship will go to either Miyazaki-ken or Fukuoka-ken. Last year Miyazaki-ken won. The folks of Fukuoka-ken are excited, praying that they will win this year. Saga-ken was third last year, and they vowed to keep the third position again. When I was in the second year and the fourth year in high school, I ran in a similar event so that I know the thrill and miss that excitement. I didn't run in my third year due to my pleurisy, and there was no race in my fifth year. Ours was a long-distance relay race between Karatsu and Saga, and it lasted about two hours and a half. The race that started today is the competition among the prefectures of Kyushu Island, and it started 16 years ago, the year I left Japan for America.

Today is also the opening of sumo wrestling in Fukuoka. This and the long-distance race are igniting the love of sports in Kyushu. . . .

Dr. Torii was on duty last night. He came around to give me my injection and told me that the inhaler now has the attachment. Today we might resume the carbon dioxide inhalation after some adjustment is done by the mechanic. I HOPE SO.

Last night I read the poems by Ishikawa Takuboku and his biography. He died at 27. His life was not a happy one. He was close to Kindaichi Kyōsuke and a number of well-known poets. His mother, his wife, and he himself all died of tuberculosis. It said that he was distinguished as eighth from the top out of 137 students in the entrance examination of his middle school. (I was the third from the top out of 150 students—ha ha ha!) After four years, Takuboku dropped down to 80-something because he was too involved in poetry and literature. (I did not drop that much. I think I was 18th from the top at the graduation. Ha ha ha!) I spent my time in sports; it is not as glamorous as writing poems! He was the son of a Zen priest. Those days Zen priests were not allowed to marry legally. He died so young, but he left such a superb body of poetry. He will live among us forever!

Akiyama Chieko-san writes on "Female Honor" in today's paper and sends a warning to Japanese women. Forgotten feminine virtues, sex without love—these ideas did not even sneak into our heads in the old days. . . . It could be the fault of the weekly magazines that write anything for money, even the neglect of female honor. I'm glad that I was born much earlier. If one got used to living a loose life, it must be difficult to settle down in a happy marriage. Have I become too old to understand contemporary customs?

From Kiyoshi, November 11.

... Last evening I resumed the carbon dioxide treatment. I pray it will work well this time. I inhaled carbon dioxide and oxygen already mixed in one cylinder. They used to put each gas in a separate cylinder and pour the correct amount into the inhaler to mix it. This time the prescribed amount of each gas is already mixed, and I inhaled it gradually—it took 10 minutes. I think it works.

Every day I spend most of my time reading. The dictionaries and poetry collections comfort me so much. Shizuma-san once brought in another patient—her name is Iura-san and she is 23 years old. She comes to see me often with her boyfriend. They met each other when they were in high school in a poetry-writing class. He is a serious young man. They told me about Higuchi Ichiyō. I was buying pocket books of poetry published by Iwanami or Shinchō, but they buy the complete collection of Japanese poets published by Shinchō, and they recommended those to me highly. One book costs 330 yen. I bought one book by Takuboku, another by Sakutarō, and one by Bokusui—three all together. They are good! When I come home, I'd like to buy the whole collection, 34 books in all. I used to look down on the pale-faced bookworms. At age 44, however, I have reached at last the mental stage of Kiyoko-san when she was 21 or 22 years old. I can see that I am so far behind. Poems are beautiful—sometimes they make me sad, but they are beautiful! They remind me of my own words, "I like Kiyoko-san so much that my heart aches."

I learn so much about the Japanese language from reading poems.

Iura-san has a round face like you. I told her about you and how we built our happiness together, quoting your words often. She was moved and said, "*Oji-san*, you are a lucky man to have such a good wife." I said, "When everything is normal, we don't realize how happy we are. But in adverse situations, like my loss of hearing, we realize how lucky we are to be able to build happiness together. But such happiness is not easy to find. Anything great demands a serious effort from us." She was grateful for my comments.

The parents of her boyfriend are opposed to their marriage. "We love each other and hope to get married next year and become a loving couple like you," she says. Her boyfriend comes with her often, and he is apparently a very nice person.

Iura-san has to undergo surgery once more. She cannot hear on one side. I'm surprised that so many people lost their hearing on one side. Tachibana-san will come back on December 14 for the same reason. Hinashi-san will be back in March. For these wonderful young people, we are the ideal couple, Kiyoko-san. They want to nurture their own love, and when they find a successful case, they are encouraged to go on. They've seen too many cases of unsuccessful relationships. *[Continued in next letter.]*

From KIYOSHI, *November 11.*

[CONTINUED FROM PREVIOUS LETTER.] These people must have acquired an indefinable fear through reading novels and periodicals. But they continue to live, get married, and hope they can avoid infidelity. Finding a happy couple like us must have helped to restore their confidence. Hinashi-san of Kyushu University said a similar thing. A serious person should look for a serious partner. It seems to me that a more educated person would respect me and follow me—a man who has lost his hearing. And everybody praises you, which makes me very happy. We are here together because of your first declaration, "We might quarrel, but we will not be fighting over separation." Since then, we have stayed together for 18 years building up our happiness.

In the dictionary of proverbs it says 疾風に頸草を知る meaning: In a gale, one finds out that a certain grass is stronger than others. It means that one's strength, fidelity, and greatness will be shown in a time of crisis. The origin is a Chinese proverb. Ask Cecilia. In Chinese it goes as follows: 故疾風知頸草　厳霜知貞木, and this describes us too. When all goes well, it is hard to see the difference between love that comes from the heart and put-on-for-show love. But the difference will become clear when something grave happens in the nation or in the family. There are many wise sayings in Chinese, aren't there? Tell Cecilia that I am very much impressed by the wisdom expressed in her language.

From now on I'm going to write one or two proverbs at the end of each letter. There are good ones in Japanese too. 独楽の舞い倒れ means: When a spinning top halts, it falls sideways. Imagine a man working alone like mad, like a spinner; when he becomes totally spent, he rolls over. Isn't it humorous? It's no use to struggle so much without outside help. And how about this one—皿なめた猫がたたかれる means: The cat that is caught licking the plate is slapped. The hidden meaning is that some other cat emptied the plate. It's satire. 犬もたのめば糞くわず means: Even a dog would not eat if it was asked to do so. A man can finish anything on his own initiative, but if he is asked, he would drag it out forever just to show his importance. He is like the dog refusing to eat in spite of being coaxed. 明日食う塩辛に今日から水のむ means: Start drinking water today to prepare for eating salted squid tomorrow. One can be too well prepared. . . .

From KIYOKO, *November 12.*

THE JAPANESE SCHOOL WAS CLOSED YESTERDAY BECAUSE of Veterans Day. I took the car to the garage because of an oil leak. The mechanic, Bob, was not there. A different mechanic asked me, as he was working on the engine, if I wanted to change the clutch too. He thought the car needed a new clutch. So I had it changed and paid $57! But it is tighter now and feels much better. I think it was worth paying that much since we are going to keep this car.

I thought I would write a letter to you while I waited, but the waiting room was so cold that I watched children play outside instead. After leaving the garage, I went to GEM to get a book for Henry for Christmas. I bought a diary written at the Vietnam front by Bob Hope, and a Charlie Brown cartoon book, coffee candy and peanut candy (the kind you like), and cookies from Aki bakery. After supper I went to San Francisco to see an academic presentation at the San Francisco Institute. I made some wrong turns as usual around Van Ness and finally came to Hirose-san's place to get correct directions to the school. I depended on you too much on the road so I have never learned to drive. I already forgot the new way to get to Post Street. On the way back I got on that broad street to the Expressway and came home easily.

The Japanese Language School at the San Francisco Institute is far better than the one in San Jose. Several students can speak like Japanese in public; one of them, a 17-year-old girl, will be going to a university in Japan. I spoke with Mrs. Hori and learned that Mr. Hori is organizing another group tour to Japan next spring. She said hello to you. I mentioned that the San Francisco Institute was good, but if we start a school of ours, it will be equally good or even better. Please think about it when you have time. I'd like to offer a class to parents too.

By the way, I saw Hirose-san in his studio. I saw that the lights were on and so I went in. There were a lot of people inside. One of them had a suit on and I could see only the back. I had a feeling that it could be Hirose-san—and it was. He turned around and was surprised to find me. Mrs. Hirose joined us, and we had a lively conversation. Hirose-san hopes that Kiyoshi-san will stop helping people there, get well, and come back as quickly as possible! He has not received a tape of the Japanese folk singer yet. He will write to you, he said. It was an eventful Saturday.

Finally I sent out the letter to Dr. Childrey today. Have I told you about the receipt of insurance money to the sum of $310.77, including the cost of prescriptions? This Friday I will mail $100 to you so that you can buy things to bring home. Yukiko wants a science kit. If you go out shopping, please be careful not to catch cold. Be sure to gargle after shopping; you might need to gargle often from now on. . . .

From KIYOSHI, *November 12.*

. . . DAY BEFORE YESTERDAY I resumed the inhalation of carbon dioxide. I had this treatment twice this week; and today it's off because the doctors are off for the weekend. Up to now it lasted 10 minutes both times, but soon it will become 15 and 20 minutes, and twice a day. I hope we see good results.

Shizuma-san went home for the weekend yesterday. Iura-san too went home last night and will be back this afternoon. She lent me a book on Hanaoka Seishū and his wife. I didn't know that Hanaoka Seishū was the first one who succeeded with the use of total anesthesia for breast cancer surgery. His wife became blind because she let her husband experiment on her to find the correct dose of narcotics. It was 1842 in America that the first breast surgery was done using ether. In 1847 another surgery was successfully done in England using chloroform. Seishū's success precedes those two by 42 years. The articles left by him are permanently displayed at the International Academy of Surgeries in Chicago along with a Japanese painting that illustrates how his mother and wife offered themselves to the experiment on anesthetics. I cannot understand why such important work and the sacrifice of the family are not cited more openly and widely as an honor for Japan.

Next topic: the relay marathon on Kyushu Island. It will be difficult for Saga-ken to hold on to the third position this year—now Saga is the fifth of the seven prefectures. As expected, Miyazaki and Fukuoka are the top two and are still competing ferociously. The first day was from Nagasaki to Sasebo; the second day was from Sasebo to the Municipal Court of Saga-ken. The first day Miyazaki took first, and the second day Fukuoka was first. As of today Miyazaki is leading by three minutes. They run today from Saga to Kumamoto. I guess I ought to stand by Saga, but now that I'm in Fukuoka, I want Fukuoka to win—a strange sentiment! The sumo match will start today.

Prime Minister Satō will start his trip to America today. People in Okinawa are anxious to return to Japanese control. When Prime Minister Satō visited Okinawa, he declared that the war cannot be finished until Okinawa is returned. But lately he has not been as firm as he was in the face of President Johnson's stiff policy. Therefore the opposition party is reviving "Return Okinawa" rhetoric, stressing the 22 years of undelivered promises. Johnson has made it clear that the return of the island will not happen as long as the war in Vietnam goes on. I don't know what will happen now.

Yesterday someone attempted to burn himself to death in front of the Prime Minister's official residence. He is in critical condition. His will has been published. Evidently his honor or reputation was hurt—but what about people around him who might be hurt because of his act? When will people really find their happiness?

The boyfriend of Iura-san teased her by saying that he would like to marry someone like "*Oji-san's* wife" and made her cross. But she reported this with a smile and said that she would like to become like you. She is not pretty but she is very intelligent. Her boyfriend is serious, but he's also gentle and cheerful—a very nice person. He is slender and she is chubby.

I might write to you again this afternoon.

From KIYOSHI, *November 12.*

. . . I JUST FINISHED READING your letter of November seventh with such delight. . . .

You say Yukiko started to show interest in science lately. I am very happy to hear that. We've been talking about getting an encyclopedia, and I think now is the time. How about getting it on a monthly installment plan? This is our best opportunity to buy one, don't you think? It will help Yukiko's interest in studying. There are many good encyclopedias like *Encyclopedia Americana* or *Encyclopedia Britannica*. Take for example crude oil—it is the source of all the modern chemical products. She will find many kinds of products made from crude petroleum: synthetic fiber starting with nylon, plastic, manufactured leather, etc; the sweetener, saccharin. She could tell you proudly what she learned from the encyclopedia—you could listen to her as if you didn't know anything—she will learn the joy of discovery. You could even start having her make a motor and generator. I think there are models for those. I would like her to grow up to be strong in the field of science and math. When I was a child before school age, I made a sound box by stretching cords on wood and showed it to my mother. It ended there because my parents were busy and didn't understand these things. I think we can give Yukiko more support and cooperation than that.

I can't say anything yet about when I can come home. It depends on the results of the carbon dioxide treatment. You mentioned a Christmas package. It would be nice to have a variety of candies to give to the nurses and aides; about 20 Lux soap bars; a set of razors for Dr. Torii. I can use those as parting gifts if I leave before Christmas. Hiroyuki-san and Noriko-san came today and advised me to have an overcoat ready if I go home between December and February. Can you send one to me?

Hiroyuki-san and Noriko-san brought tangerines and bananas. I talked to them about happiness again. The gist of my talk was: A great thing in life like happiness is not easy to find, and one has to build it up. I told them how we did it. They were so impressed by your greatness. We have to keep trying to show these young people a good example.

So Henry received a medal—I can't celebrate it with an open heart. I don't have space left for proverbs today. I'll write some tomorrow. . . .

From Kiyoshi, November 12.

IT IS STILL SUNDAY, NOVEMBER 12TH; 8:15 P.M. I WAS reading the poems of Ishikawa Takuboku but decided to write again because I feel lonely. I'm not sure if I can finish this letter tonight—we'll see.

First, from 一握の砂 (*ichiaku no suna*) [A Handful of Sand] by Ishikawa Takuboku:

東海の 小島の磯の 白砂に われ泣きぬれて 蟹とたはむる
tokai no kojima no iso no shirosuna ni ware nakinurete kani to tawamuru

> I cry—
> playing with the crabs
> on the white sandy beach . . .
> a tiny island
> in the eastern sea

This is famous and nice, but I like the next one.

頬につたふ なみだのごはず 一握の 砂をしめしし 人を忘れず
hoho ni tsutau namida nogowazu ichiaku no suna wo shimeshishi hito o wasurezu

> I can't forget her
> who showed me
> a handful of sand
> without wiping
> her tears

砂山の 砂に腹這い 初恋の いたみを遠く おもい出ずる日
sunayama no suna ni harabai hatsugoi no itami o tōku omoiizuru hi

> The pain
> of first love—
> it comes back to me
> as I'm on all fours
> on the sand hill

The one I like best is:

いのちなき　砂のかなしさよ　さらさらと　握れば指の　あいだより落つ
*inochi naki suna no kanashisa yo sarasara to nigireba yubi no
aida yori otsu*

> It's sad
> that sand doesn't have life—
> I hold it,
> but it falls dry
> through my fingers

Maybe this was the one you quoted to me a long time ago.

When I keep reading Takuboku's work such as the beginning of 悲しき
玩具 *(kanashiki omocha) [Sad Toys]*, I become unbearably sad. For example:

呼吸すれば　胸の中にて　鳴る音あり　こがらしよりも　さびしきその音
*kokyū sureba mune no naka nite naru oto ari kogarashi yori mo
sabishiki sono oto*

> when I breathe
> I hear the rustling sound
> in my chest—
> such a dry
> lonely sound

I know this too well! I cannot go on writing because I get so emotional.
Let me change the subject.

I'm going to list a few lines from the *Dictionary of Proverbs*. They are well-
known sayings, but the source is usually not clear. . . .

蚊のまつげにくもの巣をはる *(ka no matsuge ni kumo no su o haru)*
[a spider's web on a mosquito's eyelash]; 秋の日と娘はくれぬ様でく
れる *(aki no hi to musume wa kurenu yō de kureru)* [the autumn sun
delays going down like one who's marrying off a daughter];
あわてる蟹は穴へ入れぬ *(awateru kani wa ana e hairenu)*
[a hurrying crab misses the hole].

As I read the dictionary page by page, I come across many lines that I
understand. There are many Chinese proverbs. Cecilia would enjoy reading
this book. . . .

I usually read the *Dictionary of Proverbs* after reading sad poems—it helps to readjust my mind.

Poetry is so rich. Kiyoko-san, you could write splendid poems. I never forget the haiku you wrote when you arrived in America:

さみだれや 山は故郷の それににて
samidare ya yama wa kokyō no sore ni nite

> early summer rain
> the hills look the same
> as in my hometown

I like the one you wrote a few years ago:

やまかげを いだく水面の ひろさかな
yamakage o idaku minamo no hirosa kana

> how expansive it is!
> shadow of the mountain
> embraced by water

I guess this is *senryū* since there is no season word. If you can, spend more time writing haiku and poems as your muse dictates; you will have a beautiful and graceful collection, and I will recite them all the time. . . .

From KIYOSHI, *November 13.*

. . . 9:15 A.M. I HAD BREAKFAST and just finished reading the morning papers. The long-distance relay race is getting very interesting. Saga Prefecture is in the third place now—till yesterday they were in sixth—the second from the last—I am so proud! Prince Takamatsu is the official shooting the pistol at the starting line. Now for seven days to come, citizens in Kyushu will talk of nothing but this long-distance relay race! Fukuoka moved ahead of Miyazaki on the third day with a four-minute, 32-second lead. In the three-day total, Miyazaki is ahead of Saga by 36 minutes and 47 seconds. Next comes Nagasaki; and Ōita, Kagoshima, and Kumamoto follow it. The fight between Fukuoka and Miyazaki will decide the first and second positions; the question is who will take third.

The sumo match in Fukuoka started yesterday. The new *ōzeki*, Kotozakura, has grabbed the attention of the public, which is anxious to find out how far he can excel in this match.

Prime Minister Satō left for America yesterday. The National Federation of Students' Self-Government Associations had a demonstration to prevent his departure, and 333 people were injured. The one who tried to burn himself in front of the official residence of the Prime Minister died in the hospital. The public is very critical of these events. The public is also critical of the Prime Minister's position on bombing North Vietnam and his soft approach on the return of Okinawa. There is a special series of talks with the Vietnamese Communists (or Vietcong) in the paper. It says the North Vietnamese forces are equipped with American arms. The government forces are friendly to the communists in the north so they shoot at the sky in front of the American forces; they hand out American arms to the North; some factions in the government do not favor the Americans. I think America is bogged down in a quagmire. Three hundred million dollars have been spent for this war—no wonder the American people are critical of this war. Dr. Gallup of the Gallup Poll says that in the next election a candidate who can shorten this war and cut off ties with the Vietnam government will win. The poll taken in San Francisco did not succeed because of the way the proposition was stated. It was composed with the idea of "surrender"—some were against the Vietnam War, but an unconditional retreat was not acceptable to them. It would have been different if the question was a gradual withdrawal of Vietnam government forces as well as our forces. . . .

What do you think about those poems that I cited yesterday? Do you see a different me now? I cannot write poems, but I know the difference between good poems and poor ones. As I told you many times, you have a great talent for writing poems. Your talent is unique in your perception and in your expression of that perception; I respect your work. You gave me a poem on "whistle"—unfortunately you threw it away. It was so beautiful—I wish I remembered the lines. Poetry is wonderful. Why don't you start writing again? An ardent reader of your work is right by your side. I like your poems, and I like to say your lines over to myself. I want to keep whispering your poems on my death bed with your book on my chest.

From KIYOKO, *November 14.*

... YOU ARE READING BOOKS a lot. I'm glad that you are really enjoying it—it is so different from reading weekly magazines, isn't it? Just don't get too tired, otherwise the ringing in your ears might increase. I can see that we really don't know Japanese as well as we think we do. You found a good book! ...

You seem to have learned more about the high-frequency machine, and the carbon dioxide inhaler has been repaired. Now we have hope! ... I wish there was an extra inhaler set aside in case one malfunctions. The loss of time and money for the patient is enormous.

By the way, I think you have been bragging about your wife too much lately. I'm grateful for this publicity, but it is getting to be overpowering. I am what I am because of you so that if you boast about me too much it would mean you are boasting about yourself! ...

Dr. Childrey called today. He received your letter. However, since 1954 the medical insurance law has been altered and his certificate will not work in our case. He advises you to obtain a certificate from a Japanese doctor. Regarding the inhalation of carbon dioxide, he asked if you get a body flash after the treatment as a side effect. I told him that you never mentioned it, that you feel good after the treatment for a long time compared to the effect of the prescription you used to take, which was working for only a few hours. Dr. Childrey wants to know more about it and asked when you come back and what university in Japan has this machine. If it is really a good machine, America ought to get one, he said. None of his colleagues know about such treatment for the hearing-impaired. He thinks that maybe after 1954, a formerly inefficient machine was improved in Japan and Germany, and he wonders why America did not pay attention to it.

Yesterday the medicine for your mother arrived. She was pleased and said that she will send $300 to you as a Christmas present. I told her not to do so because she has already spent so much money on us that adding more will make it difficult for us to pay back. I told her that just small pocket money will do. I told her also that so far the insurance is covering the hospital expense, and if we need some more, we will ask for her help. ...

Yukiko is fine. We have a conference day at school day after tomorrow. Yukiko is preparing me for it saying that the teacher said a "C" for Social Studies is a fair grade. Her teacher hasn't sent a note home lately; maybe she is too busy getting ready for the conference. The American school system is much more relaxed than the Japanese. Here I go again—don't make me start being critical again. . . .

From KIYOSHI, *November 14.*

. . . WATANABE-SENSEI STOPPED BY yesterday. We talked from noontime to almost six o'clock. Dr. Torii, the physician-in-charge, joined us for about half an hour. Watanabe-sensei was happy to hear that you are teaching Japanese, particularly using that question-and-answer method. He himself wants to write a manual on a teaching method for the Japanese language by the time he retires in four or five years. I told him that there is no Japanese specialist in America; that the majority of teachers do not even know what a linguistic education is; that Japanese-language education will become increasingly important as 20,000 immigrants are expected to come to America; and that it is critical to have a qualified leader of Japanese-language education. I tried my best to explain to Watanabe-sensei how important this is.

He took a look at my dictionary of Japanese language and pointed out a few professors of Japanese whom he knew among the editors; one of them is from the University of Kyushu. He said that dictionaries do not offer a teaching method for languages, and that it would become a new academic field. As schools of Japanese language become increasingly important, qualified teachers will be in great demand. I suggested the founding of a Japanese Language Institute, and I asked him if he could take charge of that to educate teachers of Japanese. California expects the Japanese population to increase by up to 10,000; in 10 years it will expand to 100,000 or more. Teaching Japanese will become very important.

The state of California needs at least one Japanese Language Institute. Make it a small school at the beginning with perhaps one teacher who can be the principal as well. Let it start as a foundation. Golden Gate *Gakuen* will not be able to depend on temporary teachers forever. The same is true with the Japanese Language School of the Buddhist Association. Sooner or later they have to take constructive measures. In the Japanese Language Institute, (a) a group would train the teachers, and (b) a group would teach students learning the language. Also it would run a printing business to print textbooks, tapes, children's storybooks, etc. We will study books on the management of schools—I think it will work. Watanabe-sensei appeared to be very interested in these ideas.

Yesterday Iura-san returned from home with a box of tangerine oranges. Her family has a large orchard. She brought a huge box full because I said I loved tangerines. I gave Watanabe-sensei a bagful. Iura-san brought one branch on which tangerines were hanging like grapes. She brought it so that I could see the best ones. Her boyfriend has a new camera. I'll ask him to take some pictures of me and send them to you. . . . *[Continued in next letter.]*

From KIYOSHI, *November 14.*

[CONTINUED FROM PREVIOUS LETTER.] Harris Public Opinion Research reports that support for President Johnson dropped down to 23%. Johnson must be having a difficult time. Also reported this morning was the meeting of Johnson and Prime Minister Satō. The future of the return of Okinawa is uncertain, and the anti-American sentiment will become worse.

Now it's about Akiyama Chieko-san. She writes that the number of "high Misses" (formerly called "old Miss") is increasing because of the economic independence of single women. But that independence is threatened nowadays because married men are watching them for an opportunity to prey upon them. If a married man tells a "high Miss" that his wife cannot satisfy him, the "high Miss" takes him in, thinking that she could do a better job than his wife. Single men do not pay attention to "high Misses." The general trend is that men marry by 26 years old, and some years later their middle-age relationship begins. Men and women need each other. But the economic independence of women put the brakes on such a basic need. It is unfortunate!

The fourth day of the relay marathon ended with Miyazaki-ken first, Fukuoka second; Kagoshima, Ōita, Nagasaki, Kumamoto followed; and Saga was the last! But in the four-day total Saga is still third. I'm going to skip the Grand Sumo Match because it must have been reported in your local Japanese paper. The big news is about the four deserters from a U.S. aircraft carrier.

I wrote earlier that Iura-san brought a box of tangerines from home. I didn't do anything for her except invite her for a dinner because she does errands for me. There is a new restaurant on the first floor of the hospital—inexpensive with good food. She brought many books from home too. She wants to get married and be like us, and she asked if she can write to you. . . . I told her you would be happy to hear from her. If she writes, please send a card or a short note in return; she will be very happy—and mention the tangerines.

I got a letter from Iwama-san yesterday. She says her African violets are in full bloom. She inserted some flowers, but they were all smashed in the mail. I'll write to her in a couple of days. She says she will send me almond chocolate for Christmas. If you see her, please thank her for me. She is very happy that her son made third or fourth in his class.

Please inquire at Mills College and University of Santa Clara regarding what I wrote in English in my letter the other day. We had asked Hisayo-san's help in this, but nothing has happened so far. . . .

I want to see you. I read the poems of Takamura Kōtarō. They make me cry. My longing for you gets deeper. I miss your body too, but it is more a spiritual thirst. . . .

From KIYOSHI, *November 14.*

. . . IT'S SO GREAT TO HEAR about the raise in your salary to $595—and you got it so fast! Isn't it GREAT! It shows that your ability is recognized—you worked hard, and it was recognized. . . .

Hinashi-san comes to visit me often. He is a good friend. He calls me "*Oji-san*." He is an A student of Kyushu University—he knows the works of famous poets like the palm of his hand. He noticed my collection of books and opened page after page to show me the best work of Hagiwara Sakutarō, Takuboku, Hakushū, Tōson, etc. I was impressed. And I was awestruck when he wrote by memory the following Chinese poem by Toho!

春望　杜甫　　Hope in Spring　by Toho

国破在山河
The country lost the battle, but mountains and rivers remain
城春草木深
The castle is covered deep with spring greenery

感時花濺淚
Reminisce with tears covering the flowers

恨別鳥驚心
A bird surprises me at our parting

烽火連三月
The battle lasted for three months

家書低万金
My book collection is now so depleted

白頭搔更短
Scratching my white head, I find my hair shorter

渾欲不勝簪
All I want is to be back at the palace

Show this to Cecilia. I'm touched and grateful that someone like this genius calls me "*Oji-san*" and comes to see me so often. I haven't given him anything–even a coffee candy! He listens intently to my philosophy of life. He respects me. Today I told him about happiness not being found easily, and he agreed. It's so different from my experience of a hospital stay in America. Here I enjoy talking with these great people, including Iura-san. They are really great people.

I wrote back to Iwama-san today.

How is Yukiko? How about her school work? She loves me and thinks that I am the best father in the whole world. She tells me not to worry about losing my hearing because she is there to help me. But when children become teenagers, they become critical of everything around them. She might become self-conscious about her father being handicapped. It must be hard on her. She might feel ashamed of introducing me to others. I can't blame her. But if I work on something really meaningful, when she becomes 25 or 6, she might feel proud of her father who tried to do something noteworthy in spite of his hearing loss. I am not worried about it. I am going to try my best so that she can be proud of me. You and Yukiko are my irreplaceable treasures. I want to be a worthy husband and father.

From KIYOSHI, *November 15.*

. . . I JUST FINISHED READING the *Asahi* and the *Nishi-Nihon*—the English newspaper is delivered only at night.

I will write important things first. Last night Dr. Torii told me the following: I have no chance of getting my hearing back; I should prevent a worsening of the present symptom; the inhalation of carbon dioxide will be stopped at the end of this month. He will prepare a medication that I should take home. His suggestion is that I go home by Christmas. I felt sad because this meant that the world of sound is forever taken away from me. But I will not give up my life! I will do my best without hearing. It is the only way to answer your boundless love for me. Even if I can't hear, I will become a father whom Yukiko can respect. My future will not be easy physically and emotionally, but I must face it. I may cry, but I will stand up to it.

Please send my winter coat as soon as possible. It should reach me by December 20. Also send me parting gifts such as coffee candies, Almond Roca, Lux soap, and a shaving set for Dr. Torii as soon as possible. I'd like to leave Japan as soon as the package arrives.

I'd like to start getting things like a wrist watch for Yukiko, a rice cooker for my sister, rice buckets for Cecilia and us, albums, etc. I will ask Hiroyuki-san to mail these and my summer clothes and books. How about a camera for Yukiko? Let me know anything that we should get.

I think I should get the ultrashort-wave machine. Dr. Yasuda highly recommends it, and I am interested in it too because it will be better than taking medicine to stimulate the capillary vessels. I don't get headaches from it. Also the machine is good for other ailments such as neuralgic pain. Let me know what you think because I want to get the shopping done and out of my way as soon as possible.

Please don't tell people that I am coming home next month. It would be different if my hearing were restored.

Please be prepared for the last expense to be a fund for gift shopping [and] a few days extra stay in the hospital (beyond December 18); the expense for travel may go over $200.

I will write again later. Take care.

To my beloved Kiyoko-*sama*

From KIYOKO, *November 16.*

. . . SO MANY THINGS HAPPENED today. The train that runs behind our building had engine trouble and has been sitting there since this morning. The traffic was shut off from the south at First Street to 13th Street in the north. It didn't affect me but Yukiko had a hard time getting to school and Hiroko-san was late for work—there was a great deal of confusion.

I went to Yukiko's school conference. She started this session very well but slid back into daydreaming and sloppy handwriting. She cries if the teacher scolds her so that the teacher feels sorry for her. I told the teacher that unless Yukiko corrects her attitude right after crying, she should keep reminding her. Yukiko tends to stay up late at night so I must help her to go to bed early. I don't think she is lazy; but she is slow and gets distracted. I believe she needs more sleep. I will cut down on her evening activities and send her to bed at nine p.m. I'm sure lack of sleep is the first problem. She didn't get any As; all C's and C-'s, with just one B+; I'll send you a copy.

The teacher says that Yukiko is a happy child, has a high IQ, and is always dressed clean—but she lacks consistency in her work. When we had parents' visiting day, Yukiko was chewing gum. The teacher didn't say anything because she didn't want to embarrass her or me in front of the visitors, but later she warned Yukiko not to do such a thing; it didn't work because she was chewing gum again soon after that. The trouble is that Yukiko does not take things seriously. The teacher would praise her for her excellent work, but Yukiko fails to maintain the same high quality in her next assignment—there is no consistency in her study. It worries the teacher very much, and she wants our understanding, cooperation, and permission to help Yukiko out of this situation. I was carefree too at that age, but Yukiko is more so.

Last night I went to the one-year celebration of Tsukiji-san's store and ran into Shiro-san and his bride. Do you remember a Caucasian woman who worked at the fruit stand? She is now Shiro-san's wife. They said hello to you.

Now about Linda. In order to help her Italian boyfriend who was ordered home by the Immigration Office, she sent a paper to the authorities saying she was the wife of that man. The bureau immediately started to investigate and came to the company. Our supervisor, Mr. Johnston, was the first to be interviewed and me the next. They came to ask me a lot of things about Linda all the while taping the conversation. I was asked if I would testify in court as a witness. I said I would talk to my husband first. He said that is understandable, but if my testimony is needed, would I cooperate with the bureau. I said I would. What a troublemaker Linda is! I'll manage it somehow—please don't worry. I received one letter from you yesterday, and two today. But I'll write to you again tomorrow because I'm tired from too much excitement. Poetry is something so far from reality at this moment.

From KIYOSHI, *November 16.*

. . . I WENT TO SEE THE ultrashort-wave machine yesterday afternoon with Shizuma-san as a guide. Since Dr. Torii told me that my hearing will not recover, I want to try everything I can before accepting that diagnosis. After listening to an explanation of the machine, I tried it on my ears for about half an hour, and it felt good. When I scratched my ear, it sounded louder than before—I don't think it was my imagination. So I bought the machine, and it will be delivered to me today. I don't want to ignore the report on the clinical success of this machine at first-class universities such as Tokyo University and Chiba Medical University. The cost is 79,000 yen, about $220. I think this machine will help me.

On the way back, I stopped at the dentist and had my teeth filled and cleaned. There were 11 teeth to be filled with amalgams. It cost 13,000 yen all together. You'll be surprised to see the difference—the black color on my teeth is all gone. I was amazed to see the advanced technique of Japanese dentistry. I didn't have a bridge made because it's costly—about $150 for one.

Yesterday Shizuma-san brought with her another interesting girl. She is from Saga Prefecture, and her father has been working as a school doctor at the University of Saga. Her name is Morokuma-san. She is a second-year medical student at Kyushu University. She is quite intelligent and pretty. She uses a hearing-aid too. Shizuma-san must have told her about you and me as hero and heroine of a love story, and Morokuma-san wanted to meet me. When she heard about your inspiring words, "We will have a happy life together even if you lose your hearing," she had tears in her eyes. . . .

She told me that in the Soviet Union a study is being carried out right now using surgery to restore hearing; that the theory has been established, but the clinical technique has not been fully developed yet; and that the surgery should become common practice in four or five years so that I should not lose hope. She is following the development of this study closely because she herself is impaired with the loss of hearing. She will let me know the progress of this study as the reports come in. . . .

She said you might know her father since you went to the University of Saga. Her name is Morokuma Yoshiko and she is 22 years old. Although she will be busy with exams, she wants to see me again in December before I leave. You said once before that we don't know what it will be like four or five years later. I look forward to something good in the future—I have hope! . . .

From KIYOSHI, *November 16.*

. . . THE ULTRASHORT-WAVE machine arrived today. Yesterday I tried it at the store, and I could hear some sound. I thought it was my imagination. So today I tried it without expecting to hear anything. But I still heard sound —I think this is working—I put my finger in my ear and scratched—I could hear the sound clearly! Maybe because I am so desperate, I'm imagining the sound?

I'll wait and see. In the explanatory note attached to the machine, it says that the blood vessels expand remarkably. Am I facing a miracle, maybe? I'm going to observe it with utmost care. I'll report to you every day how it goes. According to the note, by using other pharmaceutical products, the enlargement of the blood vessels could last for about one hour. Using the ultrashort-wave machine, it lasts for several hours; and if the patient continuously applies this machine for a couple of days, the blood vessels will remain enlarged for several days.

In Dr. Shirabe's opinion, the enlargement of the vessels was caused by the heat that comes from the machine. But the note specifically points out that the effect of the ultrashort-wave machine on the capillary vessels is not caused by the heat; it is caused by the nerves that control the vascular movement. The test was performed on animals as well as humans; the enlargement of the blood vessels was observed, and with humans the said condition lasted for several hours. The note continues to say that the blood vessels did not shrink even under the effect of a strong contractile agent such as adrenalin, and this proves that the short wave lowers the tension of the nerves which control the blood vessels.

Tonight after nine p.m., I'm going to use the machine as it is recommended to use it twice a day for 30 minutes. I have never felt this good before. Arlidrin worked for about two hours, but I didn't feel good afterward. This ultrashort-wave treatment appears to be different. It may be too soon to say one way or other. I will observe it carefully and take notes. In four or five days I should be able to make a better judgment.

Today I read the poems of Takamura Kōtarō. They are good, Kiyoko-san—I couldn't help but cry. I hope you read them too. The poet's love for his wife breaks my heart. I want you to read them as soon as possible. I want to share this experience with you right now. Takamura Kōtarō loved his wife—I am not the only one who loves his wife so much.

This evening I read your letter of November 12. I'm glad you had the clutch replaced in the car. It doesn't cost much, maybe about $5, but the labor to remove a motor would cost between $30 and $40. When the motor is removed, the clutch should always be replaced.

It's a good idea to start preparing for the literary exercise at the school. The important point is to have everybody take part in it—the parents of the slow learners will be more interested in the achievement of their children. If you can, prepare for two plays. A Japanese dance, that rabbit dance, would be good too; also Japanese songs. I'll ask Iura-san to get some scripts for the plays. . . .

From KIYOKO, *November 17.*

. . . TO TELL YOU THE TRUTH, I'm not thrilled to write back to the many ladies whom you've been talking to—you are an excellent publicity man! I'll send them cards to thank them for visiting you.

I talked with the section chief today about my appearance in court on Linda's case. He said that I must comply with the summons from the government; besides Linda may need my help. I'm just unlucky to be involved in her case.

I'll try to find the quickest way to send your overcoat. Also I'll send you candies so you can give them to people as a parting gift or Christmas present. I plan to send you $100 today to buy presents for friends back home.

Could you ship by sea mail a rice server for Cecilia as soon as possible? A folding umbrella is a good gift from Japan. I'd like to have one too. How about four or five umbrellas of different colors? Select colors that might stand out in the rain.

It sounds like Watanabe-sensei has a great idea for the education of Japanese teachers. I hope he can start as soon as possible. It would be nice to have a published textbook. If the textbook is good, it can cover somewhat the inexperience of teachers, but it would help more if the teachers were well trained too, not just anybody from the street. I really hope it materializes soon.

I had Hisayo phone Mills College and Santa Clara University. She was told that there was no class in Japanese or any plans to do so. The reason was that their institutions were too small to have Japanese classes. I think it's better to write as many colleges and universities as possible from a list of educational establishments. Do you remember a Mr. Claus, a student of Hori-san in his Japanese class? He went to Japan with us once. I don't know his background. He wants to live in Japan and study Japanese on a scholarship. He could teach English while studying Japanese, but since there is no such exchange program, he has to be invited by someone in Japan. I mention this although it is totally different from Watanabe-sensei's idea.

Thank you for recognizing my poetic talent! I'll keep writing haiku from time to time. . . .

I'm going to take care of Yukiko. I told Mother not to spoil her. Last night I put Yukiko to bed at nine p.m. But she seems to need more sleep. It's hard work to be a good parent, isn't it! . . .

From KIYOSHI, *November 17.*

I HAVE NOT USED THE ULTRASHORT-WAVE MACHINE yet this morning because the assistant professor, Dr. Soda, is supposed to make his patient rounds. Otherwise I plan to put on the machine twice a day—at nine o'clock in the morning and in the evening.

I finished reading the newspapers. In the relay marathon on Kyushu Island, Saga Prefecture is holding third place, Miyazaki is keeping the lead, and Fukuoka is struggling to keep second position. The race will end the day after tomorrow. The sumo match will go on. The pro-boxing match ended yesterday with the Hawaiian boxer, Fuji, holding onto his title. He is second- or third-generation Japanese from Hawaii. He calls himself "The Soul of Japan," and that ignites his Japanese fans. But he cannot speak Japanese well. Last night he knocked out the challenger from West Germany. The old folks in Japan lament the lack of spirit in the new generations, and now the soul of Japan is brought back to them by a third-generation Hawaiian—ironic, isn't it?

This morning I read again the book by Takamura Kōtarō. Such a beautiful love story! He says, "I met Chieko—she cleansed me with her pure love and rescued me from decadence. I needed her so much that her death was a cruel blow to me. For the first several months her death gripped my heart, and in that emptiness, I lost the will to create art. I used to show my sculpture to her first; we used to examine it together each day. It was a supreme moment. She understood my work and adored it. She would keep my wooden sculpture in her bosom and walk around town caressing it. Who would love my sculpture as much as she did—like a child hangs on to her favorite toy. Now I have nobody to show my work." Chieko adored him too. Even after losing her mind, she kept mumbling, "Chieko, Kōtarō, Chieko, Kōtarō . . ." I couldn't help but cry as I was reading this book. He loved Chieko deeply, and Chieko admired and trusted Kōtarō. . . .

Us
by Takamura Kōtarō

When I think of you
I sense eternity right away.
I am here; you are here:
here is my *raison d'être.*

My life and your life . . .
lean against each other,
tangle up and melt into each other,
return to the chaos of the beginning.

You depend on me;
you live in me;
you become alive because of me.

We treasure life;
we do not rest.
We can't help but
be pushed up to the highest of heights;
reach to the farthest of the far;
go to the deepest of depths.

How bright it is . . . what a joy!!

· · ·

CHIEKO PLAYING WITH PLOVERS
by Takamura Kōtarō

On the deserted beach of Kiyūkuri
Chieko plays sitting on the rock.
Countless friends call Chieko's name,
Chii, chii, chii, chii, chii . . .

Printing tiny footmarks on the sand
plovers gather around Chieko.

Continuously mumbling something,
Chieko calls back with her hands up,
Chii, chii, chii . . .

Plovers ask Chieko for shells in both her hands.
She throws them in the air;
the plovers call Chieko
Chii, chii . . .

Giving up being a human,
Chieko returned to Nature,
her back being a solitary dot there.

In the windbreak forest two blocks away,
in the setting sun,
I stand blankly
in the rain of pine's pollen.

. . .

I wrote only two of Kōtarō's poems here. Aren't they beautiful? Love between husband and wife—I can't think of anything more beautiful than that in this world. My heart becomes beautiful when I read Kōtarō's poems.

I'll write again later.

From KIYOSHI, November 18.

. . . THE MORNING PAPER REPORTED on the front page that a member of the International Inspection Team, a soldier from India, died in a bombing. In the relay marathon, Miyazaki is definitely in the lead; Fukuoka is lagging in second; Saga is still keeping third, but Ōita is moving up; they are behind by only 19 seconds. There is no telling how this race will end. Tomorrow is the last day. The sumo match catches everyone's attention too.

I definitely feel that the ultrashort-wave machine is working for me. There is a distinct difference between before the use of the machine and after. If I can find the correct power suitable to my condition, I think it will work much better. I'll let you know. . . .

A few days ago, one of the patients by the name of Yatomi Hidehiko (age 33) came to see me. He heard about my condition and wanted to cheer me up. He is a graduate of the University of Kitakyushu. He was hospitalized for five years for a heart condition and recovered from it without having surgery. However, he too would have lost his hearing if he hadn't stopped taking streptomycin when the horrendous ringing in his ears started. He has read a lot of books on philosophy. We enjoyed talking about it. He is checking out of the hospital today. He told me not to lose hope and quoted the following lines by Romaine Roland: "Even at the moment of death, one must try to get up." It reminded me of your words: "Up to the moment of death, one must look forward." He also quoted something very close to what you said. A certain philosopher in Europe said: "Instead of chasing after what you have lost, go after the possibility that you may still have it." Kiyoko-san, you told me that I must not cry over something that I lost; I still have good eyes, a good mouth, good hands, and most of all good mental agility; I must do my best with what I have. I'm glad I met him. We went to the restaurant downstairs to have dinner together yesterday. He works in a printing company. He lives happily with his wife. He was in the hospital for surgery on his middle ear, the tympanum.

They say the Japanese have become unconcerned about others these days, but there are still many good people. Starting with Ōsedo-san, the lady who took care of me when I came here, Matsuda-san, Tachibana-san, Hinashi Yoshiharu-san, Ōtomo-san, Iura-san, and Yatomi-san, who went home today . . . I've met so many nice people in the hospital. We have the same Japanese blood in us—everybody desires to do better in life—I will try my best too. . . .

From KIYOSHI, *November 19.*

SUNDAY, NOVEMBER 19, A CLOUDY DAY. HOW ARE YOU, Kiyoko-san? There is no change around here; even the ultrashort-wave doesn't show any change; not much news in the paper either. Fukuoka's team won't be able to pass Miyazaki's team because they are 20 minutes behind. The race between Saga and Ōita for the third position is more interesting. They kept exactly the same timing for nine days—quite unusual. Today is the last day, and the goal line is in front of the Nishi-Nihon Newspaper Building.

Regarding the literary event of the Japanese Language School, I asked Iura-san and her boyfriend yesterday to look for scripts of plays and records with dancing instructions. They said there are many good scripts of Japanese nursery songs. You can present a successful show so that, after this event, Mrs. Tokutomi of the Japanese Language School of San Jose will become very famous! I asked Iura-san to keep sending us good scripts for future use too.

Her boyfriend's name is Kamiseji-san. He is an engineer. This couple respects us and wants to become like us. I told Iura-san that you majored in Japanese literature at the University of Saga. She wants me to read many poetry collections so that I can impress you! I have cited two of your haiku to her [quoted in November 12 letter]. . . . She was so impressed. Both she and her boyfriend love literature.

How is Yukiko? Please tell her to write to me.

I forgot to mention Ōsaki-san when I listed the many admirable people I met since I came here. She was the one I thought best for Yotsuo-san's wife. She is the nurse in the treatment room. She cleans my wound every day with such tender care. She is the "Nightingale" of the Otorhinology Section. Everybody, not just me, is treated the same way with utmost care. She graciously turned down the chance to become Yotsuo-san's wife in America. I believe it is her mission to serve sick people like an angel in white. . . .

From KIYOKO, *November 20.*

. . . SO YOU ARE COMING HOME this year end! Be careful not to catch cold while you travel. I'm glad that you bought the ultrashort-wave machine to bring home. I mailed $100 last Friday. Your mother had set aside $200 for your Christmas present, and she offered to mail it to you.

I have put buttons on your coat and started to get the package ready. But Almond Roca is all sold out and coffee candies too, so I packed something else. I'll see if I can get Almond Roca somewhere else this evening. If I can't find any, I'll send the coat, razor sets, and candies without the Almond Roca, which will be mailed later.

I'm worried about you catching cold and the ringing in your ears becoming worse when you go out to shop. I'm glad to hear that you are bringing home some medicine from the hospital, but have you consulted anyone about the excess noise around our house, for example the noise of trains and airplanes? Please discuss it with the doctors.

Yukiko says she is sorry about your hearing loss, but she will never stop loving you. She says when you come home you'll be hers only—you are not Mommy's Daddy. When Hisayo came to our house, she didn't know what to do or how to take your condition—and you may be afraid of a similar situation with Yukiko. But I think it will be all right. If I couldn't handle the situation, it would be different. But with our love and trust which are stronger than ever before, we can manage it without any problems. Just like a hole in your sock, you may be aware of it, but others won't even notice it. Nobody laughs at your hearing problem. If the three of us can lead a happy life in spite of your hearing loss, we will be more blessed than any ordinary family.

The most important thing is that you hold on to your high spirit to conquer your handicap—which no one else but you can do—and that will be the source of our strength. If you can maintain that spirit, we can be a very happy family. Our path will be wide open, with you as our leader and the one whom we respect. Please do not forget that you are the leader of our family even though you lost your hearing. A brain surgeon, Dr. Shimizu, said when he himself suffered from a cerebral hemorrhage, he realized that there is no other way but for the patient himself to go through the horrific passage of recovery. (*Bungei-shunjū*, September issue.) It sounds harsh, but it is true.

I'm writing now from home. We just had dinner. Today I received two letters written on the 16th and 17th. I just finished reading them. Takamura Kōtarō's poems are so beautiful. . . . He loved his wife so deeply that his sentiment was transformed into these poems that capture our heart. You've found a great poet.

I have just a little space left to write on. How about purchasing things for Yukiko, but save them for the right occasion to give her as a reward? I forgot about tracking your stoma bags. Let me know by wire if you need more right away; if not, write me so that I can mail them by air. I'm going out now to look for Almond Roca. I'll finish packing tonight with or without Roca, and tomorrow I'll take it to the post office. I've bought a card for Iura-san, but I'll wait till I receive a letter from her so that Shizuma-san won't become jealous of her getting a card from me. . . .

From KIYOSHI, *November 20.*

. . . THIS MORNING DR. KAWADA made the rounds of the patients so I asked him if he has heard of the operation that had taken place in the Soviet Union to restore hearing. He has never heard about it. Morokuma-san said she has heard of it, but maybe it was from a different source. Dr. Kawada said that the operation is not possible at the present time. I was disappointed and sad. But I told myself not to lose hope because the medical world is advancing rapidly. Morokuma-san herself has a slight difficulty with her hearing and has a keen interest in any improvement of its treatment. I will keep in touch with her.

It makes me really sad to learn that there is no breakthrough to restore hearing. I now realize that the world of sound had been a very important part of my life. I feel miserable just to think that I'm going back to San Francisco without being cured. I know I must overcome this sadness. I know that you treasure your language. I will search for new hope in the Japanese language to which you are deeply bound. With your love and collaboration, I know I can recover my footing.

The boyfriend of Iura-san brought several records of Japanese dances and games for children. I hope you like them. He said he will also look for scripts for plays.

Yesterday Hiroyuki-san and Noriko-san came to see me. I didn't know they were coming. I was having dinner in the restaurant downstairs. We didn't have much time together but talked about the packages to be shipped home. They will help me the next time they come.

Thank you for your letter, and your explanation about the telephone call from Dr. Childrey. I don't understand why he cannot simply write that the treatment is not done in America. "Carbon dioxide inhalation treatment for the hard-of-hearing caused by medication is not being done in the United States"; why couldn't he write that simple statement? If our insurance would cover at least the airfare, I could pay the debts back to my mother. Could you please talk to Dr. Childrey again?

I'm glad the medicine for Mother arrived. If it is good, I'll send another package and will bring some home with me. Have you shipped my overcoat? I want to come home as soon as I receive it.

I feel depressed; I don't know what to do with this gloomy feeling. I must change my mood. . . .

From KIYOSHI, *November 21.*

TUESDAY, NOVEMBER 21, 9:20 A.M. HOW ARE YOU, Kiyoko-san? It is a beautiful autumn day here. Today's paper covers the return of the Prime Minister Satō extensively and the fall of the British pound.

There is no change here; neither better nor worse. I can't help but feel depressed about the fruitless outcome of what we went through. Now I just want to go home. I don't want to stay here even a day more. I can't help but feel gloomy when I think of my future. I know I must live to the best of my ability, but I suspect that it's not easy. I must avoid making judgments prematurely; I must be cheerful; I must be calm. I know it is important. But at times I become worried. I know I don't want to make you unhappy, but sometimes the circumstances might make you sad. I will try, though, to live through the adversity and to be worthy of your boundless love.

I will work hard to compile a textbook for Japanese. I don't know how far I can go, but I will try my very best. I will write to the Japanese linguists for their guidance and complete my teaching method. I think it is important to seek guidance from contemporary authorities on the Japanese language, such as Kindaichi Haruhiko and Ōno Susumu. They have done respectable research in languages including English, and I would like to get to know them. I may have to alter some of my theories or put more emphasis on them, and getting to know these scholars might help me a great deal. I have to study methodically and extensively in order to make an excellent text-book. I have asked Watanabe-sensei to get books on language education for me. This is the field that I can pour my energy into now that I have lost my hearing. This is an area that one can excel in as long as he has eyes and brains and hands. I'm sad because I have to lean on you so much, and I cannot do anything for you. I'd like to become a husband whom you can respect and be proud of. I want to stand firm against hardship, have no inferiority complex, stay cheerful—and someday I'd like to be the husband and the father who became, against all the odds, an accomplished teacher of the Japanese language. Whether I achieve something or not isn't important. I'd like to keep going remembering your encouraging words to hold me up. . . .

From KIYOSHI, *November 21.*

. . . YOUR LETTER ON YUKIKO'S school conference and about Linda just arrived. Your letter is the only thing that keeps me going. Thank you so much.

We will work together on Yukiko's problem when I come home. From now on I'm going to concentrate on two things—Yukiko and the Japanese language. I'd like to help her understand the joy of studying and of getting good grades in class. I'd like to be a good father and a good example for her. This is the best thing I can do in my life. Also this is the last chance for Yukiko to learn the good study habits required to excel in school. I'm sorry that you have to work harder at your job, but I will keep the house and concentrate in Yukiko's education while I develop a teaching method for a Japanese language class. I think this is better than me having a job trying to make a living. I think it is very important for us to nurture our love and, equally important, to assure Yukiko's happiness.

Linda's case is a big surprise. Why is she not married to this man? I feel sorry for people who hang in a relationship only for the sake of pleasure. Do they think they can keep the same young love forever by just living together? Don't they think that marriage would bring a steady, happier life? Japanese weekly magazines are full of those sex stories as if they are trying to awaken young minds to the hedonistic life. Fourteen- or 15-year-olds are reading these magazines full of illustrations of the male sexual organ, and instructions on how and where to fondle it to have the best excitement—you'd be shocked. There will be many girls like Linda in the future. I want to protect Yukiko from such a wild life. I want her to find someone whom she can really love and marry him. It is we parents who have the responsibility to protect her and guide her to a happy marriage.

I can hardly wait for my departure date now that it is decided. I can hardly wait for my coat to arrive. Today a visitor from JAL came to assure me that everything is taken care of. He said he will make the reservation as soon as possible because of the Christmas rush. Ōshima-san must have written to the JAL office in Fukuoka about my departure. Anyway, I will come home as soon as the coat arrives. . . .

From KIYOSHI, *November 22.*

. . . YESTERDAY I FINISHED THE October–November insurance papers. Maybe Iura-san's boyfriend can mail it today. We had a fire in this neighborhood last night. From my window I could see the flames engulf the house, and I felt so uneasy. It was after 7:30 p.m.

Shizuma-san told me that a young heart patient upstairs wanted to meet me. So I visited her for about a half hour and cheered her up. She is 18 years old. She had surgery last month and cannot walk yet. After talking with me, she said she would not lose hope or expect too much. She would try her best. She has a dark complexion and reminds me of somebody—but I'm not sure who. She has a round face and large eyes—very cute. I hope she gets well soon. . . .

Today's *Asahi* newspaper reported a riot at San Jose State University. The students were protesting against a help-wanted ad of a company that makes napalm bombs. I felt homesick just seeing the familiar place name, San Jose. . . .

How are you, Kiyoko-san? I haven't seen you for more than four months —I can hardly wait! If I were with you, I might be more cheerful and energetic. Right now I am so depressed. But I'll be all right—don't worry. . . .

From KIYOKO, *November 23.*

. . . I SLEPT LATE THIS MORNING, went to Jane's for Thanksgiving dinner, and came home around seven p.m. Your letter of November 20 came yesterday. However, I think two or three letters were skipped—I'm sure they will come later.

You seem to be discouraged again. It is as though in your psyche you are standing on a cliff. If you want to stop these ups and downs of your psyche, you need to choose a secure foothold now. If you don't want to stop, you will keep falling. There is no reason for us to feel miserable. We are capable of finding a new way of life even if we have a handicap. You must shake off this sad feeling and step down from the airplane with a smile and confidence. Don't push yourself into the darkness of sorrow; you must steady yourself. Otherwise our hope for an ideal way of life will fade away in front of our eyes. We have always cherished life. It's not like Kiyoshi-san to think that the value of your life is diminished because you lost your hearing. Sure, it is inconvenient, but it is nothing more than that. The Kiyoshi-san whom I selected for my husband would overcome that inconvenience gracefully and cheerfully—I will be proud of him and respect him; he will be my paragon. . . .

About the certificate from Dr. Childrey: I cannot ask him again when I had already asked him to write "It (carbon dioxide inhalation) is not done in America." He told me that he could not write even that. I suspect he was concerned about how it would look to his colleagues. Otherwise I cannot think of any reason why he would not comply with our request. Dr. Childrey is a very nice man, and he was evidently sorry for not being able to help me. He called me after he discussed it with the other doctors. I couldn't help but imagine an ad hoc society of doctors. Dr. Childrey has to deal with the convention of American otolaryngology and all those temporarily assigned doctors—it's a stiff wall to face. None of the doctors will write such a certificate. Therefore, I think you should ask a Japanese doctor to issue a certificate saying, "Presently this method is used only at the University of Kyushu in Japan and one other institute in Germany." Then our insurance company will have to investigate to see if there is any institution in America that provides the same treatment. . . . In any case, we can pay back the airfare incrementally so it's better if we try not to worry too much.

Changing to a more relaxed subject—I bought a new dress for Yukiko for Thanksgiving dinner. She looked very nice. Everybody was surprised about how big she was. The guests were Uchida-san and her oldest sister, your sister's family, the son of your brother's friend by the name of Yamada-san (he is in the Air Force), and Yukiko and I—Hisayo didn't come because she had a sty in her eye. Jane's violets were beautiful. You can ask her for some when you see her.

It is getting cold here finally. I almost forgot to tell you—I shipped the overcoat the morning of the 21st. I hope you get it before Christmas. Almond Roca is still not in the store. Maybe we could mail it directly to your friends. What do you say? Let me know what you think.

I'm thinking of your homecoming every day.

Forever your wife, Kiyoko

From KIYOSHI, *November 23.*

THURSDAY, NOVEMBER 23; IT'S LABOR DAY HERE. Isn't it Thanksgiving Day in America? It is a beautiful day. I'm going to visit Iura-san's orange orchard. Kamiseji-san will pick me up at one o'clock in the afternoon. Seeing that I was so despondent lately, they urged me to come see the orchard and relax. They are such a nice couple. They want to visit America and meet you. He is an engineer, so he can save some money for the trip relatively easily. He is also a poet, and wrote the following poem when he was a student at university:

> Look at me—this frail body,
> the wind can easily blow it away.
> But I shan't be defeated ever . . .
> this body
> can bear any hardship.
>
> I'm alive;
> I'm young;
> I want to be naked.
> I want to train myself,
> I won't be daunted.

I have a dream,
a wonderful dream,
a gigantic dream . . .
I want to wrestle with it
with this body.

I can do anything—
Just wait and see.

Don't you think it's an interesting poem? Kamiseji-san is thinner and shorter than I am. He has an innocent look—a very pleasant person. I pray that they will become a happy couple like us. While we were having curry dinner yesterday, I said to Iura-san that she must not become too accustomed to being cared for and forget to care for Kamiseji-san. I told her that a man gets lonely too. Kamiseji-san must have been reminded of something; he nodded many times and laughed. I told them that I had to remind you of loving me too. I said that a woman sometimes forgets to express her love even if she is deeply in love. Kamiseji-san was happy to hear that. By the way I asked him to mail the insurance papers. . . .

The newspaper reported that Japan will adopt the Zip Code system starting next July. But the Postal Labor Union is opposing it in anticipation of job cuts. The Zip Code system saves so much because one machine can do the work of seven employees.

Yesterday's evening paper took up the problem of the weekly magazines. There are over 50 magazines on the blacklist. Shameless eroticism is shown in photos and the issues are full of vulgar articles. . . . It is time for a critical public discussion. . . .

To my precious, beloved Kiyoko-*sama*

From KIYOSHI, *November 24.*

. . . I'LL START WITH THE shopping list. But first, (1) please do not worry about writing to the patients here. You must be busy because of my homecoming. Just mention their names in your letter to me—I will pass your message to them. (2) I am anxiously waiting for the overcoat. (3) I'll buy one rice pail for Cecilia tomorrow and mail it as soon as possible. It is possible that I will arrive home before Cecilia gets the pail in the mail, but I'll bring home another one anyway so that we might end up with an extra pail as a spare. I'm going to buy two small ones and two large ones, and one small one that I'll get today and mail. (4) I'll get a high-quality folding umbrella for you, and four or five ordinary ones for others. (5) I'll get 10 thick albums like the one Tsukiji-san has (about 800 or 900 yen), and 10 thinner albums (500 or 600 yen). (6) An electric rice cooker for my sister, a watch and rain boots for Yukiko. (7) What shall I get for my mother? If her medicine is working all right, I'll get a lot of it.

I think I might need $300 more. If you've sent $100 already, could you send another $200 as soon as possible? I have 90,000 yen in the hospital office. But I may need a little more in this pay period because they are now giving me carbon dioxide inhalation. $20 or $30 for pocket money on the return trip is included in that $300.

Now I want to tell you that I joined the Academy of Japanese Language. The scholars, Drs. Tokieda Seiki, Kindaichi Kyōsuke, and Kindaichi Haruhiko are also members. Their office is on the campus of Tokyo University. Their bulletin, "Studies of the Japanese Language," is published four times a year from this office and mailed to the members. They work for the advancement of the study of the Japanese language, make contact with scholars and concerned citizens, have seminars and public lectures, and publish "Studies of the Japanese Language" and books. Members can make presentations at the seminars and publish articles in the bulletin.

The membership fee is 1,500 yen a year which includes the bulletin. The annual fee is about $5. I sent 5,000 yen because I wanted to read some back issues of the bulletin and to cover the international postage. The bulletin costs 300 yen, and they can send me eight issues retroactively. Now I can get information on the Japanese language in Japan and make contacts. I suspect that teaching methods for Japanese language classes will become one of the study subjects in the future. I'm going to work hard in that area. I spent a lot of money on books and now the membership, but I'm sure you will approve of this. Now I can do systematic research and make inquiries about the Japanese language as a member of the academy—I feel I've my energy back—I'll do my best—Kiyoko-san, please back me up!

I will tell you later about the outing to the orange orchard since there is no space left in this sheet. I had a great time. Take care, Kiyoko-san. Let me know quickly if we need to add anything to the shopping list.

From KIYOSHI, *November 24.*

IT'S STILL NOVEMBER 24. IT WAS CLOUDY IN THE MORNING, but now the sun is coming out. The area is covered with smog though—it's worse than in America.

Yesterday Kamiseji-san and I visited Iura-san at her home. We took a taxi; it cost 720 yen one way—about $4 both ways. Her house is on a hillside of Fukuoka and is surrounded by a number of orange orchards. We arrived at her house around two p.m. and leisurely walked up to the orange groves enjoying the view of the mountains. It took us about 30 minutes. The mountains were beautiful; the air was clear; the orchard was so fascinating. Kamiseji-san took many pictures; some of them were with the three of us as he had a timer. Iura-san brought a pair of scissors, and we ate so many oranges! The adjoining cedar hill is also their property. Nowadays bulldozers can make roads and highways easily. The Iuras have a truck to ship the crates of oranges. It's amazing! It was an eye-opening experience to listen to their talk on the difference of cedars, i.e. sugi and hinoki. I gathered acorns for Yukiko. I did not know akebi, *maki* (Chinese black pine) or *shii-no-ki* (Formosan oak) till they showed me. It was all new to me!

We walked around the orchard and hills for about an hour and a half; then we went back to the house to have chicken sukiyaki. I enjoyed the pickles which Iura-san's mother made. Regardless of where they are, country folks are all simple and honest and friendly. I was told to take some pickles to you and Mother when I go home. It was about six p.m. when the three of us came back to the hospital.

Japanese farmers are prosperous nowadays—everybody has a car and drives it to transport their products. It won't be surprising if they become increasingly rich.* By the way, yesterday was the three-year anniversary for Iura-san and Kamiseji-san's first date on Mount Kokonoe.

Kamiseji-san is from Kagoshima and works in a company that produces traffic signals. I think Japanese signals need some improvement so I plan to take photos in America as samples and send them to him. For example, the signals in Santa Clara are clear and easy to see even at night, but Japanese signals are not recognizable since they are often hidden behind obstacles.

The newspapers are still raising a ruckus over the sumo match. A foreigner, Takamiyama, is leading the junior class and getting ready to become a *yokozuna* (grand champion). . . .

ON NOVEMBER 23, 1967, KIYOSHI TOURED *the family tangerine orchard of Iura,
a young woman whom he met in the hospital and who subsequently visited him with her
sweetheart, Kamiseji. Photo by Mr. Kamiseji, courtesy of Yukiko Tokutomi Northon.*

I am so glad that I joined the Academy of Japanese Language. I feel that I just discovered my own path in which I can work hard to reach a sensible goal.

*In earlier days farmers sold their produce through *kumiai* (cooperatives). After the war, by eliminating the *kumiai* system and delivering produce to their customers directly, the farmers, with reduced reliance on middlemen, became more wealthy than the merchants.

From KIYOKO, *November 25.*

. . . FOLLOWING THEIR STRANGE management directives, the school [the Japanese Language School] had phoned the students telling them that it is closed on Veterans Day but open on Saturday after Thanksgiving Day. So I was wondering how many students would attend the class on this Saturday of a four-day-long weekend—two-thirds of the class was there. . . .

I'm glad that you've met various people whom you help and who help you in one way or another. You've been there for about five months; you've had some inspiring experiences—your objective of life is getting clearer. I think it has been much better than just staying home and suffering from your loss of hearing. There is a Japanese saying, "Should you lose your step, get up with something in your hand." Quite aside from the calculating nature of the saying, it is a good idea, I think.

I'm glad you collected so many good books, thanks to your friends. I'm happy to hear that you find our own ideas in those books. It seems that we have tried to live correctly. Together we will march forward, toward the same goal, shall we?

I'm glad you want my mother in Nabeshima to know about your hearing before you leave. I'm very happy to hear that. Shall we ask her to come see you in the hospital? If you want me to write to her, please let me know. I'll write to her after we've discussed it further. I think it is good to let others know about your situation one by one; the recognition of your own condition will help you too. What do you say?

Have you paid for the ultrashort-wave machine, or is it still on a trial basis? I think it's better to make sure that the machine is perfectly adjusted before bringing it home.

Mother says the medicine is not really working. How about getting a different kind? Mother gave some to Nanba-san, but it didn't work for her either. This kind of medicine doesn't give results quickly, I think.

Everybody is fine in the family; no one has come down with a cold. Mitsuko-san is doing better in school, the counselor told me. Mother started to complain about her to me but not to others, so it's all right. I don't mind anything except being summoned by the school; I hope it won't happen again. . . .

I've been thinking about this for some time now, but I wonder if Fukunaga-sensei can find a way to lower the sound waves to 45db or 50db so that you can hear us through that machine. Another way is to learn how to read lips; it is a passive approach but will help conversation. It takes time, but we will find a way to conquer our situation.

Speaking of a shopping list, I would like to have some good tea for us because it's impossible to get high quality tea around here. It is good as a gift too. We paid between $6.50 and $8.00 for the album that we bought at Tsukiji-san's store. Please be careful when you go out shopping.

I worry about the overcoat; I hope it arrives soon. If you cannot keep your reservation on that flight, you should cancel it as soon as possible so that you won't cause trouble at the JAL office. If you wait too long, you may have to pay a cancellation fee. Ōshima-san would take care of the situation, but it's better not to put him to such trouble. Please figure it out by the arrival of the candies from Iwama-san; I mailed the coat to you a week after sending the candies.

I dreamed of your warm body last night. I can hardly wait. . . .

From KIYOSHI, November 25.

. . . NOVEMBER WILL BE GONE in five days. If I can leave here on the 15th, I have 20 days left. I will be happy to see you again; at the same time, I can't deny my sense of disillusionment. I am disappointed, but I'm going to disappoint others too. I cannot accept that easily. We spent so much money on me, and it failed—to whom shall I apologize??? How will Yukiko take this? Will she feel ashamed of me? That is the hardest to swallow. . . .

From KIYOSHI, *November 25.*

. . . I RECEIVED YOUR LETTER of NOVEMBER 20 with $100, and one from my mother written by Mitsuko-san, I guess.

Thank you so very much for your letter and $100. Mother says she will send $200 too. This will take care of my expenses for the trip home and funds for gifts as long as the departure is on or before December 15. You mentioned a camera for Yukiko in today's letter. If we are going to get a camera for her, we'd better pay at least around $50; but the present budget cannot cover that. If we pay that much, we can get a good one that will last till she goes to college. It is better than buying a cheaper one now and replacing it later. Besides, if we buy a 35-mm camera, we can use it also and make slides as well as prints. The same camera would cost more than $130 in America. If you think we should get one now, let me know, and send me about $50.

Mother thinks I should stay and continue treatment till March next year. But I'm coming home next month because the doctor has a negative opinion and the carbon dioxide inhalation is not showing any improvement. I think the ultrashort-wave machine was working, but I wrote to the manufacturer because the ringing in my ears increased. They will send someone here on the 27th to show me how to use the machine. I've stopped using the machine for now.

You worried about the noise of the train. Kiyoko-san, my hearing is gone now; I can't hear anything. The index showed 55 when I came to Japan; it went down to 45 at one point; now it is down up 60. Maybe if the inhaler did not get broken down—well, it's no use now. The last hope is the short-wave machine and how much I can restore my hearing with it. . . .

I'm glad to hear that Yukiko does not mind that I have this condition. As you say, I should not succumb to my fate; I should live with confidence facing this adversity. . . . Because I cannot hear, I can concentrate in my work. This is a blessing, not a handicap. Instead of a grim resolution I will keep a cheerful attitude. I have everything to keep going because I have Kiyoko-san! . . .

From KIYOSHI, *November 25.*

. . . IURA-SAN CAME BACK from shopping. I asked her to get a rice pail, an album, and an umbrella as samples of gifts. The rice pail looks good. I'm sure Cecilia would love it. It has a tray and a tiny rice scoop. Iura-san bought a large and a small pail as samples, but the price is the same, 750 yen for each. The large one does not have a tray. But both of them look very nice.

An album costs from 500 to over 1,000 yen. The style of the 500 yen album is better than the more expensive ones, so I'll get 10 to 15 of them. The umbrella cost 2,500 yen. It is very nice and will be for you. For the others I'll get four or five cheaper ones (about 2,000 yen each). If you need anything else, let me know right away. . . .

I realized that I had not included the cost of the medicine that I have to bring home when I leave here. I'm paying more than $50 a month for shots. (You can give me these shots.) Dr. Torii said I should take home enough shots to last for three months. Since it is covered by the insurance, I'd like to bring home as many as possible. Could you please send me another $200 for the prescriptions and the shots? I am so sorry that I forgot to include this earlier.

As I was finishing the last letter, Tachibana-san came to see me with a folk doll made of sea shells which she bought on her school trip. She started to cry when I told her that I was getting ready to go home to America. She is such a naive and unspoiled child! . . . I couldn't help but pray that this 17-year old girl will keep her beautiful disposition as it is and will not become spoiled. She brought me postcards and pressed flowers. She will become a good friend to Yukiko. She insists on coming to Itatsuki Airport to see me off. She herself is scheduled to be back in the hospital on December 14. She had a beret on today and looked very cute. I asked her to get another beret like hers for Yukiko. . . .

From KIYOSHI, *November 26.*

. . . NOT MUCH NEWS TODAY. The members of the new Satō Cabinet have been introduced: the Minister of Construction is Hori Shigeru of Saga Prefecture; the Minister of Home Affairs is Nabeshima Naonori, and he also heads the Bureau of Science and Technology as well as the Atomic Commission. I'm sure this has already been reported in the *North America Japan*. . . .

Before coming home, I want to see *Okā-san* [Kiyoko's mother] of Nabeshima. I'll ask Hiroyuki-san to tell her and Masayuki-san [Kiyoko's older brother] and his wife about my condition the next time he goes to Saga. Otherwise everybody will talk about it, including the children, and Tokunaga-sensei and his family might find it out. I have to be careful.

It is a sad situation. It will make your mother terribly disappointed to have her daughter married to a deaf person. I am mortified just to think of her disappointment. But what can I do? . . . I tell myself that as long as I keep my head and eyes and my right arm intact, nothing can stop me from achieving my goal. I know I can do it.

I must not forget how lucky I am. There are married couples with perfect health and yet their life is cold and empty. I have a wonderful wife who stands by me with her love and encouragement . . .

From KIYOSHI, *November 26.*

. . . I SPENT THE DAY READING the *Japanese Language Dictionary* and the *Dictionary of Fables and Proverbs*, flipping pages here and there. I needed to check out the general instructions on how to study the Japanese language. The *Japanese Language Dictionary* lists the items that students must learn starting from elementary school, then middle school, and finally high school. . . . I can write my American textbook based on the instructions in these dictionaries. I will use words, ideographs, verbs, particles, auxiliary verbs, etc., that are distinctly suited to each grade. The literature on particles and auxiliary verbs is very good. . . . So far I haven't found in the *Japanese Language Dictionary* any references to a teaching method. I would be interested to know how much work has been done by English-speaking teachers of the Japanese language. Ogawa Yoshio-san (president of the College of Foreign Languages in Tokyo) and his group offered a short course in Hawaii which Mrs. Hori attended. Apparently teaching methods for English were applied to the teaching of Japanese in that course.

Definitely this is a new field—I can't help but get excited! Kindaichi Haruhiko-san also teaches at the College of Foreign Languages in Tokyo. I look forward to making contact aggressively with these scholars. I came to realize lately that it is impossible to teach complex Japanese using English-teaching methods. We have to have a teaching method designed specifically for the Japanese language. For example, according to the English method, a modifying verb is considered to be one of the adverbs. You cannot teach Japanese that way. One has to be fully versed in the structure of Japanese. I will treat the Japanese language with much more reverence. Could we use the $25 from Akizuki-san to buy reference books? I want to study them. . . .

From KIYOKO, *November 27.*

. . . THE RAIN STARTED THIS afternoon. It is winter here. I'm writing on this old air letter because Yukiko has used up the new ones. . . .

Three of your letters were waiting at home; the first, your visit to the orange orchard; the second, a shopping list of souvenirs; the third, acquiring a membership in the Academy of Japanese Language. The last one was the best news of all the news that I've ever received!

Kiyoshi-san, nothing has pleased me this much so far. I even enjoyed reading the newsletters from the Japan Association. The bulletin from the Academy of Japanese Language will give me such pleasure that I can hardly sit still! You bought so many books and now you have become a member of the Academy of Japanese Language—it looks as though you took my place! Actually, however, by the merger of these two assets you help achieve your original objective of teaching Japanese. I didn't expect this to happen now, but I am so happy!

An investigator from the Immigration Bureau came this evening to record my statement on Linda's case. I feel a load is off my shoulders now. The investigator was nervous and smoked too much during the inquiry. He appeared to be uncomfortable in coming to the house when the man of the house was away. But this seems to be my last duty so that I feel relieved.

Linda has a boyfriend whom she wants to marry. She simply wanted to help a friend of her boyfriend. But her good intentions went awry when she made a wrong decision. It made me think that there are many kinds of friendship and good intentions, but if they are not correctly directed, we might as well not have them. One tends to be swept away by the present problems and forget the larger scope of things. . . .

We have to do something to lower the Customs duty on those souvenirs from Japan. The best way is to prepare several packages of up to 44 lb. with a variety of articles in it, or limit the cost of articles in the package to about $10 and send them on different days. But we don't have the luxury of time to space out the dates. Just avoid packing a great quantity of the same articles. We don't have to be so fussy if we are not concerned with paying high taxes. Just remember that the limit for bringing in articles without paying taxes is $100. If you pack them carefully, they should come through Customs easily. I added tea and seaweed in the last letter. How about a knife for cutting fish and another one for vegetables—do you think you can add them? What about something for Mother? I wrote to you about her medicine—that is not a good idea. I'll think about it and let you know quickly. Have you bought an ice shaver like we were talking about last summer? If not, it's all right—maybe we can get one here. Anyway, please do not overwork yourself packing—your health is more important than souvenirs.

I miss you so much. . . .

From KIYOSHI, *November 28.*

. . . A RAINY DAY. I HAD A fever yesterday, so I took aspirin. I feel better today.

Yesterday, I had Shizuma-san send the rice pail by air. You might be surprised to hear this story. I gave Shizuma-san 2,000 yen to cover her transportation and pocket money. At the post office, she was told that it may not reach its destination before Christmas. So she sent it by air. The cost was 1,885 yen! She came back by tram car. What can I do—she did it with good intention! I had told her that it was your Christmas present to your friend, and she remembered it. As a result, the rice pail for Cecilia cost us 3,135 yen. . . . That pail cost us so much—let's hope it will arrive in one piece. . . .

Watanabe-sensei came to see me yesterday. He is sorry that I am going home like this. He brought a reference book on the teaching methods of languages written by Palmer. He cannot give it to me, but I can take it home and study it. I'm so grateful for his help. I'm going to make copies of this book as soon as I get home. This is a priceless book. We talked from four o'clock to seven o'clock. I showed him your letter—he was pleased to learn that you were happy and said that he would like to observe the classes in the Japanese Language School in America. He suspects that a drastic change is needed there. He was pleased to know about your stance of passive resistance. He would like to observe your class at the Buddhist School first, and he suggests that you and he together draft a teaching plan for the class. Then you invite the teachers of Japanese language to observe the class and then offer them a short training course after that. He and I suggest the title of the course to be "Popularization and Improvement of Japanese Language Education for the Sons and Daughters of Japanese in America." Perhaps we could ask JAL and the Sumitomo Bank to become sponsors of this plan. Also we should ask the Consul General of the Japanese Embassy to invite Watanabe-sensei to America. The University of Kyushu is known to be one of the best universities in teaching Japanese, and Watanabe-sensei himself is one of the few specialists in the area of teaching methods for the Japanese language. With the proper approach, I think this can become a reality. . . . [Continued in next letter.]

From KIYOSHI, *November 28.*

TO CORRECTLY START OUR PROJECT, WE WILL WRITE letters to the Consul General, JAL, and the Sumitomo Bank pointing out the importance of education in the Japanese language. I will draft the letter as soon as I come home. Watanabe-sensei will be the right person to be the pioneer and the leader in the field of Japanese language education. It will be a great joy for us too. I myself always loved the Japanese language, and now I feel it more important to learn the language correctly. This is different from the study of Japanese literature or Japanese culture in the university; this is the propagation and improvement of the education of the sons and daughters of Japanese-American families in the States. I know you have a keen interest in the Japanese language which was your major in college; so do I. If we work together as partners, I'm sure we will succeed. We are Americans, but the Japanese blood runs in us. Japan is the country where our parents came from. We should respect their language. If we can become a bridge between the two countries, it would be great. It is not necessary to vow loyalty only to America just because we have American citizenship and to become antagonistic to Japan. It is not wrong to be loyal to America as well as to Japan and pray for the prosperity and friendship of both countries—in fact, there is a big responsibility laid on the shoulders of Japanese Americans.

Maybe I've been talking too seriously. In any case, along with the rise of the Japanese position in world politics, in the world economy, in education, and in industry, their language also will become important. In America, as the Japanese immigrants increase, their language will certainly become important. When I was a child, some of us went to the Japanese language school after the regular school closed for the day. I think our plan will be like that. It will enable parents to keep working till evening without worrying about the safety of their children after school. Stretching it further, the idea of a Japanese language school can be applied even to kindergartens and nurseries because the education of language should start when children are young. The future of the Japanese language is certainly bright. . . .

From KIYOKO, *November 29.*

. . . YOU SEEM TO BE VERY busy preparing to come home. And I am anxiously waiting to start our life anew. You are now looking straight at your bodily limitation and have decided to overcome all the difficulties and inconvenience without cowering, but with cheerful acceptance. You have stopped depending on your hearing and listening to the sound of your environment. Instead, you will use only your eyes to comprehend your surroundings—I look forward to our future life! You still can talk, see, think, walk, and do many more things—you and I can live together very happily. Your healthy mind is my best possession! So, no more tears—let's walk into our new life with great hope for the future. Please remember this when you see my mother. Tell her that the medical treatment didn't work, but next time she'll not have to use paper and pen to communicate because you'll learn to read lips. Then everybody will feel relieved about our future. Don't tell her that you feel sorry for me because I married you. She wouldn't know how to respond to that kind of apology; besides it does not change anything. Tell her that Kiyoko doesn't cower before anything; instead, she pulls everybody together in the family with firm leadership so that you feel at ease in spite of losing your hearing. It will work. . . .

Yukiko's camera is expensive. Perhaps you should get it only if there is some money left after taking care of everybody else. You could get a Polaroid for her for now and later get a nice 35mm camera. It's up to you. Your mother doesn't know what she would like to have from Japan. She says she will think about it. Hisayo wants a small electric rice cooker to give to her colleague (a math teacher). I will send $250 by air mail. If Hisayo has time, she may be able to mail it tomorrow. I'll ask when she comes home.

Please tell me what your plan is as soon as possible because I'd like to start preparing for a vacation when you come home.

I am a part of you and you are a part of me. No one can separate us now! . . .

From KIYOSHI, November 29.

. . . I GOT YOUR MESSAGE about the letter from the Japanese doctor. Today's letter tells me about the situation more clearly than your earlier letter. I thought maybe you didn't explain clearly enough to the doctor, or you could have said to him simply that this treatment was not available in America. If you had explained clearly like in today's letter, I would have understood better.

You might have cut your explanation short because it takes time to explain it to a person who is deaf—this might cause an unexpected misunderstanding or become a cause for mistakes which could lead to an irreparable situation—all of which are likely to happen in the future.

You might say that you didn't mean to, but it will be too late. I'm so sorry to say this—I'll try hard, but you too please cooperate with me. Fortunately nothing serious has happened up to now. But I mention this now so that we can prevent a misunderstanding that might happen in the future.

Thank you for mailing the overcoat on the morning of the 21st. I hope it arrives within one month because I'd like to leave here on the 20th or the 23rd. I could send Almond Roca later. What else did you put in the package? I know that you put in a razor, an overcoat, and Life Savers. How about Lux soap bars and peanut candies? I'd like to know because I'm making a list for the distribution of these gifts. Please let me know. It'll help if I know what the contents of the package are.

This is not a pleasant letter—maybe I should tear it up. I know that I'm just asking my own wife about the contents of a package, but I hesitate. Ever since I asked you for an extra $200 for the take-home medicine, I have felt uncomfortable asking you for anything. On top of it, I asked you to be more precise when you write to me and to cooperate with me, etc. I hate to be so base. I've been telling myself not to become like this. I'm turning out to be a mean person—I am miserable—I feel so uneasy even with my own wife.

I will write again. Forgive me for this letter. I am sorry.

From KIYOSHI, *November 29.*

FORGIVE ME FOR THE WAY I WROTE TO YOU EARLIER. Since I've been bothering you so much, I turn base and despicable every time I have to ask you to do more. I should quickly get rid of feelings like this, but it's not easy. Please forgive me. I'll try to look forward and be cheerful. You said in the letter that came yesterday that on an imaginary cliff in our mind one can make a foothold where one can choose, if he wants, to stay put there; unless he chooses to stay put, however, he might slide down into a bottomless pit. You are right—if one wants to find that foothold, he can find it anywhere he chooses. . . .

I've been reading Palmer's book that Watanabe-sensei loaned me. It is very helpful. It was written to teach English to Japanese students, but it is an excellent reference book. I'm very much encouraged because there are quite a few passages similar to what I've been thinking. I wrote to you several days ago about a guide to the study of Japanese language, i.e., what sort of words, what type of expressions each grade should learn. Palmer, too, lists necessary words that the beginners should learn, especially verbs. Some time ago I told you that besides the format "No, no, no—then what?" there should be "Yes, yes, yes—no!" I'm so glad to find this form in Palmer's book. I was right!

In this book there are many other subjects that I've been thinking of—it's amazing! I can write a good textbook on the Japanese language using the exercise on "は、が、も (ha, ga, mo)" for an example. I'm going to study this very carefully. It was good that I joined the Institute of Japanese Language. It doesn't have to be for the study of classics or old Japanese—it could be just looking at Japanese and its grammar. I think formal study is necessary in order to really understand Japanese, not just to satisfy your curiosity and become skillful in handling the language. We now have a new scholar like Kindaichi Haruhiko who studied other languages extensively. Japanese has to become one of the world languages, and it has to be studied comparatively. The knowledge of Greek and Latin is necessary to the study of the European languages. A similar scientific analysis is needed in the study of Japanese. It cannot stand alone anymore, and it should be done by Japanese natives. . . .

From KIYOSHI*, November 30.*

THURSDAY, NOVEMBER 30, THE LAST DAY OF THE MONTH—it's amazing that months go so fast. We get old fast too. It's a cloudy day. . . .

Yesterday I asked Dr. Torii if he could have his assistant professor write a letter according to the draft that I prepared as shown below:

> To whom it may concern:
>   This is to certify that carbon dioxide therapy for hard-of-hearing patients due to medication is only being done at Kyushu University Hospital in Japan and in West Germany.
>   Truly yours,
>   Asst Prof. Soda, PhD, M.D.
>   Dept of ENT
>   Faculty of Medicine
>   Kyushu University

Dr. Soda agreed to do it right away. First I asked for a professor to write the certificate, but Dr. Torii preferred to have an assistant professor do the job because it's difficult to ask professors to do this kind of work. I will get the certificate written and mail it to you soon. . . .

Using the ultrashort-wave machine doesn't show any improvement, but the electrostatic therapy is working—I put it under my sleeping mat. This is to stimulate the cellular tissue of the blood vessels. Now when I move my finger in the left ear, I can hear a slight sound. It would be great if this sound becomes steady and louder. This machine has three settings—the ultrashort-wave length, low frequency, and static electricity. I started to use the machine on the lowest setting four days ago, and it is working. I'm surprised to hear the sound.

As I was writing about the sound, Ōtomo-san stopped by. She came to the hospital for her one-month checkup. We didn't have much chance to talk because she was with her friend, but she looked fine. She left around three o'clock. Then the technician of the short-wave machine came. It is 4:30 p.m. now. The technician said that usually the user feels uncomfortable at the beginning, but it will get better eventually. I'm going to continue with the electrostatic setting since it is working. I'll write again this evening if I have no interruption. . . .

From KIYOSHI, *November 30.*

. . . I COULDN'T FINISH WRITING the letter this morning because Ōtomo-san came to see me after having a monthly checkup. I'll mail it together with this letter.

Ōtomo-san gained weight, so much so that I didn't recognize her at first. She came with her friend, Shiraishi-san. Her mother sent some homemade *inari-zushi,* and the three of us enjoyed it for lunch. Shiraishi-san is also suffering from hearing loss, but hers is not as advanced as mine. She has had surgeries twice. As a result, her facial nerves were damaged—her mouth is pulled upward toward her left ear. Otherwise she would be quite beautiful. She is 22 years old. She is happy that her hearing is gradually getting better. She has an electrical massage every day, and it is working. I didn't see many deformed faces in America, but particularly here in the Nose and Ear Department, I see many. I feel sorry for them. In Shiraishi-san's case, nobody notices it until she talks. I feel sorry for those whose faces become deformed before they are of marriageable age.

Shizuma-san had surgery yesterday so that she will be forced to stay inactive at least four or five days. But in a week or so, she will bounce back like a vigorous weed. Ōtomo-san wants to see me off at Itatsuki Airport; it's a two-and-a-half-hour trip from her home. Both Tachibana-san and Ōtomo-san are nice girls; Iura-san too. I'll send you Iura-san's photo.

In a week the University of Kyushu will have in new office paper with the University's letterhead. Dr. Soda says he will write the certificate on the new paper.

My hearing is better today than yesterday—the sound is getting stronger. I'm eating a lot of the tangerines that Iura-san gave me. This might help to clean my blood.

Mother's $200 arrived today. Please thank her. . . .

To my dear wife, Kiyoko-*sama*—with endless love

Kiyoko Tokumori
490 N. 5th St.
San Jose, Calif.

福岡市大字里粕三七六
九大病院中央五階病棟
五三三号室

德富燁様

（博多局区内）

FIRST FOLD

AÉROGR

JAPAN

December

..

[THE *Sound* OF *One Hand Clapping*]

From KIYOKO.

DECEMBER FIRST. WE STAYED UP TILL TWO O'CLOCK IN the morning to finish Yukiko's homework. I was so sleepy, but it was a busy day in the office too because today was the last day for my supervisor.

I received one letter on Thursday—it looks like the continuation of a letter. I thought the first part might come today, but it didn't. I guess the post office is already getting busy with the Christmas mail. I'm going to wait for the first section to come, and then write a reply. . . .

I'm sorry for this short letter. Staying up till two o'clock and having a very busy day made me exhausted. My supervisor deserved a large farewell party after serving almost nine years, but she turned down the suggestion. Instead of a party, I designed a nice card and gave it to her. Some people said they expected I would do this, and they helped me. I asked everybody to write a farewell note on various papers that the company uses and paste them nicely on the card. After that, the Department Chief invited the retiring supervisor and me to lunch. That made me feel like I was some important person! . . .

From KIYOSHI, *December 1.*

... THIS IS THE FIRST DAY of the last month of the year—it feels like Christmas and New Year's are just around the corner. It is 9:30 in the morning, and I just finished reading the newspaper. Since yesterday the first page is covered with the news of the resignation of Secretary of Defense McNamara. Ted Kennedy insists that the real cause of McNamara's resignation should be told to the American people. Other interesting news is the International Marathon Race which is to be held on the day after tomorrow.

How are you, Kiyoko-san? My mind is filled with deep emotion now that I'm coming home as soon as I get my overcoat. If my hearing were back, I would be so much happier. But as I was leaving America, you told me to look forward to coming home even if the treatment didn't work. Also your encouragement that is expressed in your letters has been my great support at this homecoming. ...

Last night after the lights were turned off, I was thinking of the uniqueness of the Japanese language. For example, we don't have to use a verb for an expression like the following: "*akai, akai, ohisama akai*—Red, red, the sun red," or "*ohisama wa akai.*" These sentences are perfect without verbs. But from the point of English grammar, it is unthinkable. "*yukiko ga ōkii, ōkii*—Yukiko is big, big," or "*yukiko wa ōkii ne*—isn't Yukiko big!" To write this statement in the third person, it would be "Yukiko is big." In conversation, even when you are facing Yukiko, you say "*Yukiko-chan wa ōkii ne,*" which is close to "Yukiko is big, isn't she?" and it is a statement in the third person.

The question of the verb "*desu*" [is] whether to add it to the above sentences or not; the answer is that it is a second person statement but it is expressed in the form of a third person. It would be interesting to study the differences between these expressions. There is a distinct difference in the Japanese language between conversation and written forms. But there is some similarity too. I think it would take a great deal of study to place the Japanese language along with foreign languages.

I don't think comparisons with foreign languages have been studied enough. In English, it is the second person, "You are big." In Japanese, on the other hand, the subject of the expression "Yukiko-chan is big" can mean both second and third person. It is a matter of feeling. Most languages have a distinct difference between second and third person sentences. Why does the Japanese language not have that distinction? I guess the use of *"desu"* started not so long ago. It could be the key to understanding modern Japanese conversational language. . . .

From KIYOSHI, *December 1.*

. . . THIS MORNING PROFESSOR Kawada made his rounds, but no treatment yet. I don't know what will happen. . . .

The evening paper reports that Senator McCarthy will be a candidate for the presidency on the Democratic ticket; he opposes President Johnson's Vietnam War. The unwritten law in America is that as a courtesy no one from the same party will challenge a sitting president. McCarthy is going to break that tradition and the repercussions are expected to be great. Even Robert Kennedy has been declaring not to run and is supporting Johnson. McCarthy may not have a chance to win. Besides, the Democrats will be divided; so is the sentiment of the nation. To Johnson, this must be a great shock—particularly the timing of it being immediately after the resignation of Defense Secretary McNamara. What is going to be the reaction of the American people?

I had the treatment finally. Dr. Torii was apologetic about not treating me often enough because he was busy operating on other patients. A Japanese doctor's life is not easy; they are paid poorly and work so hard. But others are even worse off. A bowl of ramen costs 70 yen including the delivery to the hospital; this means the bowl of ramen itself costs 20 cents—still it makes a business. Sometimes I order a special ramen with plenty of meat. A grown-up man delivers it with a courteous salutation—I wonder how they ever make money. A woman who graduates from high school can earn about 15,000 yen; a man about 20,000 yen. Suppose the daily income is 700 yen—it makes me wonder about how much ramen costs. Everybody dresses nicely and most people have a car. A lot of women with a 15,000 yen salary are wearing nice, well-fitting dresses—better than Kiyoko-san's. And not like in the old days, they go to dance halls and enjoy life. I wonder where they get the money. I make jokes and tell them that they can treat me to a dinner. Among themselves, they pay for their own dinner. How about when they are with a boyfriend? Iura-san says that one out of three dinners, she pays for her own, and she laughed. Still I think they are doing very well. . . .

From KIYOKO, *December 2.*

. . . TODAY THE MAIN PART OF the letter which I received the day before yesterday finally came. Also *ohitsu* arrived, only a few days later than the letter relating the episode about its shipping. It was worth paying the higher postage. The contents of the package were in good shape; it was worth paying 3,135 yen for postage in order to be in time for the Christmas gift exchange. If it were sent by regular mail and I ended up buying something else because it was damaged, it might cost us more than double the 3,135 yen. . . . Shizuma-san did us a great favor because we would have to pay far more than $10 if we had had to buy it in America. I'm very happy about this, so don't worry about the cost. It is a clean-looking, beautiful gift. It is larger than I thought. If you have not bought the other *ohitsu* yet, please get one or two the same size as this. About tea leaves, be sure to get the best quality.

So, Watanabe-sensei came to see you at the hospital. I must write him and thank him. Soon after you come home, the winter break will be over at the Japanese Language School. With your help, I'd like to make a fresh start with a new teaching plan. I'm getting more used to having two grades in my class, but it's not easy because the ratio is 29 students to four students. Lately I'm barely able to keep the class in one body because I'm so busy with other things, and my enthusiasm has lessened (partly because of the increased absences on account of the holidays). The second semester, however, will be different because I myself have some new ideas. The class will be divided into groups and leaders will be selected; each group will practice conversation on a given subject. Then the whole class will do the exercise in the textbook. One who cannot write well is our Yukiko, and a couple of other children. The rest of them can write fast so the practice of conversation is needed the most. By the way, Yukiko does not practice reading at home. She just goes to the Japanese Language School because she is given 10 cents for that. However, I found in the reading test given today that she is as good as the older students. I was pleasantly surprised and pleased. She used to put a pause in the sentence at random wherever she pleased. I wanted to correct it, but that habit is gone since she started to attend the Language School. There is no student who can say in one breath *tanjōbi ni katte kudasaimashita* (this was bought on my birthday). Most students can say *boku no otomodachi o tsure te asobi ni kimashita* (I brought my friend to play with) if the sentence is cut into five phrases. A notable tendency is to skip the particles and move on. It is so important to introduce Japanese correctly at a very young age. It seems that my students started out ignoring particles. I thought you might be interested to know this tendency. Tsukiji-san came at break time and asked me how I teach *ya* and *yaya*. I said that I stick to the form in print because new students may get confused otherwise. I mentioned our plan to invite a specialist in methods of teaching Japanese to the teachers. Tsukiji-san was glad to hear that and said he wanted to have a textbook that is easy to understand, easy to teach, and introduces good Japanese. He says he is sick of Naganuma's textbook. I feel the same way with the book I use and want to question the editor's intention in using certain examples. Both the textbook and the teachers need improvement. So you showed my hurried letter to Watanabe-sensei? What can I say—I break into a cold sweat!

I'm going to attend the presentation at the Golden Gate School on December ninth; it may be helpful to us because school and education may become our future work. I'm happy about our future. Take care and come home safely. It's getting cold here too—I can see snow on the mountains. . . .

From KIYOSHI, *December 2.*

. . . MR. GOLDBERG, AMBASSADOR to the United Nations, is reported to have decided to resign. He is the last Vietnam moderate in President Johnson's cabinet after McNamara resigned. The situation will get worse.

It is reported that this year's crops of seaweed in Saga Prefecture dropped down to three to five percent of the average year's harvest. Ariake Sea is the best seaweed producing region, as I mentioned earlier, and Saga Prefecture produces one third of the total production at five hundred million sheets of seaweed a year. But this year it faces huge damage due to a disease rotting the algae. I thought the farms were around Morotomi, but actually they stretch to the Shioda River—and probably to the rivers near Ariake Sea. . . .

Everybody seems to have a huge bonus this year end. The employees at the department stores get two or three times their monthly salary. It would be nice if this happened in America. I wrote last night that Japanese youths spend money like rich folks do. I read the following sketch in the newspaper column: A passenger on a plane to Hawaii saw three teenagers in the cabin and asked them about the purpose of their trip; they said they were going to spend a week swimming at Waikiki Beach. The passenger was shocked. A university professor has to ride back and forth in a jammed tram car to go to work; the students drive their family cars. When they take trains, they ride in a special second-class car. What's going on—so says the newspaper. . . .

Tōkyōdō published a wonderful book entitled *Development of Infant Language*, written by Ōkubo Mitsugu of the National Japanese Language Research Institute; the price is 2,800 yen. One child was observed continuously for six years before he reached school age, and in that period the author collected a great number of words. Through recording, arranging, and analyzing, he studied the development of words, particles, conjugation, inflective words, questions, and composition by the child. Also attached are "The Record of Life with Words," a "List of Reference Books on the Study of Infant Language," and a "List of Language Used by an Infant." I'm going to buy this book because it will help me a great deal when I write a textbook on the Japanese language. Tōkyōdō is a good publisher. I may buy some more books from them. I'm going to do some well-organized, respectable research before I write my book. I'm so grateful to you, Kiyoko-san, for your understanding and support of what I really would like to do. If I put my effort into this project for three years, I should be able to write a respectable textbook. I'll get in touch with well-known scholars in the field so that I will not end up with a book of self-taught ideas. I'm a lucky man to be looked after and encouraged and loved by Kiyoko-san. . . .

From KIYOSHI*, December 2.*

. . . I RECEIVED YOUR LETTERS written on November 25 and 27. I was so delighted to hear that you dreamed about me. I took a rest because I wanted to dream about you too. . . . I rested with such a happy feeling, and I'm writing this letter now feeling refreshed. I haven't seen you for so long. . . .

I'm delighted to hear that you like my decision to join the Academy of Japanese Language. Also I was encouraged to hear you saying, "Let's walk together even if the road is rough." . . .

I think it's better to have Hiroyuki-san explain my condition to your mother. I'm going to ask him to do that when he comes today. After that, please write to your mother. I'll let you know when would be the best time.

I would rather not go see her because I don't want to meet many people there, and also it will be hard on my health. I would like to see her here in the hospital.

Please don't worry about the shortwave machine. Every day I use its electrostatic application, and it's working well. The store that sold it to me is very conscientious and comes here often to give me advice. I'm not using the ultrashort-wave application even though I was told that the ill effect may be only at the very beginning. I don't want to take a chance. I will use the electrostatic application as much and as far as I can. It cost us 79,000 yen.

Evidently the medicine for Mother is not satisfactory for her piles. I'll get some other medicine and send it to her. I bought the first one with the idea of trying it for a long period. Did she give it away to someone? That kind of medicine takes time to show good results. . . .

From KIYOSHI, *December 2.*

. . . I EXPECTED HIROYUKI-SAN today, but he didn't come. I'm so disappointed. He could have phoned me if he wasn't able to come. I have no way to give vent to my resentment—I just feel so angry. . . . Not only did Hiroyuki-san not show up, but also the lunch I ordered out for was delivered more than one hour late—I'm in a very cross mood—it irritates me. However, my anger wouldn't affect the restaurant keeper one way or another—it's my loss. I'm sorry that I made you the target of my irritation.

I was skimming through the pages in the *Dictionary of Japanese Language*. The particles and the auxiliary verbs are listed as a peculiarity of the Japanese language—I was so happy to see that. I was right! The National Institute for Japanese Language publishes a magazine monthly entitled *Language and Life*. I'm going to subscribe to this. A bulletin named "Language" is published by the Linguistic Society of America and is considered to be the best printed information on the Society's movement. Also it has started to include research papers on Japanese, Korean, Chinese and other Asian languages. I'm going to look into it when I get home. Someday I'd like to publish my research paper in this bulletin, which concentrates on theses and critiques. I must do extensive research worthy of the attention of first-class Japanese scholars. Also the *Dictionary of Japanese Language* is really an excellent book—it has so much information in it.

I wrote the above paragraphs last night. Today is Sunday, December third, a wintry day. I've been reading the newspaper, and it's already 10 o'clock in the morning. This is the first day of the International Marathon in which universally famous runners compete. The world's interest is focused on this race because of the 1968 Olympic Games in Mexico.

Under the title "Suspicious of the U.S.," one of the members of the South Vietnam government exposed the news and said that the U.S. was negotiating unofficially with the communists of North Vietnam. This is reported in big headlines on the second page.

Japanese workers are poorly paid, but they get big bonuses twice a year. The average bonus for teachers is 130,000 yen; for executives, 200,000 to 300,000 yen. This is why people buy expensive coats, shoes, suits, and cameras, etc., at bonus time. This may explain why they are well-dressed. When they retire from a job, they receive a certain amount of their monthly pay plus a retirement allowance. If the monthly pay is high, the employers have to pay more at the time of retirement. Therefore the employers increase the bonus but keep the monthly pay low; this makes the employees happy because they feel that they have extra income. Besides, the amount of the bonus does not affect the retirement pay so that the employers are content. This system makes both employees and employers happy. . . .

From KIYOSHI, *December 3.*

. . . AS I WAS WRITING A LETTER to Hiroyuki-san asking for his help with packing my stuff, he showed up just before the visiting hour ended. He was involved in a three-car collision, and his neck was covered with thick bandages. (Don't worry—he had been checked by a doctor specializing in whiplash due to a car accident and had been told that it was not a serious hit.) It happened on the 21st of November; he was hit from the back, and it was not his fault. After the x-rays, the doctor told him that he was OK. He has been back at work for three days now.

Whiplash is spreading in Japan. If it is serious, it causes horrendous headaches and ringing in the ears. The best preventive method is to install a headrest on the seat. We'd better have headrests in our car. This type of injury is caused by a collision from the rear. Please install headrests right away.

Also, get a signed note from Hiroko-san which states no contest in case of accident. Type the following note and have her sign:

> To Mrs. Kiyoko Tokutomi
> I will never complain at all whatever happens to me in your car.

Tell her about the accident your brother went through, and then you keep the note. Hiroko-san may not complain, but her husband will.

In any case, install the neck rest right away. It is reported that one can end up with a terrible illness from whiplash—almost becoming an invalid—so that it has become a social problem in Japan. You are so precious to me that we have to prevent it no matter how much it costs.

I asked Hiroyuki-san to call your mother on the phone. Next Sunday, she and Masayuki-san will be at Hiroyuki-san's house, and I will be there too. . . .

I feel relieved now, but Noriko-san could have phoned me and let me know about Hiroyuki-san's accident. Anyway I'm glad it wasn't too serious.

Take good care of yourself, Kiyoko-san. Don't forget that you are so important to me.

To my precious and beloved Kiyoko-*sama*

From KIYOKO, *December 4.*

. . . RECENTLY THE MAIL DELIVERY has become so irregular that today I received seven letters from you all at once! You say that you received one letter about the package with gift items. I was going to write you about the contents of the package after getting the Almond Roca but failed to do so because it was so difficult to get that candy. The coffee candy that I used to send you is also sold out. But I got a different type of coffee candy and coated peanuts that you like, five packages each—maybe three packages of coffee candy—I forget. . . . I couldn't find individually wrapped Lux soap —instead they were all economy packs of five soaps each. So you will find 20 Camay instead.

Then finally I found Almond Roca and bought four medium-size cans. I thought that I might mail them separately on the 27th but decided not to because it won't reach there before your departure. Instead of taking a chance, we could send Almond Roca to the doctors and nurses from home. I was waiting for your instructions. Then, I re-read your earlier letter and found out that the Almond Roca can wait till you come home.

If the static electricity is working better, it's a lucky discovery. Nothing is better than home treatment. I wonder if the mat that Koyanagi-sensei invented follows the same theory—maybe I should use it on my chair. A few days ago I read in the newspaper that a Japanese scholar received a prize from the American Academy. It was Dr. Hara who discovered a therapy that cures many difficult illnesses with high-voltage electrolysis, which he studied for 40 years. If you treat a patient with 100,000 volts, his blood gets ionized, its acidity is alkalized, and the illness that medicine and surgery couldn't help is cured.

I sent you two week's worth of newspapers in the package, and the rest I kept at home. Mother sent you $200, and I had Hisayo mail $250—$50 more to allow you to have a safe and comfortable trip. I wish I could send you more, but please try your best with this. For Cecilia's husband, how about a folding umbrella, or a tie of Hakata weave, or some photo equipment because he likes to take photos or a record cleaner because he has many records. I know he wants to get a small TV made by Sony, but it would be too expensive. It would be good if we can find something small that shows Japanese scientific excellence. . . .

I can hardly wait to read the books together with you. I wish I could retire from work right now. What you are going to do with the Japanese language is what I want to work on too. It makes me so happy. It doesn't matter even though you lost your hearing completely—I have great hope for our future life. It will be so much more joyful than those days when you worked hard to make money. Your decision to immerse yourself in the research and the study of the Japanese language makes me very happy. The money from Akizuki-san should be spent for it. I have a salary from the Japanese Language School which we can spend for our mutual goal. I'll be content with our honest poverty. I would rather be rich in my heart than in my pocketbook. . . .

From KIYOSHI, *December 4.*

... I HAVE A NEW PHYSICIAN-in-charge starting today. It is unthinkable but that position has changed quite often. The other day Ōtomo-san said that she had eight different physicians-in-charge in a year. She was disappointed too. We cannot expect successful treatment in this kind of a system. The new physician-in-charge is called Dr. Miyahara. I don't need a Gillette razor for him! You must be disappointed too; but let's not think about it anymore. I just want to go home. Mechanization and systematization may be necessary in order to improve the world, but it's a pity that the relationship of doctor and patient or teacher and student is affected by it. If the patient dies, they just say, "Can't help it—too bad." What a sad world we have created!

Let me stop complaining. Today's newspaper, the *Nishi-Nihon*, carries an article on whiplash. It is about a whiplash patient who killed himself leaving the following note to his wife: "It was a short but a happy four years (of marriage). Thank you. But I can't continue (living) with this pain. Please take good care of our child." The man killed himself by inhaling gas. What a sad story. . . . Please have headrests installed in our car as quickly as possible. If something like this happened to you, I would follow you because I cannot keep living without you. It doesn't matter how much it costs—protect yourself for me—I need you!

The next big topic is the International Marathon Race. First place was a 25-year-old Australian runner, Clayton—he made it in two hours, nine minutes, and 36 seconds, breaking the wall which was two hours, 10 minutes. Second place was a 22-year-old runner, Sasaki from Saga—his time was two hours, 11 minutes plus; the new world record is now one minute faster than the existing record of two hours, 12 minutes. The runner from Ethiopia made it in two hours, 12 minutes, 11 seconds. This race will be a great attraction in the Olympics in Mexico. Sasaki ran the course in spite of a cramp in his belly. I didn't know that Saga Prefecture had produced such a good runner—he ran 26 miles with the speed of a 5,000-meter dash. . . .

From KIYOSHI, *December 5.*

. . . A WINTRY SKY. I FINISHED breakfast and read the newspaper. Today's big news is about the transplant of a human heart—I'm sure it was reported in America too. The surgery was done in the British Commonwealth of South Africa. If the patient continues to live for 10 to 20 days, the surgery will be called a success. It would be a great development if we can replace a damaged heart with another heart. The problem would be where to find a healthy heart as replacement. Some say from the speedy execution of the criminals on death row; others strike back saying that one so heartless as that [recommending a speedy execution] should be used as a heart donor. This is a difficult social problem, but a remarkable advancement in the medical world.

The newspaper here reported on a young man in Sunnyvale who burned himself to death protesting the Vietnam War. Did you read it in your paper? The man died in the San Jose Hospital.

Two men with guns in hand tried to rob the Saga Bank. The safety of the customers was a big concern. But it turned out to be just an exercise for the police force.

As for the shopping, I've done everything except the albums. I couldn't find an ice shaver for Yukiko because it is winter now—I should have bought it much earlier. I'm sure Yukiko will love the watch I bought for her; it is a Seikō. Her rain boots are very nice too. I have to talk to a pharmacist about the medicine for Mother.

By the way, the chocolate from Iwama-san arrived yesterday. Maybe the overcoat too will arrive in time. I'm thinking of reserving a seat on JAL leaving on the 20th from Fukuoka. In two weeks, I'll be on it—I can hardly wait. Unless you hear from me otherwise, please don't write after the 14th. If you post it around noon of the 14th, it'll reach me on the 19th. I plan to leave the hospital on the 20th and take a taxi straight to Itatsuki Airport. The checking-out process at the hospital will be finished the day before. The packages will be shipped out next week—I'll have only a suitcase to carry.

I've bought seaweed, tea, and a knife. I have six umbrellas, including yours. Don't tell anybody about the umbrellas. You take a look at them and decide whom you want to give them to. They are all good. With the new features added, the rice cooker for my sister is much better than ours. I'm expecting $200 from you for medicine that I'll bring home. If I'm left with

30 or 40 dollars out of it, I'll get a camera for Yukiko. But first I have to pay about $50 for the extra stay in the hospital. Don't tell Yukiko about the camera because I may not be able to buy it at this time. . . .

Today marks the 143rd day since I arrived in Japan. . . .

From Kiyoshi, *December 5.*

. . . I wrote a letter to the Fukuoka Branch of JAL and asked them to arrange my departure on the 20th. I plan to check out of the hospital on Tuesday the 20th. It will take half a day to go through the last checkup, paperwork, and payments, etc. Then I'm going to rest in the hospital overnight and go to Itatsuki Airport the next day.

Ōtomo-san will come to Itatsuki Airport from Ōita; Iura-san and her friend will also come. Hinashi-san will come depending on the departure time because he has a class to teach. Tachibana-san will come for sure; so will Shizuma-san. The other day Yatomi-san came to see me from Kitakyushu— he is a good man. I told him not to come to Itatsuki because it's so far away from Kitakyushu. He was the one who talked about Romain Rolland and the European philosophers. I'll write a parting note to Matsuda-san who lives in Ōita. These are a bunch of really good friends. It was nice to be adored by women friends. But friendship with men whom I respect is something different—it is tightly bonded and long lasting. Ōtomo-san, Iura-san, and Tachibana-san had a sincere affection for me, but it is different from the feeling I get from Hinashi-san, Yatomi-san, and Matsuda-san. Women friends will see me off with tears in their eyes—but not the men. But I feel my blood runs together with these men. Isn't it strange? I know you will understand.

In two weeks I'll be home! . . . I can see Yukiko's joy and your smile. . . .

Shizuma-san had surgery on her ear; now ringing has started to bother her. Sometimes it's better not to have surgery. Ringing in the ear is hard to get rid of. She had been strong as a weed—not now. . . .

On the 14th please send your letter in a regular envelope so that it will be handled as express mail. It costs a little bit more, but this will indicate that it is your last letter. I'll keep writing till a day before my departure date.

My precious Kiyoko-san, take good care of yourself. Say hello to Yukiko and Hisayo-san. I want to see you—I can hardly wait! . . .

From KIYOKO, *December 6.*

. . . CHRISTMAS IS APPROACHING. I wanted to finish my project early this year, but not so—I'll be busy till the very end. Your letter written on December second came yesterday. I feel that finally we've made contact because you answered many of the questions I sent out. . . .

Our happy-go-lucky Yukiko forgot to bring her textbook home in spite of her having a homework assignment. Not only happy-go-lucky, but also this lazy child played until dinner time, and then told me that she had homework but forgot her book at school. I told her to go to her classmate's house on Fourth St. and either borrow the book or copy the pages for her assignment. But I ended up taking her to the friend's house and copied the pages for her. I don't know how to spark her up—no wonder her teacher becomes irritated at her. I grew out of that, thanks to my mother, although I still often oversleep. Come home quickly and help me, Kiyoshi-san. We have only one child, and I cannot handle her alone!

While I was copying the homework from the textbook, the TV was featuring a golf champion who has no arms on the program called "You Asked For It." The man lost both arms when he was a young boy; he was waiting for his mother at a railway station and fell from the platform. The train was unable to stop. He overheard a visitor at the hospital saying, "He will be selling newspapers at a train station," and he made up his mind to do everything that normal men do. Now he can type at the typewriter, pick up the telephone with his neck and shoulder, play golf, and enjoy card games; he was showing all this on the television. He is married happily and introduced his wife and four fine boys. I wanted to tell you about him particularly when he said, "There are many handicapped people in this world. But they are making themselves handicapped when they start to think of themselves as handicapped. If they don't think they are handicapped, they are not handicapped." I was very impressed. He was utilizing all his remaining faculties and kept doing things better than ordinary, healthy people do.

With the above story in mind, I wrote the following haiku:

三日月の
冬空に高く
夫（つま）の留守

mikazuki no
fuyuzora ni takaku
tsuma no rusu

the new moon
high in the wintry sky
absence of my husband

After the rain everything was clean including the sky. As I was walking in the parking lot on the way home, I was thinking about Kiyoshi-san and looking at the new moon. Please enjoy this haiku. I think I like to write haiku better than other forms of poetry including tanka. Haiku is not easy, but other forms of poetry are even more difficult. . . .

Tonight a rain cloud is hanging low and the wind has become chilly. I am remembering your look and now close this letter.

From KIYOSHI, *December 6.*

THERE IS NO WIND AND THE WINTRY SKY IS COVERED with smog. We don't see this kind of sky in San Jose. It is 10 minutes before 10 o'clock now, and I just finished reading the newspaper. The popularity of President Johnson has been slightly higher, according to the Harris survey. Other than that, there is no big news today; the paper is covered with advertisements for the year-end sales.

In two weeks I may be leaving Japan. I intend to enjoy these last days here.

The heart transplant patient in South Africa is reported to be in good shape—he even asks for food now. He has been on liquid food and has now moved up to soft-boiled eggs. I hope he keeps improving. There are heart patients in this hospital too. They are all doing well. The rate of failure is as low as that of an appendectomy. There is a girl by the name of Matsumoto Hiroko in the picture I sent to you. She had to quit a junior college to have a heart operation on the 13th. Shizuma-san took me to visit her. She is taking it lightly as if she is going to have an operation on her appendix. I hope it goes well. She is 19 years old.

The high-school girl whom Shizuma-san took me to is already recovering and even walking around now. The improvement in medical science is amazing. . . .

I have not heard from Yukiko for some time now. How is she doing? How about her school work? When I come home, we will work together on Yukiko's study habits. You will be going out to work; I'll be home to oversee Yukiko's studies. I'd like her to have an interest in studying without being forced. She is our only child. I'll do my best to help her build good study habits. Willie Mays once said that his first job was to help his son to grow up correctly, and his second job was baseball. I thought he made a great statement. He adopted this son. It is so great to be responsible for the future of a child, be it his own or not. He was the one player who never challenged the umpires on the field. He was a noble individual and a great thinker. . . .

From KIYOSHI, *December 6.*

. . . I RECEIVED NINE VOLUMES of the *Dictionary of Japanese Language.* They are great—I can hardly wait to show these to you.

I received the following flight schedule from the Fukuoka Branch of JAL:

Leave Fukuoka	December 20 18:20	Flight No. 370
Arrive Tokyo	December 20 19:40	
Leave Tokyo	December 20 22:50	Flight No. 036
Arrive San Francisco	December 20 14:50 (San Francisco time)	

Above are all direct flights. . . .

You wrote in the letter of the 29th that you look forward to building our life together. What a great idea you speak of! You cannot imagine how much your words lifted my spirit—they are much better than some wordy sympathy for my condition. Don't worry, Kiyoko-san—I won't have an inferiority complex, I won't lose my dignity, I will be relaxed, and I will enjoy life. I will treat my treasure, Kiyoko-san, with the utmost care. . . . I won't feel inferior when I meet your mother and brother. I won't feel tragic over my condition; instead I will live with bright hope. Together we will make our life rich with love, and I will see how much I can accomplish without my hearing ability. . . .

The dictionary that came today is so wonderful. You will be surprised. Chapter 66 is about the use of the particles の (*no*), が (*ga*), は (*wa*) and the application of existing grammar to the Japanese language. I have not read it yet, but I think it is close to my own theory. I think this dictionary will help

Watanabe-sensei and his research. It quotes English examples too. I think this is the first publication that treats Japanese academically. . . . I am so encouraged. I can write my research in English too. I have Kiyoko-san, who thinks I am great, who believes in me and has great expectations for me. It will take a few years, but someday we will rejoice hand in hand and cry for joy at the completion of my research. . . .

From KIYOSHI, *December 7.*

. . . THE MAIN POST OFFICE IN Fukuoka is facing the busiest time of the year now. A postman wanted to take a day off because of his stomach ulcer, but he was made to work, which he did in spite of the pain. At the end of the day's work, he was told to work overtime. He felt sick while working after hours and lay down on a sofa. He then spit up blood, was carried to a hospital, and operated on. His colleagues wanted to help him, but they were shouted at to stay put because it was still working hours.

The above episode has become the talk of everyone as an example of the neglect of human rights. The labor union joined the newspapers to attack the post office. Japan is still behind in modernization. The executives are arrogant, and their workers humble themselves too much. It is getting better, but equality in the workplace is still overlooked. In the Ears and Nose Department of the hospital, the doctors prostrate themselves before Professor Kawada. (I asked Dr. Torii if he was afraid of the Emperor; he said "Yes.") This doesn't mean, however, that Dr. Kawada is a mean person. This means that there is a clear distinction of the upper and the lower group. Watanabe-sensei told me that younger people call him "Sir," and he laughed. It is improving—but come to think of it, a certain distinction may not be too bad. . . .

According to JAL, the minimum charge to ship by sea is 25,000 yen, about $70, for up to 800 kilograms (the charge for packing is not included). I'm going to send mine by parcel post as gifts—then there will be no tax for up to $100. I'll put my stuff in five packages and mail them a few days apart. . . . The books may be heavy, but I'll find a way to distribute that weight. . . .

Tell Mother that I'm OK.

From your happy husband, Kiyoshi,

to my dearest Kiyoko-*sama*

From KIYOSHI, *December 8.*

. . . IT WAS SNOWING EARLY this morning—the first snow. . . .

Yesterday Hiroyuki-san brought four cardboard sheets to make boxes. I still have to buy 20 albums, a rice cooker for Hisayo-san, Mother's medicine, and a camera for Yukiko. Your $250 helps me a great deal. But since I didn't include the cost of shipping packages—between 15,000 and 18,000 yen—it will be very tight financially. I'm wondering if I should ask you for an additional $50 to be sent by wire. But we may not have time. Perhaps the best way is to send it to Hiroyuki-san and ask him to send the five or six packages after receiving the $50. It will be impossible to take six packages in my luggage. I have to send some clothing in a package so that I can hand-carry the shortwave machine. . . .

I almost forgot it, but this was the day when the Pacific War started. . . .

I'm leaving Japan at 6:20 p.m. on the 20th and arriving in San Francisco at 2:50 p.m. on the same day. It is a Wednesday. I hope you can take a whole day off that day. It would be even better if you can take another day off. Maybe you cannot take off so much because it is the year-end. I will be content if you can have one whole day off on the 20th. It is a nonstop flight to San Francisco so that I have to go through Customs. I couldn't decide about the camera, but I will get it here. Please send a money order [for an extra $50] by wire to Hiroyuki-san. . . .

From KIYOKO, *December 9.*

. . . I JUST CAME HOME FROM the Language School. I'm getting ready to go to the presentation at the Golden Gate School after a quick lunch.

A letter from Iura-san came on Thursday together with your three letters including the one on Hiroyuki's accident. I wrote back to Iura-san on one of the cards. She wishes that she could do more for you—but Shizuma-san does everything. I thanked her for her part. I was going to write to you last night but couldn't. Not only did I have to prepare for today's Japanese class, but also Yukiko was coming down with a cold. I put her in bed and gave her noodles and hot lemon water as she asked. She will be OK because we caught it early enough. She did her homework on Thursday after having a good chiding from me. I wish she would learn to do homework without being forced.

You seem to have finished all the shopping for gifts. What are you going to give Yoshimitsu-san? Your mother asked me that last night. I said maybe an album, but it would be nice if you can find a book on bonsai for him. Mitsuko-san sent Mother some dried seaweed cookies called 塩つべ, and she liked them. So Mother wants more of that. She also wants a medium-size rice cooker for her friend. Hisayo wants a small-size cooker, just in case I haven't mentioned it. Mother will send you money and ask you to get three cookers, but I think you won't have time. . . .

Forgive me for this hurried letter—I'll write again this evening. Please don't get sick from working too much. I'm thinking that tomorrow is the day you go to Hiroyuki's.

To my dearest Kiyoshi-san,

from your happy Kiyoko

From KIYOSHI, *December 9.*

. . . I'VE SLOWLY STARTED TO PACK. Iura-san and her friend will help me today with shopping for albums and a rice cooker for Hisayo-san. The camera will be the last item to purchase. I can get the medicine for Mother at the pharmacy across from the hospital. . . .

I'm so anxious to get home to you. While I pack, while I read books in bed, you are in my mind all the time. I miss you, I long for you, and I want to see you right now—that's all I can think of!

Every day I'm reading the bulletin from the National Institute for Japanese Language. It is really great! I'm sure you will enjoy this. Mr. Iwabuchi Etsutarō, the head of the National Institute of Japanese Language, says that it is important to make it easy and efficient for foreigners to learn Japanese. I learned a great deal from Ms. Oyama's thesis on the particles は (*wa*), が (*ga*), の (*no*). She must be a great scholar. But she doesn't go into a teaching method that is easy and effective—and that's what I can do! I am encouraged! In this bulletin so many first-class scholars in linguistics and literature are presenting research work, essays, and critiques. I'm anxious to show this to you. . . . I must study systematically—it is true that a frog in the well knows nothing of the great ocean, as the saying goes. I am glad to have this book.

Your mother and Masayuki-san will come to Hiroyuki-san's house tomorrow. But I'm about to come down with a cold because the temperature dropped suddenly since yesterday. I'm not sure if I should go out without an overcoat; if it gets warm, I will go. But I had Shizuma-san call Hiroyuki-san and ask him to bring your mother and Masayuki-san here if I don't show up there by one o'clock. Either way, I will see them tomorrow. I've not seen your mother for 15 years—I'm sure we will have a lot to talk about.

The latest big topic here is the discovery of the diary of Prince Konoe. Another one is the teachers' refusals to perform night duty at the schools. The problem was doubled when one school had a fire with a student doing night duty as a side job. . . .

From KIYOSHI, *December 10.*

. . . I WAS GOING TO BE AT Hiroyuki-san's house today to meet your mother and Masayuki-san. But I decided to ask them to come to the hospital because my treatment has not been done yet, and I had a little fever yesterday. Hiroyuki-san just phoned, and I asked him to come around one or 1:30 this afternoon. . . . I look forward to seeing them! . . .

A man from the JAL Fukuoka branch office came yesterday and took my passport so he could issue the final tickets with the December 20 departure date. They are so helpful—I don't know how to thank them!

You must be busy with extra work at the Language School. Please take good care of yourself. I'm glad you talked to Tsukiji-san about the uniqueness of the Japanese language. I'm going to see Watanabe-sensei once more before my departure, and I'll mention it. Every day I've been reading the *Dictionary of Japanese Language.* It is great! There are many excellent theses, e.g., on intransitive verbs and transitive verbs. I'm learning a great deal!

In 10 days I'll be with you! I can't wait—I'm so happy! I'm anxious to see Yukiko, who has grown up a lot by now. She will be so excited to have her Christmas presents, a watch and a camera! But the camera will be shared with Mommy because Yukiko didn't make good grades. I hope to write again tonight about my meeting with your mother and Masayuki-san. . . .

From KIYOSHI, *December 10.*

. . . I JUST SAW YOUR MOTHER and Masayuki-san to the elevator.

I'm so glad to have seen them. They were happy to see me too. It was a very pleasant get-together. Masayuki-san told me that I looked just like in the old days and didn't show any sign of impairment. Your mother said that her heart was choked up, and she didn't know what to say. But she was happy. On her obi she had a clip that I gave her a long time ago. She looked exactly like she did in the old days. Masayuki-san showed some aging. We talked and talked from two o'clock to six o'clock—I feel a little bit tired now. But don't worry. Masayuki-san suggested that I should meet, at least, with Kondō-sensei; so I'll meet him this Sunday, December 17. I'm so glad to have spent some time with your mother and Masayuki-san. Your mother was so pleased to see me, and that made me very happy. . . .

I'm going to get a folding umbrella for Cecilia's husband. It is about $10. I gave 3,000 yen to Hiroyuki-san for taxi and train expenses. I hope you understand that. Besides, they are planning to see me off at Itatsuki, I think.

From KIYOSHI, *December 10.*

. . . REGARDING THE NEWSPAPER ARTICLE about Professor Hara receiving recognition from the Academy of America—actually, the machine that I bought uses his theory to combine short- and low-frequency waves. I was astonished. This treatment using static electricity ionizes the blood, alkalizes its acidity, and supplies nutrition through the cellular tissues. According to the literature that came with my machine, it is a method that uses a pair of high-voltage currents—the figure 30,000 volts is mentioned. No wonder it is working on me. I'm now renting a machine at 1,000 yen a week from the store where I bought the other machine. This is a high-frequency machine, and its moderate use has cured ringing in the ears of some patients. I've been using it for a couple of days, and it seems to be working. I use it for 20 minutes before going to sleep and in the morning around 9 o'clock. I've started to hear some sound.

This machine is supposed to bring life back to the cells which have already stopped functioning. In my case, however, the hairy parts of the ear have to come alive first—so it might take longer. At least now, I can hear a repetitious sound in the inner ear. I wrote it down in today's diary. I've been using this machine since the evening of the eighth. My diary records, "I can hear it a little," on the eighth; "I can hear it," on the ninth; and today I wrote, "Surely I can hear it well." This machine only produces ultrashort waves, and it is to be used only on low. . . . I rented it for a week because it costs 6,000 yen. If I see some improvement after one week, I'm thinking of buying it. That means I have to cut corners on my spending in order to squeeze out about $16—it is not impossible. I don't know if Dr. Koyanagi's theory is similarly based on the method of high-voltage currents. But this small machine that I sleep with (setting it at its lowest) seems to be the one that you wrote about some time ago. It seems that the combination of ions and the ultrashort wave is producing a good result. But I'm not going to jump to conclusions right away—I'll wait for a few more days and see the result. Thank you, Kiyoko-san, for letting me know about it. . . .

From KIYOKO, *December 11.*

. . . I WENT TO BED LAST night around 10:30 p.m. after the usual busy activity of a Sunday. I had a dream of being in the hospital with you helping you to pack and prepare to leave for Itatsuki.

I was so moved by the three letters that came today. I saw you in them —your determination to fight back against this disadvantage. Mother offered to wash the dishes so that I could read the letters. So, you will fly back on the 20th! You tell me about that sad story of a postal worker; however, I can't help but pray that the package with your overcoat will arrive in time. I saw my supervisor today to request a vacation for 13 days starting from the 20th (counting weekends and a holiday plus six days of my own vacation time). I told her that if need be I could come to work half days. It was approved right away. There will be no problem even if your flight is delayed for a couple of days.

If you bring the short-wave machine as your carry-on luggage, be sure to have a doctor's certificate on it so that it won't be taxed. It is a tiring flight straight to San Francisco. Be sure to rest well in the plane.

I've arranged for Sumitomo Bank to remit $50 to Hiroyuki. This is for him to pay for the shipment of your packages. The bank transfer by telegraph costs $5.75; therefore I asked Mr. Nagasaki to send it by air mail. He says that the money should be in the Sumitomo Bank-Fukuoka Branch on Monday the 18th. Have Hiroyuki telephone the bank on Friday, the 15th, or Saturday, the 16th, and ask the bank to call him as soon as the money arrives.

It's better to send everything by postal service. Not only will packing and shipping by sea cost about $70, but also we will have to rent a truck to pick it up. It's much better to make the packages small although it takes more time to pack them. How about writing "not for sale" on the package of books? Use Hiroyuki's name as the sender and address it to Hisayo, or me, or you. Well—I wrote too much on shipping—I may dream about it tonight!

I must write a thank-you note to Watanabe-sensei. You wrote about your friends who are planning to see you off, but you didn't mention him, right?

I sent you the insurance documents using my company's envelope. The articles related to your case are marked with a red pencil. I think you should state that you could not be an outpatient because you had a hearing problem. Anyhow, we have to give some good reason to choose hospitalization rather than being an outpatient. Your doctor might be able to help you on this. Earlier on, some doctor used the letterhead of the University to write a certificate for you. Please get your doctor's help and prepare the application for insurance coverage while you are still in the hospital.

You might be writing right now about the meeting with my mother and my brother. I'm going to write them after reading your report about it.

It is getting cold now. I turned the heater up to 80.

I hope you can get one more rice cooker—this one is for your mother—she wants to give it to somebody. She phoned me to say that she had not sent money to you. But she wants at least one cooker for her friend. Have you found something for Cecilia's husband? I'm sorry that you were kept so busy with these gifts—maybe that's why I dreamed about helping you pack. I'm sorry that I can't help much. Please don't tire yourself. If some of your friends offer help, please take it.

I'm anxiously waiting for you.

From KIYOSHI, *December 11.*

. . . I WAS USING THE ultrashort-wave machine starting at 9 o'clock; then my treatment began around 11 o'clock. I spoke with the physician-in-charge about the static electricity and the news on the Academy of America. I was surprised to hear Dr. Miyahara, the new physician-in-charge, encourage me to use the machine. It's amazing to find that the doctors are not in agreement, in that both Dr. Shirabe and Dr. Torii flatly deny the validity of the machine while the instructor, Dr. Sakamoto, says that I can use it, but I have to pay for it because the university does not have the funds to support it. (By the way he is on leave and went home to help his ailing father.) Dr. Yasuda read several books about the machine. He told me that I could use it until the carbonic acid inhaler is repaired. The inhaler could not be repaired after all so that I have not been able to use it for more than three weeks. I didn't tell you this because you might be disappointed. If Dr. Yasuda could have stayed, I might have started on this machine and had some improvement by now. But perhaps he felt he could not go against the physicians who were his superiors. . . . I asked Dr. Torii to certify the use of the machine so that I can take it home, but he refused to do so because he doubts the validity of the machine. I asked Dr. Miyahara, and he OK'd it— what a difference! I'm going to give the Gillette shaving kit, when it arrives, to Dr. Miyahara, together with cookies and a soap bar. If I have the certificate of a doctor, our insurance will cover the cost of the machine.

The static electricity and the low-power short wave seem to be working. This morning I heard a sound clearly. It may take a long time, but I think I will get my hearing back. I'm so glad that I talked to Dr. Miyahara this morning.

It is snowy now. The high mountains on the horizon are all white. I am so glad that I saw your mother yesterday. I told her that I was hesitant to see her since I lost my hearing. She comforted me and said I was wrong. I could see her joy—I can't describe how happy I was! She has not changed her love for me, her son-in-law—I could feel it. She said that she should have been told about me sooner. She may be right. I told her that next time I see her in America, I will be talking to her without paper and pen. I want to save money for an airplane ticket and invite her to America. I was surprised because she had not changed much in the past 15 years. She has some wrinkles around her ears, but that's all—it's amazing! We talked about Hisayo-san too. I said she works hard and has gotten promoted; she's risen so much so that she might not be able to find a husband—everybody laughed. Masa-yuki-san added that she was always a hard worker. I told them that I was happy to see Hisayo-san feeling at home in our house.

I had such a happy afternoon with them. Your mother will come again on the 17th. . . .

From KIYOSHI*, December 11.*

. . . IT HAS BEEN A BUSY DAY. In the evening when I was having a haircut, Hiroyuki-san brought three more boxes. I now have seven boxes—I think six will be enough. . . . I'll do maybe two boxes a day to avoid getting exhausted. . . .

The physician-in-charge, Dr. Miyahara, came today to see my machine. He said if this machine helps me, there is no reason not to continue using it. He said he would write a certificate and asked what I wanted him to write. I showed him the following note:

> Ordered for Kiyoshi Tokutomi's inner ear treatment.
> Dr. Toshiyuki Miyahara, PhD, M.D.
> Kyushu University Hospital
> Department of E. N. T.

He wrote this on the back of the receipt. I was surprised that he wrote PhD after his name—and in spite of such an impressive background, he didn't mind writing the certificate! In contrast, Dr. Shirabe and Dr. Torii refused my request flatly. Dr. Miyahara knows about the ultrashort waves and the enlargement of the capillary vessels. Also he knows about static electricity, and he asked me if I had side effects. He was pleased to learn that I didn't have any ill effect from the static electricity. People tell me that Dr. Yasuda is also a conscientious doctor. Dr. Miyahara doesn't show off the airs of a PhD holder. Once I learned that he had a PhD, my respect for him went up because he doesn't pay much attention to his looks. Earlier, when I asked Assistant Professor Soda to write a certificate on something else, I said, "Please add PhD, if you have one." So when Dr. Miyahara asked if he should add his title or not, I said, "Do you have a PhD?" I thought he was kidding. It was a rather disrespectful question, but he took it nicely. He gave me his business card, but it says only "Miyahara Toshiyuki, Kyushu University

Hospital, Department of E.N.T." I like him. I'm going to give him the Gillette shaving kit. He doesn't care about his appearance—his shoes need to be shined. He is reading books all the time and he is unsociable. But the other day he wrote in a note that if I could hear, he would learn English from me. It surprised me. . . .

From Kiyoshi, December 12.

. . . Eight days before departure. It's a beautiful day. Every Tuesday they change the sheets so I couldn't write earlier. There isn't much to report from the newspaper.

I'm thinking of going out after lunch to shop for an umbrella for Cecilia's husband.

How are you, Kiyoko-san? Did it take time to write Christmas cards alone this year? I didn't write at all. Maybe today my overcoat will arrive—until I get it, I can't sit still. . . .

We have been separated for almost six months—it was so hard to bear! I couldn't have done it unless I wanted to have my hearing restored. I pray we don't have to be separated ever again. I want to be with you. I might meet good friends, kind people, but they cannot fill the big hollowness that your absence creates. . . . At night in bed, I called your name silently so many times. . . .

I had my treatment from Dr. Miyahara. I thanked him for his visit yesterday and got his permission for my outing this afternoon. I'm going to get medicine for Mother too. I will look around for a camera. It is my last item to buy—I'd like to study it carefully first because it'll cost about 20,000 yen. Also I'll stop by the post office and get some tags for packages.

I cannot stay composed now that I know I can see you in several days. . . .

From Kiyoko, December 13.

. . . Since yesterday it turned cold and windy in San Jose. I've been in bed with a cold. Yukiko had one last week, but now she is all right in spite of this wind. She said that she passed her cold on to me and laughed. I don't have much fever because I took a preventive shot for a cold. I'll be all right by the time you come home. . . .

I planned to fill up the crevices in the windows today but I gave it up because it is so cold.

Your packages will not arrive home for a month. You must rest after your long trip. We have lots of things to talk about after half a year of separation. That is why I wanted to have a long vacation from work, and it was approved. . . . Yukiko will be home too because the school is closed. Night is the only time when we can be alone.

Everybody is anxious to talk to you so I will finish the evening chores fast and will be ready to go to bed early. I am so happy that I can see you face to face and touch you. That's the best part. Also there will be some work cut out for us to do together. I really look forward to it. On top of it we can make love to each other—what more can I ask? I'm so happy, so much so that I have forgotten about your ear problems. Or, should I say that we will not be troubled by them anymore.

If this were in Japan, there are hot springs everywhere, and we could go there during vacation. Let's talk about it when you get home. We will be together even though there is family around. But we must find time to be alone. I want to hold you tight. . . . I [am] craving . . . your kisses—it's been so long without your touch. [We] went through the pain of separation. And now I want to be so close to you that we can forget everything in our ecstasy.

I'll come to San Francisco with [only] Mother and Yukiko because our car is small and we have so much stuff. Everybody is looking forward to seeing you return home—so be cheerful—don't feel that you are being left out. I know you are happy to come home—so I'm not going to say any more. . . .

I will bring some money to the airport just in case you need some. We'll be standing just outside of Customs so if you need cash, please come get it. I'll see you soon!

I love you forever, Kiyoshi-san. . . .

From KIYOSHI, *December 13.*

I HAVE ONE WEEK TO GO BEFORE LEAVING HERE. Your letter [with your haiku] was waiting yesterday when I came back from shopping. . . .

I like it! "The absence of my husband" matches well with "the wintry sky." You say you like to write haiku, but I think . . . if you had plenty of time, you could write beautiful tanka, or poems, or anything. I know your talent in poetry better than anybody else—maybe better than you yourself.

I went to town shopping yesterday. Dr. Miyahara recommended a high school student to accompany [us]—Shizuma-san, who just had an operation, and me. We went to Iwataya. Originally I was going to buy a camera after shopping around, but I found a nice one, and I had money with me just in case. It is a Canon QL 17; it cost 25,100 yen, a surprisingly good camera. Everything is automatic—exposure and focus—everything. You don't have to do anything after setting the camera on automatic—just focus on the object and press the shutter release. Of course, you can set everything manually. Even then, exposure is indicated in the view finder automatically—you can't make a mistake! I thought this camera was great so I bought it. A flash attachment and a case are included. I think this camera should be for you. It is too good for Yukiko—she will have to wait for . . . a camera like this. You can take this camera to work. The lens is f/1.7 so it is very fast, much faster than our old Rolleiflex which is f/2.8. It is about $20 more than I planned, but I think I can manage. Please don't worry because I don't need more than $5 once I get on the plane. This is a really good camera—I can't believe that it costs only a little over 25,000 yen and it is a Canon. Wait till you see it!

For Cecilia's husband, I bought an umbrella that can be folded two times —it's very small when it is folded—it's between 20 and 20.5 cm—much less than one foot. I'm sure he will like this. I picked deep blue, instead of black, because he likes blue colors. We'll give the umbrella along with an album for the couple. Also I bought a set of GO to play with Yukiko. The stones are magnetized so they won't get lost easily. This game is very popular in Japan, and there are big competitions.

Thank you for your story about the handicapped man. I must try hard to be like him. . . .

I'm going to see you in one week, Kiyoko-san! . . . I'll be home with a big smile. I can't wait!

I love you so much. . . .

From KIYOSHI, *December 14.*

... WHAT WILL IT BE LIKE, setting my foot on the ground in San Francisco? I can see your smiling face, and Yukiko's—she will run into my arms shouting, "Daddy!"

The overcoat has not arrived. But I will come home with or without the overcoat. I'll be all right without it. I went out shopping without a coat, and it was all right.

Yesterday Ōtomo-san came to see me. She had talked with the nurses the day before yesterday and had permission to take me out to show me around the city. She arrived around one o'clock. We talked for about two hours. Then she took me to the West Park and the East Park by taxi. Her mother felt sorry for me since I could not go out much due to my hearing problem. Since her daughter also had hearing trouble, although it is much better now, the mother suggested that she show me at least the town of Fukuoka before I leave Japan. Ōtomo-san's thoughtfulness touched my heart—she would hold my sleeve tight when we crossed busy streets. She is young but her tender attention to me was thorough. I was very moved. She had spent three hours traveling from Hida, Ōita-ken, to show me around before I leave the country. Her mother gave you and me something as a souvenir. I owe them so much. I tried to give Ōtomo-san 3,000 yen to cover some of the cost. She accepted it after some persuasion, but it was not easy. She wants to see me off at Itatsuki. I don't think I can stop her. I pray that she will find a good husband and have a happy life. I'm sure she will.

Tachibana-san will check in to the hospital today. She is the descendant of a feudal lord. She is a nice girl too. I'll take a lot of pictures. I took about a dozen pictures yesterday. . . .

The Department of E.N.T. (Ear, Nose, and Throat) of Kyushu University Hospital reported in the newspaper that the medical cases of children without ears have increased markedly. It is caused by the mother's use of contraceptive pills. I saw a number of children without ears in this hospital. They are here for plastic surgery. There are so many of them—such innocent kids—it makes me sad. We are lucky that Yukiko has a perfect body. . ..

I look forward to seeing your mother and Kondō-sensei this Sunday. . . .

From KIYOSHI, *December 15.*

. . . I HAD SO MANY VISITORS yesterday. The day before yesterday, Ōtomo-san came. Yesterday Tachibana-san came. (She had to go home and wait for a room to become available.) As I was seeing her off at around three o'clock, Watanabe-sensei arrived; then Hinashi-san came while we were talking, and soon after Iura-san came with her sister. Until about eight o'clock, guests came in one after another, and today I feel a little tired.

Hinashi-san did not stay more than 30 minutes since Watanabe-sensei was with me, but he will help me the afternoon of the 20th as it is the last day of school. After that the Iura sisters came, but I asked them to wait outside for a while as Watanabe-sensei was about to leave in order to attend some meeting. I talked with Sensei till about 5:30 p.m. He gave me a wrist-watch made by Seikō—it would be worth more than 13,000 yen—I couldn't find words to thank him. He helped me so much, yet gave me a watch with dates and days on it!

I showed Watanabe-sensei the bulletin of the National Institute of Japanese Language, and we talked and talked. He was very much interested in the bulletin and said—what do you think he said? He said, "Let's write a book together." I was so encouraged by this. I am so elated. I'm so grateful to Sensei. He said if I select a unique subject on the Japanese language that only I may be able to handle, it will surely be in the bulletin. This is a bulletin of the highest order in the academic circles of Japanese language. You know that it is such a difficult process to be accepted by academic bulletins, and you know also that it is the highest authority in the field. Watanabe-sensei pointed that out to me after he read the essays written in English. He wants to be my preceptor. I am so encouraged. I am to go to his house tonight from seven to nine o'clock, and we will discuss how to compile textbooks and other subjects. I declined to be a co-author of a textbook in order to maintain its quality, but I agreed to collect and analyze the data. I told him that I would be satisfied if he mentioned my name in the introduction as the contributor of the data. Before I start writing a text, I'd like to see my essays in the printed matter of academia, receive recognition from the Institute, and have stature of an authority in the field. I think this is the correct order. . . .

Yesterday Mrs. Ōshima came to see me from Saitama-ken. She gave Yukiko a doll. . . . I'm going to write a thank-you note to her today. I already wrote to Mrs. Matsumura and her father. I'm going to stop here and start packing. . . .

From KIYOSHI, *December 16.*

. . . FOUR DAYS TO GO. I'M BUSY with sorting out my stuff. It is a big job to pack. Shizuma-san is helping me because the box is big. We are breathing heavily because it's heavy too. I'm exhausted! . . .

Watanabe-sensei suggested that he and I do research on the English that Japanese Americans (particularly the first generation) use and jointly present it to the National Institute for Japanese Language. I was impressed by his focus on the subject. There are many research papers on dialects in the bulletin. The research on English used by the first generation of Japanese Americans will be very interesting, particularly as it correlates to their schooling, age, gender, profession, and length of time they have spent in America. We can present this research to the Institute. I told him that I will help him with the collection of the above data. Then I told him that after finishing the above project, you and I would like to do research on the Japanese language used by the first, second, and third generation of Japanese Americans. It is like the survey that JAL had at one time. After a thorough study of the subject, I will make a questionnaire. We will collect the facts on a tape-recorder. It's OK if it takes several years—we want to find out what kind of Japanese language they use. After a thorough analysis, we would like to present the study to the Institute. After you read the *Study of Japanese Language* and the bulletin, you will want to take part in this, I'm sure.

I was inspired by Watanabe-sensei last night. Mrs. Watanabe was very nice too. I took some pictures. As we were parting, she thanked me for the perfume that you gave her. Of course Sensei will see me off at Itatsuki. . . .

I'll talk to the doctor about the reason for my hospitalization—the advanced nature of my case and the necessity of close care, etc. I'm sure Dr. Miyahara will write the certificate. . . .

From KIYOSHI, *December 17.*

. . . IT IS A STRANGE AND wonderful feeling—I can't describe it well enough —in three days, I will see you, Kiyoko-san! The package has not arrived yet. It doesn't matter anymore. I'm going to leave for home on the 20th with or without my overcoat! . . .

I wish I could have gotten a rice cooker for Mother. She should have told me sooner. Tell her that the packages are already closed and ready to be shipped. But I will see if I can have a cooker sent directly to her from the store. The money will be squeezed out of the medicine fund. If the store cannot ship it directly to Mother, I will give money to Hiroyuki-san and ask him to ship it. I cannot carry it with me. . . .

Tell Yukiko that her letter made Daddy very happy. . . .

From KIYOSHI, *December 18.*

IT'S A BEAUTIFUL DAY. YESTERDAY I SAW KONDŌ-SENSEI. Your mother and Kazume-san came too. Kazume-san has grown up. She startled me because she looked very much like you—her eyes, her mouth, the shape of her face—everything including her manner and her walk—I was even shocked! She was so dark, and now her skin is white. She was the biggest surprise of yesterday.

Kondō-sensei has not changed at all. Maybe after 40 years of age, old men don't change. Hiroyuki-san and Noriko-san were here too, but they left around four o'clock to go to his company's year-end party. The rest of us continued to talk till five o'clock. Everybody was in this room and former patients came in and out too after hearing that I was leaving. One was Nonaka-san who gave me a flower vase; the other was Ōsedo-san, the lady who was very kind because I was new here and had difficulty with my hearing. I wrote to you about them at least once. Everybody is so kind! Otomo-san writes every other day to cheer me up—she wants me to go home with happy thoughts. She is really concerned about me. I hope that she gets completely well quickly. She writes: "My mother worries over me because I am sick all the time. I am going to get well so that she will feel relieved—I want her to have a life free from anxiety." I pray that will happen very soon. . . .

Thank you for calling me on the phone today. I read your last letter sent in a regular envelope. It made me feel even more anxious to return home; it is as if I'm now equipped with a rocket engine! . . .

I'm closing this letter now. Wait for the real Kiyoshi, not a letter. . . .

KIYOSHI, KIYOKO, AND YUKIKO TOKUTOMI, *February 1968.*
Photo courtesy of Yukiko Tokutomi Northon.

Epilogue

· ·

FINALLY CONVINCED THAT his hearing loss could not be reversed, Kiyoshi and Kiyoko began to restart, as Kiyoko said, "our life with 'he can't hear a thing.'" Kiyoshi continued to work on developing his method of teaching the Japanese language in collaboration with Kiyoko, who through her classroom teaching in the Japanese Language School was able to test his methods. However, neither this work nor his research on the history, development, and comparative language analysis of Japanese was ever published.

One of Kiyoko's ideas was to introduce Kiyoshi to haiku. She hoped that at literary gatherings, where the focus was on the written language, Kiyoshi would be able to participate more easily with others.

She took him to a local meeting of the Yukuharu Haiku Society, which had headquarters in Japan. To Kiyoko's delight, Kiyoshi enthusiastically embraced haiku; it was his idea to teach haiku to English-language writers. Together they founded the Yuki Teikei Haiku Society (at first it was called the Yukuharu Haiku Society, English-Language Division) in 1975, the same year that Kiyoko joined Kari, the Japanese Haiku Group of Shugyo Takaha, also based in Japan. Thus began her years of writing haiku in both Japanese and English.

They conducted the Yuki Teikei haiku meetings as a team. Kiyoshi would introduce an idea for discussion, and Kiyoko would follow the discussion, translating the cogent points for him by air-writing in Japanese on her hand and forearm, which she would hold up like a tablet for him to "read" the invisible strokes as she wrote. This was their usual method of communication: Kiyoko listening to what people said, Kiyoshi reading what she wrote either in the air or on paper. Friends and students would often take up the pen themselves and write directly to him, and he to them.

Kiyoshi had a consistently upbeat attitude. He celebrated being able to walk around the block—a most arduous task for him as he grew ever weaker. Kiyoko, always attentive to his needs, tried to make arrangements that would

THE TOKUTOMIS WITH KAZUO SATO *on the occasion of a Yuki Tekei Haiku Society ginko at Vasona Park, Los Gatos, California, September 8, 1979. Professor Sato was the representative of the Haiku Museum in Tokyo; he edited the "Haiku in English" column for the* Mainichi Daily News *in Japan. Photo from the collection of Patricia J. Machmiller.*

enhance his creativity. On warm summer days, for instance, in their house on Eighth Street in San Jose, where they had moved after he returned from Japan, she set up his writing table outside under the shade of an oleander, where she hung a small wind chime. Even though he couldn't hear it, she said, just seeing it would make him feel cooler.

Kiyoshi died in 1987. Kiyoko continued with the work they had started together in the Yuki Teikei Haiku Society. Her leadership style was more indirect. She tended to listen, to give encouragement, and to offer guidance when asked. In 1997 she was invited to speak at the Haiku International Conference in Tokyo about what she and Kiyoshi had accomplished. She continued to write haiku in Japanese and English and in 1999 was named *dojin* in Kari, a designation in Japan given to the most accomplished members. Until 1998 she had also continued her teaching at the Japanese Language School.

In 2000, the Yuki Teikei Haiku Society celebrated its 25th anniversary. Speaking at the dinner celebrating this event, Kiyoko modestly gave credit for the success of Yuki Teikei to its long succession of presidents starting with Kiyoshi, and to Kiyoshi's early decision to pass the torch to others. Kiyoko attributed the Society's ability to attract and retain creative talent to this decision, which is based on the more democratic American model of organization rather than the Japanese model of retaining leadership under one person.

In August 2000, Kiyoko learned she had cancer. Through the next two and a half years, weakened by the cancer treatment and the onset of Alzheimer's disease, she continued to write haiku. Her book *Kiyoko's Sky: The Haiku of Kiyoko Tokutomi,* translated from the Japanese by Patricia J. Machmiller and Fay Aoyagi, was published in December 2002. On a very stormy night she read from the book for the first time at the Yuki Teikei Winter Party with her daughter, Yukiko, and oldest granddaughter, Nicholette, present. She died two weeks later, on Christmas Day, 2002.

KIYOKO TOKUTOMI WITH JON SHIROTA, *author of* PINEAPPLE WHITE, *and Mr. Akizuki, reporter for the* Hokubei Mainichi *newspaper, San Francisco, California. Original photo in the Haiku Archive of the California State Library, photographed in turn by June Hopper Hymas.*

The YUKI TEKEI HAIKU SOCIETY *in San Jose, California, c. 1976, with Teruo Yamagata, member and now director (2009) of the Yukuharu Haiku Society of Japan. From left, front row: Kiyoshi Tokutomi, Kiyoko Tokutomi, June Hayashi, Teruo Yamagata, Beth Martin Haas, Bohumila Falkowski; second row: Dr. Edwin Falkowski, Hal Dumas, Lillian Giskin, Patricia Machmiller, John Hickok, Susan Soss, Elizabeth Gilliam (not pictured: C. Joy Haas). Photo from the collection of Patricia J. Machmiller.*

Appendix: THE *Families*

SHIBATA FAMILY:

Mother: Matsue Miyazaki Shibata; b. Jan. 23, 1906, Japan; d. Oct. 26, 1996, Japan.

Father: Hideji Shibata; b. July 31, 1898, Japan; d. May 13, 1956, Japan.

Masayuki (m): b. Sept. 11, 1926, Japan; d. Jan. 19, 2009, Japan; married to Mineko Tsurumaru; four children, Setsuko, Kin'ya, Akiko, Yasuaki; lived in Nabeshima, Japan.

Kiyoko (f): b. Dec. 28, 1928, Japan; d. Dec. 25, 2002, Ben Lomond, Calif.; married to Kiyoshi Tokutomi in 1957; one child, Yukiko, m. Jeff Northon, three children, Nicolette, Alissa, Jason; lived in San Jose, Calif., and later Ben Lomond, Calif.

Mitsuyo (f): b. Sept. 19, 1931, Japan; married to Akira Tao; three children, Glen, Paul, Alan; lives in Watsonville, Calif.

Hisayo (f): b. Dec. 10, 1934, Japan; married to Katsuji Hirahara; two children, Arthur and Ann; lives in Santa Clara, Calif.

Hiroyuki (m): b. Jan. 5, 1937, Japan; married to Noriko Kuroki; two children, Masayuki and Hirotaka; lives in Fukuoka, Japan.

Kazume (f): b. July 26, 1940, Japan; teacher, lives in Kurume, Fukuoka, Japan.

Masayoshi (m): b. Sept. 17, 1943, Japan; married to Sumie Yamato, 1972; three children, Tomomi, Ayako, Satoko; lives in Kōriyama, Japan.

Tokutomi family:

Mother: Sada Haraguchi Tokutomi; b. March 3, 1897, Takakise, Saga, Japan; d. Oct. 24, 1981, San Jose, Calif. (Interned at Heart Mountain, Wyoming, 1942-45.)

Father: Tatsuichirō Tokutomi; b. Sept. 1886, Yae-machi, Japan; d. Nov. 9, 1931, Berryessa (now San Jose), Calif.

Mitsuye (f): b. March 3, 1921, San Juan Batista, Calif.; married to Hiromichi Hoshino; three children, Henry, unmarried; Frank, married, with twins Jade and Jasmine; Lily, married, with two sons, Samuel and Gregory, from husband's previous marriage; lives in Sunnyvale, Calif. (Interned at Heart Mountain, Wyoming, 1942; left the camp to work as a maid at the U.S. Navy Japanese/Oriental Language School in Boulder, Colo.)

Kiyoshi (m): b. Oct. 3, 1923, Watsonville, Calif.; d. June 6, 1987, San Jose, Calif.; married to Kiyoko Shibata in 1957; one child, Yukiko, m. Jeff Northon, three children, Nicolette, Alissa, Jason; went to Japan to study in 1931 after his father died; lived in San Jose, Calif.

Yoshimitsu (m): b. April 1, 1926, Watsonville, Calif.; d. 1985, Sunnyvale, Calif.; married to Jane Uchida; two children, Eric and Ken, both married; lived in Sunnyvale, Calif. (Interned at Heart Mountain, Wyoming, 1942; left the camp by joining the U.S. military.)

Sachio: b. 1928, Berryessa, Calif.; d. June 7, 1929, Berryessa, Calif.

Kikuyo: b. 1930, Berryessa, Calif.; d. Dec. 31, 1931, Berryessa, Calif.

Glossary

akamutsu—warm water fish found south of Tokyo in the Pacific and near Niigata in the Sea of Japan; the fatty meat is best served roasted with salt

arigatō—thanks

Asahi-shinbun—one of the oldest and largest Japanese national daily newspapers; published in Japanese and English

Bon—a festival to remember the deceased on certain days between August first and the 25th; the most popular practice in Japan starts on the eve of the 12th when the spirits of the family ancestors revisit the household altar, and ends at dawn on the 16th; also called the Feast of Lanterns, as the spirit of the deceased is accompanied on the journey back by lantern

bon-odori—folk dance performed during Bon Festival

bonsai—potted plant; hobby that creates a view of trees and plants in nature in a portable container

botamochi—a rice cake dumpling covered with a sweet bean jam

Bungei-shunjō —a literary magazine

-chan—suffix for young child; term of endearment (see *tō-chan* for comparison of degrees of formality in Japanese forms of address)

chicken-rice—rice cooked with chicken broth and diced meat

chōdai—give me, please!

CYS—Community Youth Service

daikon *yakusha*—idiom referring to an actor who looks as plain as daikon, a large white radish, and who cannot act well

daimyo—feudal lord; early in the days of the shogunate, it meant one who is influential locally; later it meant a samurai who had property and subordinates

donburi—bowl made of porcelain; food, especially rice, served in a bowl

funa—fish in the carp family; Shiga prefecture is famous for sushi made with *funa*

gakuen — school

gakuin—school with slightly higher standards than *gakuen*

GEM—a discount store in the U.S.

Ginza—an entertainment and shopping district in Tokyo; also a restaurant in Japantown, San Jose, California

gomennasai—I'm sorry; forgive me

gumeshi—rice seasoned with meat and vegetable

gyoza—an appetizer; meat and vegetables in a thin wrapper made of flour and served boiled, fried, or steamed

Hakata doll—one of the traditional Japanese dolls made of clay; originated in Hakata area in Fukuoka Prefecture around 1600; became popular as an export item after 1800

hiragana—one of two sets of Japanese syllabaries of the kana system, having a cursive style of script

Hōji-shinbun—a newspaper in Japanese

Hokubei Mainichi—a San Francisco newspaper in Japanese

inari-zushi—rice ball coated in thin fried tofu the color of fox (*inari* refers to the fox-deity who protects the harvest)

itsutsusaki—name of a local fish in Saga

Iwanami—a Japanese publishing company

JLA—Japanese Language Association

kaibun—palindrome: a word, verse, or sentence (as "Able was I ere I saw Elba.") that reads the same backward or forward

kana—a general term for the syllabic Japanese scripts, hiragana (ひらがな) and katakana (カタカナ), as well as the old system known as man'yōgana, all based on logographic characters of Chinese origin known in Japan as kanji

kanji—a Japanese system of writing based on Chinese characters

kasutera—a pound cake introduced to Japan by Portuguese missionaries in Nagasaki in the Muromachi Period (1336-1573)

katakana—the simplest of the Japanese scripts, a fragmentary kana derived from components of kanji characterized by short, straight strokes and angular corners; a kana used for writing foreign words or official documents, e.g. telegrams

ken—prefecture

kimono—a loose wrap-around Japanese robe with wide sleeves and sash, worn by both men and women

koharu-biyori—Indian summer

kokeshi doll—a limbless wooden folk doll

konbanwa—good evening!

LIFE—a U.S. magazine featuring full-page photographs of current events

machi—town

Macy's—a U.S. department store

Mademoiselle—a glamour magazine published in the U.S.

Mainichi Daily News—national Japanese newspaper published in English

Man'yō—the period of the oldest *waka* collection compiled between the middle of the 7th century and the middle of the 8th century

Man'yō-shū—the oldest surviving *waka* anthology in Japan (see *Man'yō*)

myōga—an herb, *Zingiber mioga*

Nagamochi-uta—the title of a folk dance that originated in Saga Prefecture

NB—Nicheibei Bussan, a gift and dry-goods store in Japantown, San Jose, CA

Nichibei-news—a San Francisco newspaper

Nihingo News—newsletter of the Nihongo Society

Nishi-Nihon-shinbun—a newspaper in Kyushu, Japan

oba-sama—honorific expression for a woman of middle age; also for a sister of one's mother (see *tō-chan* for comparison of degrees of formality in Japanese forms of address)

obi—broad Japanese sash wound around the waist over the main kimono; usually tied at the back

Obon—see Bon

ohitsu—a rice tub

oji-sama—honorific expression for a middle-aged man (see *tō-chan* for comparison of degrees of formality in Japanese forms of address)

oji-san—uncle; middle-aged man in general (see *tō-chan* for comparison of degrees of formality in Japanese forms of address)

okō-san—mother (see *tō-chan* for comparison of degrees of formality in Japanese forms of address)

onigiri—rice ball

origami—colored paper for folding

ōzeki—a wrestler of the highest rank and immediately under the grand champion

ramen—noodles cooked in pork-bone soup; originated in Kyushu area

saba-zushi—raw mackerel with bite-size rice ball seasoned with vinegar

-sama—suffix with respect after a name

san/-san—suffix with familiarity after a name

Sanseidō—a Japanese publishing company

sashimi—sliced fillet of raw fish

sayonara—good-bye

senryū—a Japanese verse form similar to haiku, free of season, with a focus on daily life and the human condition, especially human foibles, often with a slightly comical air

sensei—a teacher, a master, a doctor

shi—city

shihan—school; teacher

shinbun—newspaper

Shinchō—a Japanese publishing company

shiso—an herb, beefsteak plant

shogun—military governor of Japan before the mid-19th century revolution with power exceeding that of the emperor

shogunate—the government of a shogun

shoyu—soy sauce

Shunjū Yoroku—Newspaper column of light commentary

sumo—Japanese form of wrestling in which a contestant loses the match if he is forced out of the ring or if any part of his body, other than his feet, touches the ground

sushi—seasoned rice served in a bowl or rolled with fillet of fish

tai—a fish, gold bream

tai-ryōri—food prepared with gold bream

tai-no-sashimi—sliced, raw gold bream

tanka—a Japanese poetry form in 31 sounds, typically arranged in phrases of 5-7-5 / 7-7 (see *waka*)

tō-chan—informal address for father; *otō-chan*, slightly more formal; *otō*-san, more formal; *otō-sama*, formal

Tōkyōdō—a Japanese publishing company

tonkatsu—breaded and fried pork

uchiwa—Japanese fan

umeboshi—pickled plums

waka—the name coined in the Heian Period (794-1185) to refer to a genre of Japanese poetry to differentiate native poems from Chinese poems; tanka (meaning short poem) with the 5-7-5 / 7-7 count became the sole sub-form of *waka* in the beginning of the Heian Period

washi—Japanese paper

White Front—a U.S. discount store

ya—expression of surprise; My goodness!

yaya—to some degree

yokozuna—sumo grand champion

Yomiuri-shinbun—largest national Japanese daily newspaper; publishes Japanese and English editions

yukata—summer kimono

Glossary of Medical Terms

ATP—adenosine triphosphate

Arlidrin—A pharmaceutical brand name for the drug nylidrin (see nylidrin below)

Arturo-gold—Apparently an over-the-counter medication sold in Japan, as mentioned in one of Kiyoshi's letters. It was supposed to be helpful for a number of maladies including high blood pressure, dizziness, constipation, ear ringing, numbness of the limbs, etc. There is no evidence of Arturo-gold ever being sold in the U.S.

Chitomakku-P (Chitomac-P)—A macroporous beaded chitin; we were not able to determine how it was used in treating Kiyoshi.

electronic medicine—Treatment in electronic medicine was based on a hopeful theory that electric currents or electro-magnetic energy would have the ability to control organs of the human body and in some way provide a cure for disease. No one has found electric or magnetic treatment helpful for either the form of TB afflicting Kiyoshi or the permanent hearing loss caused by streptomycin.

ENT—A clinic that specializes in ears, nose, and throat medicine.

high voltage duplet—The term duplet implies a pair; for example, the sound produced by two musical notes played simultaneously is termed a duplet. One might assume that a "high voltage duplet" machine would produce a pair of high voltage electrical currents applied simultaneously as some form of medical treatment. There is nothing, however, in the Western scientific literature that describes or even mentions this particular treatment.

histamine—A naturally occurring active protein found throughout the body and best known for its role in human allergies. Histamine also plays a role in the transmission of signals along nerve pathways.

kanamycin—An antibiotic related to streptomycin that also has a toxic side-effect that can lead to loss of hearing. (See streptomycin.)

karikurein—(together with *kininogenin*, *kininogenaze*, Kallikrein EC 3.4.21.34·EC 3.4.21.35): A kind of enzyme that breaks down protein and is related to lowering blood pressure. There are two groups—serum and gland. As for the protein, it is classified into *serinproteaze* and *endoproteaze*. We were unable to determine what function it served in Kiyoshi's treatment.

Leeben—A German commercial brand name for alfalfa saponin, a glucoside usually used as an emulsifier.

metastasis—The transmission of disease from an original site to one or more sites elsewhere in the body, as in tuberculosis or cancer.

nylidrin—This common medication has been used as a vasodilator to help increase the circulation of blood throughout the body; used for treating strokes, poor leg circulation, cramps, Alzheimer's disease, etc.

otorhinology—The study (ology) of the ears (oto) and the combined nose/throat area (rhino). The term otorhinology is a variant of several commonly used terms describing the field of doctors who specialize in treating diseases of the ears, nose and throat.

PAS (para-aminosalicylate sodium)—An anti-tuberculosis agent used in combination with other anti-tuberculosis agents to treat clinical tuberculosis.

stoma bag—Internal organs will occasionally develop a passageway through the skin to the outside of the body. The term given to the actual opening in the skin is stoma. A stoma bag is simply a plastic bag designed to seal around a stoma and collect drainage from the internal organ. (Kiyoshi had a stoma in his chest, an opening purposely created by surgeons to allow drainage from his TB-infected lungs. He used stoma bags to control the drainage and prevent the soiling of his clothes.)

stratigrams—Two or more x-ray images taken at different angles for evaluation of internal organs or areas of disease. The size, shape and volume of an internal image can be roughly determined by comparing the various x-ray views; i.e., the total area of TB involvement in a lung can be judged with this technique.

streptomycin—This was the first antibiotic found to be effective for tuberculosis. It was considered a miracle drug at the time and saved the lives of thousands of people ravaged by the disease. Streptomycin was a powerful antibiotic and consequently had powerful side-effects, one of the most notable of which involved the vital nerve tissues in the ears. Deafness occurred in approximately 20% of patients treated with streptomycin, as a result of permanent nerve damage. No way has been found to reverse the damage or restore the loss of hearing. The deafness often appeared to occur suddenly, without warning, and there was no way to know in advance which patients would be affected.

TB—tuberculosis.

thoracopathy—English translation of the term used in Japan for the medical science of studying chest function and chest disease.

tinnitus—A ringing sound in the ears usually caused by internal damage to the auditory nerves. The sound can be perceived as loud and persistent and is often of great annoyance to the sufferer.

Index of Names

A note on names as they appear in the letters: The Tokutomis used the Eastern custom of writing the family name first and the given name second with no comma. Often they used only one name and that was generally the family name, such as Hinashi-san or Watanabe-sensei. First or given names were used mostly for people in their immediate family, for instance Yukiko or Hisayo-san. In this index we have listed such names in the Western style, alphabetically by last name, but also by first name with a cross-reference to the entry by last name. There are a few people mentioned in the letters whose place in the world or relationship to the Tokutomis we could not determine; they are listed without additional information. **Boldface** numbers indicate photographs.

About THE *Translators*

BORN IN TOKYO, TEI MATSUSHITA SCOTT lived, worked, and painted in the Washington, D.C., area for more than two decades before moving to California, where she maintained a studio. She now works in New York.

She received an M.A. in the humanities from the University of New York in Buffalo, where she combined her studies in the arts, literature, and philosophy. She actively exhibited her paintings in galleries in Manhattan and abroad until 1970 when she took an extended sabbatical to devote time to her family. In 1987, she resumed painting full time.

She is an avid student of English, Spanish, and Japanese poetry, and paints in abstract forms to express the emotions found in these written words. Deeply influenced by Far Eastern calligraphy, she uses brushstrokes with "relaxation and tension" to convey her feelings.

Tei Matsushita Scott (www.matsushita.com) took on the translation of the Tokutomi letters because she felt that she and Kiyoko Tokutomi had similar histories—born in Japan, educated in both Japan and the United States, married to an American, and living her adult life in the U.S.

PATRICIA J. MACHMILLER WRITES HAIKU as well as western lyrics and poetic criticism. Her book of haiku, *Blush of Winter Moon*, was published by Jacaranda Press in 2001. With Fay Aoyagi she translated Kiyoko Tokutomi's haiku published in *Kiyoko's Sky* (Brooks Books, 2002). She co-edited with June Hopper Hymas *Young Leaves: 25th Anniversary Issue of Haiku Journal,* a collection of essays on haiku and haiku writing by Clark Strand, James Hackett, Patricia Donegan, Jane Reichhold and Makoto Ueda, to name a few of an extensive list of contributors, herself among them. She and Jerry Ball write a highly regarded column of haiku commentary, "Dojins' Corner," for *GEPPO,* the newsletter of the Yuki Teikei Haiku Society (published six times a year).

Her poems have appeared in *Northwest Review, the Santa Clara Review, VOLT, Caesura,* and *Denver Quarterly.* She won a second place award in the Montalvo poetry contest for her poems "Boundaries" and "Whale Watch." A manuscript of longer poems, *Blue: Like this Hour before Dawn,* is looking for a publisher.

A brush painter and print-maker (see her work at www.patriciaj-machmiller.com), she has a B.S. degree in mathematics and chemistry from San Jose State University and an M.S. in Systems Management from the University of Southern California.

Autumn Loneliness:
The Letters of Kiyoshi & Kiyoko Tokutomi
[JULY–DECEMBER 1967]

Project coordinator and editor: JACKIE PELS
Book design and production: DAVID R. JOHNSON
Typography and composition: DICKIE MAGIDOFF
Proofreader: LEAH H. PELS

Printed and bound at MCNAUGHTON & GUNN, Saline, Michigan
Alkaline pH paper (Natural Offset)

HARDSCRATCH

HARDSCRATCH PRESS
2358 Banbury Place
Walnut Creek, CA 94598

phone/fax: 925/935-3422

www.hardscratchpress.com